"RED by

James Hogan"

"RED by James Hogan"

DiaryUnlimited.com

ISBN 978-0990857006

Library of Congress Control Number: 2015901514

A CIP catalogue is available at the British library

www.DiaryUnlimited.com

Design and Layout by Tom Norwood

Book coordinator: Alex Altman

"RED by James Hogan"

Painting on the cover: "The Bleed" by James Hogan from the "RED by James Hogan collection". 14 paintings have been conceived based around the "RED by..." concept.

The paintings are part of a collection for a feature film, an interactive play and opera set in the 18th century at the court of King George the Third... A metaphor for the madness of 21st century broadcasting.

CONTENTS

Chapter IV

The near death of investigative journalism and the economics of self-censorship

Chapter V

Jimmy Savile and the psychology of self-censorship

Chapter VI

Invisible TV

Part II

Screenplay to the feature film documentary and TV programme

Epilogue

By Nick Peterson

DEDICATION

TO WHOM IT MAY CONCERN

"RED by James Hogan"

INVISIBLE TELEVISION

A great number of today's documentary features are based on access -rigged television. They are good at showing the visible. What's missing is the invisible.

James Hogan. March 2015

FOREWORD

Broadcasting: Back to the Future?

Television was undoubtedly one of the major technological and cultural breakthroughs of the twentieth century. In spite of many prophecies of its impending demise, it has proved to be a remarkably durable medium and remains a central part of national culture. It has long transcended its nationally based roots and is now an important globalizing force through the spread of TV shows and, more recently, popular formats.

James Hogan provides a lively assessment of the current state of television. In doing so, he skillfully traverses from the mid-1990s to the current era. The result is a fascinating blend of retrospective sense making and up-to-date and provocative analysis.

The book explains a broadcasting world that has changed beyond all recognition. It is remarkable to recall that a mere thirty years ago there were only four channels in the UK: BBC1, BBC2, the ITV network and the then youthful Channel 4. James Hogan was part of that broadcasting world, as a BBC current affairs producer and editor at the legendary Lime Grove studios in West London.

The story he has to tell is of a broadcasting world that has changed out of all recognition from a generation ago. Hogan grapples with the big themes of broadcasting and the book provides fascinating insights into the changed ecology of broadcasting where Sky, the BBC and a vertically integrated ITV are broadcasting giants and much of the content is provided by 'super-indies'.

As a former current affairs producer it is perhaps of little surprise that Hogan highlights the decline in investigative journalism in British television. His argument is that British television has largely lost its capacity to conduct investigative reporting. The book strikes a balance as Hogan also highlights the growth in programme genres – such as factual entertainment – and the dramatic improvement in the coverage of others, such as sport and news.

Hogan's fascination with television endures and the central message in the book is that quality television matters, not just in terms of entertainment but as a fundamental building block of a healthy democracy. Television is undergoing a revolution and James Hogan is asking us to pause and ask ourselves what kind of television do we want from our broadcasters and from programme makers? If television is an important manifestation of our society, what does contemporary television say about us as a society? In a perhaps paradoxical way, James Hogan is re-stating many of the virtues of traditional Reithian values at a time where they increasingly seem to be part of a world that has vanished. His central argument is that television must re-claim Reithian values to help educate, inform and entertain in our turbulent, time poor and digitalized age.

Of course it is not possible to turn back the clock: merely lament the loss of a golden age of television is little more than a quixotic nostalgia trip. The message I take from James Hogan's provocative book is that television is incredibly important but finds itself at a very dangerous juncture. His book calls for a re-imagining of television for the 21st Century that hybridizes the very best of the Reithian tradition with lively new formats and new technology.

Professor Chris Carter, University of Edinburgh

March 2015

PREFACE

By Alex Altman, publisher

James Hogan's powerful and insightful essay has only one aim: not to kill TV, not to downgrade it but state a point about the crazy world of 21st century broadcasting and the democratic deficit.

The cover is from a painting by James Hogan set in the 18th century at the court of King George the Third... A metaphor for the madness of 21st century broadcasting.

RED being King George III's favourite colour, RED for anger and RED for censorship.

March 2015

"RED by James Hogan"

Chapter I
Whatever happened to "television"?

Communications at the start of the 21st century involves a type of insanity that threatens to make madmen of us all. Fearful, we do our utmost to keep up - pretending to be always available, constantly monitoring everything in our midst. Frightened to admit that we actually sleep or in some cases even eat. The ever accelerating treadmill of communications spewing out limitless amounts of information can be likened to the collapsing world of George III and his relapse into madness. Deaf and blind, it is recorded that he spoke total none sense for 58 hours non-stop towards the end of his life. Endlessly repeating himself. Unable to cope with the bombardment of light, sound, images and imagery all around him. A swollen brain in shut down. Sounds familiar?

The historical data for this book is based on 50 interviews conducted over 20 years with senior figures in the television industry including broadcasters and producers interviewed for my LSE study published in 1996, which by general agreement has stood the test of time. For the first part of this book I have faithfully updated the LSE study with four long interviews conducted at the end of 2014 and the start of 2015 (with another 13 full-length interviews on camera for my feature-documentary during 2015). The four interviews were with Lord Grade, former BBC chairman of the governors and chairman designate of the BBC Trust, ex-Chief Executive of ITV and Channel 4; Roger Bolton, the former editor of ITVs flagship hard-hitting documentary series This Week and today the presenter of BBC Radio 4's Feedback programme; Peter Ibbotson, the former editor of BBC TV's flagship Panorama and one of the shrewdest observers of UK broadcast history; and John McVay, the Chief Executive of the trade body that represents UK independents, the Producers Alliance For Cinema and Television, PACT. In each case, I asked them to comment on the changing face of television, the state of independent production and the plight of investigative journalism, and to reflect on the BBC's self-censorship of the BBC TV Newsnight investigation into allegations of historical sex abuse allegedly carried out by the BBC Children's presenter, the late Sir Jimmy Savile.

The text that follows is not a gripe against television. It is a piece of analysis and a call to arms from someone who loves television. Always will. As I say in the text there is a lot of good to be celebrated –notably the vastly improved quality of TV news thanks to 24/7 coverage; the vastly improved quality of TV sports thanks largely to Sky; and the quality of accessible factual entertainment. However my argument is that the almost exclusive emphasis on entertainment has come at a very heavy price. In particular I argue that the economics of broadcasting have brought about a form of self-censorship squashing investigative journalism on terrestrial television and the spirit that characterised the birth of the indies in the 1980s 'Let A Thousand Flowers Bloom'. The latter was an impossible dream that was hugely wasteful and doomed. The re-birth of the indies after 2003 also came at a huge cost. Desperate, the indies no longer offered a torrent of ideas only to be refused. Instead they turned the system on its head. And like the CEO of a leading supermarket chain they asked the broadcaster: "What exactly do you want?", then gave it to them at a price they were willing to pay. So they learnt the hard way. The result is a quite dramatic democratic deficit which needs to be addressed -especially by the BBC given its charter and the scale of its resources. The need for the BBC to respond appropriately is all the more important in view of the uncertainty of the party political outlook in the UK and the need to ensure democratic accountability in such conditions. Red Alert.

In making my case, I am aware the system of unfettered commercialisation in television started in the US. So, a question: do we really need to be worried about the democratic deficit I identify in British broadcasting? After all if it's good enough for America surely it's good enough for the UK. In fact I don't believe you can treat British broadcasting in the same way as the US. We are two very different countries with two very different broadcast systems. The US shares with the UK the benefits of twenty four hour news. But it doesn't have the public service tradition we cherish in this country -in the same way we value the National Health Service. We in Britain have also always placed a high value on culturally authentic television programming. So I contend that points of comparison are very limited and beyond a certain point meaningless. America went straight to commercial from its inception. We didn't. Nor should we have. And certainly not without safeguards.

Everywhere I go, people ask me: whatever happened to television? Although television is everywhere -omnipresent- there is a sense of loss, bereavement. Many people say: "There are too many channels but nothing to watch on TV". Of course this is an overstatement. Indeed in one way television or rather "video" is bigger than ever before- the driving force behind the internet, social media and Google TV. There are also still some good, at times outstanding TV programmes being made. There have been some great turn around stories: the reincarnation and re-energising of both STV and ITV. The strong revival of STV as a terrestrial broadcaster has allowed it to add to its public service output at a vital time in Scottish politics. Television audiences have proved to be very resilient –the crash did not occur. Television wasn't killed by the internet because it merged with it. But there are reasons why so many people feel somewhat indifferent towards the television of today and disengaged from it: the loss of "transmission" –or sense of occasion. The loss of "impact". The dilution of TV. The loss of the sacred. The move away from being "special" to being simply "ordinary". Everywhere and nowhere. When I went to New York in the 1980's, I was struck by the fact that television was everywhere - like traffic noise. Yet people didn't seem to be viewing or even listening. TV was in shops, offices, hotels, supermarket checks outs but the viewing public had already checked out. So it is today in the UK. Yes the figures look good but the public is indifferent. Television is a backdrop. This is hard to comprehend for the UK Citizen for whom it is counter-intuitive. After all we are meant to have the best Television in the world.

The atomisation of TV audiences which has accompanied the atomisation of society in the UK has been driven by economics and the overwhelming concentration on entertainment. Television has become like a tap you can't switch. The nostalgic amongst us crave the time when it did stop. When it was time to go to bed. To go to sleep. To switch off. To stop consuming. No such thing is possible in the television world of today. It is ceaseless. It knows no boundaries. It is universal. This feature of the new TV mirrors modern capitalism. I worked in the City for seventeen years after I left broadcasting. I can tell you capitalism doesn't care about yesterday –or even today- very much. It cares about tomorrow: the promise of future earnings. It too is non-stop.

It is not an accident that television has morphed into Google TV. Google TV is a magnet for every type of entertainment and a mass of consumer data. The constant emphasis is on consumption and a blizzard of communications targeted at the consumer. There is an insanity to the sheer volume of information being sent out often by people or organisations you don't know or care about and with whom you don't necessarily want to communicate. Each day the gathering storm intensifies threatening to make lunatics of us all if we were fool enough to try to read it all, let alone respond. Viewed in this context the endless cycle of repeats on digital TV is either a reassuring presence harking back to the good old days when the likes of Only Fools and Horses or Last of the Summer Wine were first transmitted, or evidence of a sort of dementia in which you ask yourself why are we watching the same programme over and over again? Or maybe I am imagining things. Maybe I have forgotten. Maybe it's me not them. There is something delusional and crazy about labelling Last of the Summer Wine and Keeping Up Appearances as documentary as some digital channels do. Not so long ago, I sat at home on a Saturday evening with some friends -some young, some middle-aged. Despite having a choice of hundreds of channels and a state of the art TV, we could not find anything we wanted to watch. We ended up watching the repeat of one of the BBC's 1974 general election specials which we enjoyed but... Really.

In the crazy world of proliferation and exploding data people are constantly on the run. 3 words a second on TV, 140 characters on Twitter. Demented looking people apparently speaking to themselves on earpieces, lost in a crowd. Hermetically sealed, yet all at sea. People sitting cheek by jowel in offices sending each other e-mails. 'Hi! Remember me? How are you? Are you free for lunch?' In such an environment television needs to be a comfort - a sanctuary. A source of reassurance. Assurance that in the midst of it all our democratic freedoms are being safeguarded.

The economics of the new television are crucifying. After all if you ask the average person to choose between watching their favourite sport, movie, sitcom or a special on the latest political situation in Northern Ireland, we all know the likely outcome. Like democracy we get the television we deserve. Actions have consequences. When there were just a few channels -before satellite TV- the commissioning editors at the BBC, ITV and Channel 4 were strongly committed to public service broadcasting and were not under economic pressure or the pressure to make the size of audience their number one priority. Television was sheltered by the lack of competition and the regulatory regime at the time. It is no longer and it no longer offers shelter.

The killing field is terrestrial television. That is where the nation congregates. It is also where the bulk of quality television is first produced and transmitted. The large audiences that the likes of ITV can attract guarantees them advertising revenue some of which can be ploughed back into funding more original programming. However, the economics are tight and the competition fierce. Commercial television has been exposed to the ferocious force of the market place with the arrival of satellite television with very deep pockets and literally hundreds of purely entertainment-led channels delivered on a variety of different platforms including over the internet. As a result there has been a sustained flight away from investigative journalism on terrestrial commercial television. Compare the entertainment-led schedule on ITV in peak-time today with that of the past. In a previous generation when there were just 3 or 4 channels and the public service obligations of ITV licence holders were rigorous, a permanent feature of the ITV schedule were two very tough investigative strands: World In Action and This Week. They have long since gone and the economics of commercial television means that they are not coming back.

The experience of Channel 4 and its response to the new age of entertainment is instructive. In the work I published in 1996, I characterised the spirit around the launch of Channel 4 and the enthusiasm of the independent producers who were to make its programmes in the declaration: 'Let A Thousand Flowers Bloom'. Then as now Channel 4 was committed to documentary not least because of its statutory remit. It is not an accident that Channel 4 has stood by its long running strand of documentary, Dispatches. In the early days, the anarcho-syndicalism of Channel 4 allowed it to capitalise on the fact that it was different from BBC and ITV. On and off air the channel and its suppliers could think and act in a counter-cultural way. This allowed Channel 4 to deliver highly innovative programming in the 1980s and to create a unique identity. It could take risks and it did. However, over time the economics of broadcasting started to bear down on the dream. The arrival of hundreds of new TV channels chipped away at the unique identity of Channel 4. Gradually the dream started to fade away. The swash buckling neophytes who were to supply Channel 4 -at its inception- the ideal type were not entertainers but serious documentary makers who believed in television as plural democrats- learnt they could not make a living out of producing the odd documentary here and there. They faced a stark choice. Change or die. So they changed. Many changed utterly. Many simply disappeared. Economics killed them off. The people who survived were the Darwinists. They worked out that the only way to survive was to give the broadcasters what they wanted. After all they were the customers. As the customers their needs changed when the market changed. By the late nineties there was really only one type: entertainment. Of course serious subjects could still be tackled but would need to be wrapped in an entertainment format. Thus factual entertainment became the dominant genre in the new age of television. A 'soft' form of programming that looks good, and is cheap to make and popular with audiences. A win all round. As such it passes the economic test. The programme ideas that fail the economic test never get off the ground and these days are usually strangled at birth. The process -a type of informal censorship- has two steps. The broadcaster informs the indies what they want. The Darwinists give it to them. After all, what would be the point in offering the broadcaster something they don't want and would never buy? Innovation can and does take place but in a cocoon. I argue in chapter 3 that the indies were reborn at the beginning of the 21st century but the price tag was a form of self-censorship rooted in economics and involving the same process I observe in the near death of investigative journalism. Thus in the new world of television hard-hitting documentary has largely been replaced by factual entertainment. In turn a lot of factual entertainment has been redefined as documentary. Travelogues and gardening programmes along with cookery shows are often categorised by the broadcaster as documentary. These are not the documentary of yesteryear. On the whole they are the offspring of the entertainment era.

By the time Channel 5 came on air it had no choice except to turn itself into an entertainment-led channel even though it is a public service broadcaster. Over time it scaled down its original ambitions and became a niche player strongly focused on entertainment. In this guise it became relatively successful in recent years. The trick was to give the audience what it wanted. In effect it held a mirror up to the face of the new television audience and beamed it back at it.

A by-product of the economics of self-censorship is the ghettoisation of what was once called current affairs. Whereas such programming was once scheduled in volume and in peak-time when there were just three or four channels, today it has been chased into one of two habitats. Either rolled into rolling news or as current affairs in the form of studio debates scheduled at weekends and either early in the morning or late night. Looking at the schedules the message from the broadcaster is clear: if you want news there it is: if you want old style hard-hitting documentary -an angle, analysis, an in-depth look- look away from terrestrial TV. By and large it's not for you. Go digital. Go HD. Everyone and every taste is catered for there.

I decided to test some of the observations I have made in the previous paragraphs by taking a close look at the schedules of the public service terrestrial broadcasters. I took January and February 2015 which I believe is a very fair sample to choose. It is the middle of the television year when the majority of people are at home and a captivated audience. It's probably the highpoint for the roll out of original programming or one of them. This is what I found:

"RED by James Hogan"

As ever the TV schedules were dominated by the leading soaps: Coronation Street, EastEnders, Emmmerdale, Hollyoaks, and Neighbours. In between Breakfast News and the early Evening news, the schedules were plastered with cheap and cheerful factual entertainment: Escape to the Country, Flog It!, Four In a Bed, A Place in the Sun. In the run up to peak time, 24/7 News became a significant feature in terms of quality. And then at the weekend Sky Sports. In so far as the democratic function of television was evident, it made its presence felt in the cut down version of BBC TV Panorama on Monday nights and Dispatches on Channel 4. Channel 5 continued to deliver watchable tabloid documentary. The show I used to edit, Question Time, remains at the heart of the BBC1 schedule providing topical debate. The main features of the weekend schedules in terms of factual programming were the breakfast and lunchtime chat shows which for a long time have been there to deliver the big set-piece political interview intended to set the political agenda for the week. In summary there was an abundance of entertainment and old style documentary was a scarce commodity. Economics determining the outcome. Democracy suffering as a result.

As someone who worked in television and financial public relations for many years, I think the grammar of the new television in relation to business reporting deserves some reflection. In a nutshell it is picture-led and light on words. It's hot, not cold. It seeks instant recognition by name and brand. In the world of financial TV, once driven by newspaper journalists and heavy on statistics, today's business TV adores brands because they don't require any explanation and attract instant viewer recognition. It isn't an accident that major corporates and consumer brands get a hugely disproportionate amount of scrutiny: British Airways, British Telecom, BBC, BP, Tesco, Virgin etc. Self-explanatory is the order of the day. By and large individuals and individual endeavour are only interesting to the new television if they involve house prices, mega-deals, the mega-rich, criminals, and crisis.

It is interesting to do a controlled test on my thesis by comparing BBC TV with BBC Radio and in particular to compare BBC 1 with Radio 4. The nature of talk radio is that it tends towards the factual. In the absence of visuals, radio needs to conjure up ideas and imagery using words. This fact and the sheltered nature of say BBC Radio 4 has made it a desirable habitat for several programmes which would otherwise be extinct. Programmes like In Touch, Today in Parliament, From Our Own Correspondent, even In Business and Money Box fall into this category. It is also hard to imagine BBC TV or ITV for that matter replacing their Breakfast shows with the Radio 4 flagship The Today Programme. The latter is essentially an old style current affairs format which simply would not fit with entertainment-driven TV. Let alone commercial breaks.

The net effect of the economics of self-censorship is to create a sense of absence. Distrust. With this thought in mind, I wanted to understand what lead the BBC to self-censor the Newsnight investigation into Jimmy Savile -dropping what would have turned out to be a world exclusive while leaving various planned tributes programmes to Savile in the schedules. Why dropped? Why not shelved? Was it just a very bad decision or was it a reflection of a wider malaise? Was the trend towards entertainment-led television and away from hard-hitting documentary a factor? In Chapter 5 I quote from the findings of the independent report produced by the former Sky News Editor, Nick Pollard. It is an excellent and devastating account of what actually happened. I also quote from the transcripts of the interviews I conducted on this issue and explore the possible role of the sub-conscious in the decision-making process.

Chapter II
The Democratic deficit

In my 1996 LSE study I charted the birth of the UK's independent television production sector and the political forces behind it with an eye to its democratic potential. I explained that the emergence of the indies was a long time coming. Like the birth of Channel 4 itself. The breakthrough in what proved to be a protracted debate about whether Channel 4 should be, in effect, ITV 2 or an entirely new concept that would add to the plural democratic mix, came with the Annan Report in 1977 which paved the way for the 1980 Broadcasting Act which in turn laid the foundations of Channel 4:

'...We see the fourth channel as a challenge to broadcasters... we do not see the fourth channel as an addition to plurality of outlets, but as a force for plurality in a deeper sense. Not only could it be a nursery for new forms and new methods of presenting ideas, it could also open the door to a new kind of broadcast publishing...'

I explained that both the New Left and the New Right in the 1980's were attracted to independent production due to its anti-monopolistic and anti-bureaucratic character in which the role of the individual as opposed to over-mighty corporations was emphasised. Thus the publisher model and Channel 4 were born, in 1982. The key feature of the publisher model was that it would commission programmes from outside the organisation. In theory the wide open nature of the publisher model compared very favourably with the producer broadcaster type typified by the BBC and ITV at the time and promised to be a powerful new source of plural democracy.

The new publisher broadcasting model, it was believed, would also help to achieve what had been impossible in the age of monopoly: the decentralisation of the television industry. In a world in which there were going to be hundreds of channels and even more independents who could set up shop wherever they liked, there was no reason for the television industry to be so heavily concentrated in one place. Nor was there any reason for the new television fraternity to be so tied to the broadcasters. The makers of television programmes should be set free to revitalise British broadcasting. It would be good for them. Good for the economy. Good for democracy.

Not surprisingly, the arrival of these newly enfranchised, free-thinking, anti-monopolists was hardly greeted as good news by the broadcasters whose power they sought to usurp. Bloody battles were bound to ensue and it was an unequal struggle; the broadcasters had all the power, the independents none. The publisher model gradually got off the ground eventually spreading its tentacles to the BBC and ITV.

In fact, the publisher model was not without its problems -as the indies were to learn to their cost. While power was very distilled in the producer-broadcaster model, the publisher model promised more than it could deliver. The new breed of commissioning editors proved to be immensely powerful in relation to the independents from whom they were to buy in programming. They controlled the airwaves and the funds. In practice the independents were hopelessly exposed. There were too many independents. Too few outlets. The system was totally unbalanced.

In response, the indies decided they wanted a place at the table where the voices of people that mattered were heard and they were determined to get it. This meant targeting the body politic. The broadcasters were never going to give up their power lightly or without a fight.

At first the quest for institutional power for the indies focused on the proposal to introduce a 25% independent production quota. The idea was that the terrestrial broadcasters would be forced to buy in 25% of their programming. It was anathema to the broadcasters and sent shockwaves through organisations like the BBC when it was first mooted. However it was music to the ears of Tory Prime Minister Margaret Thatcher in whom the indies found a willing champion. Commissioned by Mrs Thatcher, the Report of the Committee on Financing the BBC published in 1986 chaired by Professor Alan Peacock characterised British broadcasting as a 'comfortable duopoly' - BBC and ITV. It proposed a 40% independent production quota to apply to both. The Peacock Committee sensed the dawning of a new age in which a plethora of new television channels and electronic publishing would liberate the viewer and the production process itself. To paraphrase Peacock the new consumer sovereignty would put the viewer in the driving seat for the first time. They could buy programming from the widest possible array of sources and options.

Peacock viewed the indies as a key driving force in the political and economic revolution he envisaged. In economic terms the independents would promote competition and diversify supply. In political terms, he thought they would help to bring about a more mature citizenry based on consumer choice. The indies skillfully persuaded the Thatcher government they were like-minded. While the 40% quota was not implemented following lobbying from the commercial sector, in 1987 the Home Office issued a directive stating that the BBC and ITV would have to buy in 25% of their programmes and to reach that target within 5 years. The BBC and ITV complied. By 1992 the percentage of ITV programming supplied by the indies reached 22.3 %. By 1994 the BBC figure was 24%.

The definition of qualifying hours and independence under the quota were set out in the Statutory Instrument The Broadcasting (Independent Productions) Order. Under the Order qualifying programmes were defined as all categories of programming except repeats and news. Independent productions were programmes not made by people employed by broadcasters.

Controversially independents wishing to qualify under the quota were not allowed to have a shareholding of more than 15% in a broadcaster or vice versa. While this measure was intended to maintain vertical disintegration, it limited the ability of some indies to grow. In 1995 the rule was changed to allow indies to own 25% of a broadcaster and vice versa.

In tandem with the UK initiative, in 1989, the European parliament introduced its own system for original television and film production shown in Europe, Television Without Frontières. Under the Directive, TV stations were to be obliged to ensure that the majority of the programmes they transmitted, either original productions or acquired purchased programmes, came from European programme makers and that at least 10% of new programmes made by independent producers were of European origin.

While the 25% quota gave the official stamp of approval to the indies, it failed to give them the rights to ownership of their own material. Once the broadcaster had bought the programme from the indie broadcaster, under the new rule would be free to sell it on elsewhere, licensing its use to anyone he chose and for his own gain. This was a fatal flaw.

Charles Denton the former Chairman of PACT and **CEO of Zenith Productions** speaking to me in the 1993/94 period and quoted in my **LSE study**:

"RED by James Hogan"

'...If you don't have Rights you're in a business which is working for fees -and production fees are on a pretty tight basis and look like continuing on a pretty tight basis -you are on a bicycle riding on the spot- attempting to keep balance -attempting to keep the next production coming through the door and really barely feeding the overhead of most independent producers...'

Many indies hoped that the new Broadcasting Act 1990 would provide an additional boost. In fact it proved to be a mixed blessing. Its legacy is still felt today. The Act introduced the idea of competitive tendering for the ITV terrestrial licences coupled with a blind cash bid. Overnight it increased the amount of money that the ITV companies as a whole had to pay to the Exchequer from £126 million to over £300 million. This had two effects, neither very helpful to the indies. Following the introduction of the Act and award of licences, there was a squeeze on costs and a concentration on entertainment programming to maximise ad revenue. While two of the successful bidders were publisher broadcasters -Carlton TV and Meridian- old style documentary was clearly on the wane. Thames had lost its licence. The mix of genres narrowed. As a result the shrinkage of old style documentary went on unabated. The City had taken over commercial TV. No surprise the indies were in for a very rough ride.

The impact of the 1990 Broadcasting Act was felt immediately. In its wake, I recorded the following observation from two commercial broadcasters at the sharp end that I quote in my 1996 study:

Robert Southgate, Managing Director of Central Broadcasting at the time from my LSE study:

'The broadcaster is very much more conscious of what in his schedule works, is much more conscious now than he ever was three or four years ago of the demographics that he has to satisfy. He's much more conscious of presenting and promoting all the tricks we have, in order to satisfy the advertiser. We are much more reliant on research, research before programming at the ideas stage -getting through the pilot stage- putting the pilots out to research. All these things are a product of the fact that we are much more commercial than we used to be...'

Roger James, at the time, Controller Facatual Programmes, Central Television from my LSE study:

'... one is aware that one is operating in an environment where there is more financial realism... one doesn't always have the resources to throw at difficult investigative programmes... when you take those things on they cost you a lot of money in defending yourself in court... if they go wrong they cost a lot of money in paying up damages... I think it is unrealistic to think one isn't influenced by those things...'

In my LSE 1996 study, I analysed the democratic potential of the indies and compared it with the economic reality at that time. I wrote:

"RED by James Hogan"

'It is demonstrable that independents are a potentially very valuable source of democratic expression yet they are also a very weak and vulnerable one'

'The ability of independents to extend democratic representation and accountability is severely limited by the political economy in which they operate.'

'Independents juxtapose what they view as the monopolistic and bureaucratic nature of the broadcasters with their own strongly individualistic imperative. The value of that imperative lies in the importance it places on the ability and willingness to think and act for themselves. They are a natural source of diversity and plurality. They are spiritually well-suited to playing the part of critical witnesses.'

From a democratic perspective it matters who makes television programmes, why they make them and how. After all, provenance denotes meaning and bestows political legitimacy.

In my 1996 study I noted the fact that the flat and open-ended character of the typical indie and the independent spirit embodied therein increased the number of points of entry into the industry, lowered barriers and increased the number of new faces and volume of new voices. The LSE study:

Alex Graham, Managing Director, at the time managing director, Wall To Wall productions from my LSE study:

'... for many years there were basically two types of programme-making cultures in this country... there was the BBC culture... largely Oxbridge-dominated... television run very much like the civil service... selection based on ' the right kind of chap'... 'chap' being the pejorative word in many cases... then you had the ITV culture... slightly more 'jack the lad', slightly more Essex man approach... to television... that became accentuated in the 80's...'

Christopher Hurd, at the time, Joint Managing Director, Fulcrum Productions from my LSE study:

'... It has allowed a lot of new people to enter the industry as programme makers or as producers, or as programme idea generators. We have employed quite a lot of people who have no qualifications for the job in terms of formal broadcast qualifications... with researchers, it's sometimes a policy to employ people who have never worked in television before but who have specialist knowledge and the right approach to the job... that would have been absolutely inconceivable ten years ago...'

"RED by James Hogan"

I also quoted **David Elstein** (at the time with **BSKYB)** who put his finger on the ever-present tension in the relationship between the independents and the broadcaster:

'It is in the interests of the tiger to have deer for lunch. That's the nature of the industry. Not to encourage deer to grow horns and sharp teeth and indeed eighty mile an hour running speeds. Tigers would not flourish.'

In 1996 the indies were struggling. The new licencing regime which I describe in Chapter 3 had not yet come into being. In those days the sector was divided into two very distinct segments which I described in the following terms, noting that the economic conditions in which the independent production sector operated placed severe limits on its ability to promote democratic representation and accountability:

'The picture in 1996. It is clear from the evidence compiled from the files on well over two hundred independent production companies held at Companies House and the data supplied by PACT that the overwhelming majority of independents in the United Kingdom are producers of entertainment programmes of one sort or another... While companies operating at this level have injected a great deal of creative energy into broadcasting, adding choice and innovation, even they are limited by the flawed economics of 'stand-alone' independent television production... '

'The problems experienced at the top of the market are visited with a vengeance on the lower orders of independent production which are populated largely by factual programme makers. Those operating at this level tend to be unable to command big budgets and are in no position, by and large, to invest in broadcast outlets of their own or even to retain the rights to the programmes they make which, in any case, have very little value in the secondary market. The bulk of the independent community is made up of tiny companies which are little more than conduits for freelance producers who specialise in factual programming but who have very little freedom of manoeuvre to think or act independently. They are, in truth, very dependent on the power and patronage of the broadcaster who has the daunting task of sorting through thousands of programme proposals every year and choosing, at best, approximately four percent.'

These are some of the comments I gathered from the first wave of independent producers who were acutely aware of their plight:

'There are a lot of independent production companies. There are so many scrabbling for work. They resemble the pathetic dockers struggling for the last jobs in 'On The Waterfront'.'

'I've seen, particularly small independents behave in an extraordinarily timid way with commissioning editors... you are so dependent on the next commission that the great danger is that you aren't independent at all.'

'The whole customer-client relationship is a difficult one and it puts an awful lot of pressure on independents to be amicable... not to cause a fuss... not to argue... one has resisted going into battle because one is anxious about the next job'

'...the weakness of independents is that there is such over-capacity... particularly in factual programmes... I don't know how you find the good ideas... identify the good ideas from the bad and more importantly... how you sustain the good independents... how you give them enough business to cultivate them... let them develop their talents... that's a major problem...'

'...the BBC and ITV haven't yet come to terms with independents... they deal with us... occasionally we think that we may graduate from being something on the bottom of their shoe... but not just yet...'

'...the hall mark of these relationships is that they are very unequal basically and that inequality between who is, if you like, buying the programme and the person who is trying to sell it, is greatly enhanced when you look at the relationship between independent companies and publisher broadcasters... And the more pressure that there is on costs then the greater will be the degree of disadvantage to the weaker partner...'

In its first incarnation, therefore, the independent production sector was so weak it could not realise its full democratic potential. The people best suited to realising its potential were the crowds of factual documentary makers who were the weakest of all in economic terms. The economics of broadcasting kept the great majority of them pitifully enfeebled in terms of their relationship with the broadcaster and shut them out. 'Let A Thousand Flowers Bloom simply didn't happen. It would be better re-named 'The Era of Lost Souls'.

'...the first thing that hit me when I went independent was how lonely it was -just three of us- I took my then secretary with me and hired another secretary and we sat in this little office and looked at each other all day. And when you go to the lift, there is no one you know coming out of it. It sounds daft and quite pathetic but it's very, very important. You miss crowds of people. I worked in a company with getting on for sixteen hundred employees in the building... You miss brain-storming... you miss the adrenalin of people...

'You don't notice people vanish. They just vanish. A lot of small independent producers are gone... a lot of people have left the business... not just producers and directors... but a lot of support people, production managers, wardrobe people, all that side of things...

"RED by James Hogan"

'A lot of people have gone, a lot of disenchanted people...'

When the floodgates opened up in the eighties and in theory anyone could pitch ideas to the broadcasters notably Channel 4, it was mayhem. The system could not cope either because it didn't want to because it was against the interests of those in power, or simply because it was overwhelmed. There were many casualties.

The early independents were great enthusiasts. They wanted to believe that the independent sector would grow and grow and that there would be plenty of work to go around. The spirit of the times was captured by the admirable **David Lloyd who as Senior Commissioning Editor for Channel 4** pioneered the 'Let A Thousand Flowers Bloom' philosophy. **This is what he told me in my 1996 LSE study**:

'...there is a growing type who will prosper in the current circumstances... people who don't carry much infrastructure or cost with them... who have a great variety of manners of working... they will go to a medium size company and ally with them... to get a more sellable product... sometimes a full-scale colour feature for The Sunday Times... in their case it will be varied and adventurous by which I mean it will be enterprising... they will probably have a rather profitable time because none of

the true headaches of independent production are their problem...
a lot of Dispatches work is conducted by such people... people
who are trained journalists... although this is not the only or even
the main paradigm it is a very interesting example of who is
fitting into this industry...'

Eternal optimism was endemic. Added to which was the fact that
the all-consuming nature of the TV production process tended to
make them focus on the job in hand rather than looking out and
beyond. A quote from **Denise O'Donoghue, founder of Hat Trick
Productions** speaking to me in the mid-90s **from my LSE study**:

'The intensity of production means... you get a commission...
you're in production... you think it's going to go on forever...
you've got your idea off the ground... you don't see life beyond
that... production fee... which you've probably compromised on in
the first place... the production fee that is supposed to sustain
you... the pathetic margins we get are swallowed up before you
look around... most producers don't know what they need to
survive...'

This story recorded in my LSE study makes the same point only
more dramatically;

**Bernard Clark, Executive Producer, Clark TV from my LSE
study**:

'One particular fateful day which, from memory was October 4th
1991 -the day when the franchises for ITV were announced for the

beginning of '93- suddenly TVS was not there. We had done a lot of work for TVS. Within one minute it was gone. On that one day, I basically lost three and a half million pounds of our turnover. *On that one day* we were gone... the company. '

Economic dependency has always tied independents very closely to the broadcasters. The consequences of falling out of favour or disappearing from the scene are dire for people who are in charge of such companies. When that happens people disappear. Past awards and accolades amount to naught. A friend of mine - once one of the country's top and toughest investigative TV producers - who I bumped into in 2010- told me 'Everyone I know is unemployed.'

The steady erosion of the independent spirit got underway in the 1990s. The economics of broadcasting had effectively self-censored the indies who had to come to terms with the fact that television was becoming a very largely entertainment-led medium and that if they wanted to survive the independents would have to service the needs of the new system and in particular the specific requirements of the broadcaster whose eyes would always be on ratings and revenue in the years ahead. In the following chapter I chart the re-birth of the indies after 2003 as a much stronger economic force but one that remains vulnerable on its democratic potential.

With these issues in mind I recently conducted the following interview with **Roger Bolton the former Editor of BBC TV Tonight and BBC TV Panorama, ITV This Week and Today presenter of BBC Radio Feedback**. I worked with Roger at the BBC. I know him to be a thoroughly honest man and a fearless one in pursuit of the truth. In my experience he has always understood the important role of television in a democracy. After he left ITV, he too became an independent factual programme maker.

This is what he had to say:

What developments have you seen in independent production in the last 10 years and what's changed?

'When independent production started, obviously there were some people who saw it as a way to make money but, mainly, it was a banked up series of people with ideas they wanted to explore and, perhaps, a more opinionated programme they wanted to make; and they felt constrained, too constrained, by the departments they were in. But, within a relatively short time those so-called left wing radicals, and there were some right wing radicals, but left wing radicals, had become preoccupied with making money or, in some instances, just staying alive, if you like, in commercial terms because it became very clear, very early on, and particularly in the last 10 years that there is no money whatever to be made in individual investigative documentary programmes and they are extremely difficult to make and you usually lose money.

"RED by James Hogan"

So, effectively, unless you are given a long running series by a broadcaster, for example like Unreported World, it's virtually impossible to have a significant sized indie doing current affairs. Two reasons. One is the sheer difficulty of doing it. You can't deliver easily to a fixed budget because of various reasons. And the second is because it has no value, subsequently. Usually it's perishable, very quickly. And so in terms of making money, having secondary broadcast and whatever in various outlets, it's a no, no, really.

So, the people who've tended to do it insofar as they do it, have been loners, one-offs, freelancers whose companies exist, as it were, only for that individual programme and even they have found it extremely difficult. '

I wrote, in 1996 about -when I covered the growth of the independent sector- I talked about the desire to let 1,000 flowers bloom. Have those flowers died?

'Most of them have died. There will always be the maverick who finds working within a large organisation difficult. But, those mavericks tend to go and work for a number of independent companies where possible and if they are outstanding, absolutely outstanding, will find backing.

It's very difficult to find mavericks running independent production companies now because the difficulty of actually staying in business is so great that your maverick tendencies have got to be severely curtailed.

If I take my own company, for example, Flame Television, which ran for about 10 years and I had another company beforehand, we never made a profit until the last three years. We kept going but we kept going by having a very small core staff and recruiting people when we could. And it meant that even one year making good programmes was no guarantee of the next. The only time we started to make money was when we got into daytime programming, particularly doing something called Heir Hunters which was successful, low-budget. It worked in daytime so we would get an order of 40 for the following year. You can start to employ people on long term contracts. We then started to make money out of that because we had, seven or eight series of that. They get repeated. You make money on the music and so on. So, you start, for the first time, to make a profit and for a first time to be able to offer people reasonably long contracts and to build a team together for about the first time.

So, the salvation for us was making daytime programming and, therefore, the only one-offs that we ever made after that were the ones where we really cared passionately about a particular subject and it became a sort of loss leader and they were possible because we were making money elsewhere. But, until that point we'd only just survived despite having, you know, winning odd awards and things like that.

I think what has happened, which maybe was always the case but has become clearer now, is that any suggestion that independents have any real power over commissioning in the factual area is virtually nil. The only power you have is if one was backed and you have an immensely successful programme, at which point you have an element of power. But, until that moment the power entirely resides with the commissioning editors. And if you have the good fortune to find in a broadcaster a commissioning editor who wishes, has ambition for the form, not in terms of just for ratings and their own career, and they're rare to find, then it's possible to prosper. Prosper in a real sense of doing good work. Without that, without that patron, if you like, it's nigh on impossible.'

Has documentary morphed into factual entertainment?

'Yes in the last maybe 10 years, slightly longer... documentary can be very popular and it can be relatively cheap compared to drama and other forms of entertainment. But, then, that documentary tends increasingly to be about -how shall I put it- about some of the most... either about the most extreme forms of human behaviour or the most extreme moments in life.

I mean, you look at something like 24 hours in A&E which is now being done with sort of rigged television, you would have to say on any level that is superb. It's a very fine documentary series. It combines very intimate observations of what happens in A&E together with human stories which are, by any standards, touching...'

Now, the danger is that it is starting to become much formatted. On the other hand it is good documentary, it does reflect life, it does take you places that surprise you and, although you know people are being chosen to a degree because they conform to certain stereotypes, in a way the individuals are dictating the coverage. Whereas, in most documentaries now, it seems to me, the commissioning editors have a view of the elements they require, the people they require and, therefore, you go out to find those things in people which will not, as it were, reflect reality but reflect the pre-conceptions of the commissioning editor. Or, they will say to you –which was notoriously the case with the series about people swapping wives –there has to be a crisis at the end of Part 2, and there has to be this at the end of Part 3, so you are structuring reality to fit the format needs of television. So, you still get… on the other hand, again to qualify what I've said, the change in technology has meant that you can get people with a camera, operating in the most extraordinary circumstances and producing documentaries which are remarkable because of access.

But, I think I would say of that type of documentary, is that it essentially shows the visible. And the visible at times of crisis. The less visible, shall we say, of the invisible; or the change over time that occurs, that becomes more difficult. And, certainly, the really interesting and opinionated and challenging documentary in terms of ideas is extremely rare.

The power is in two hands; the commissioning editors and those who have the talent that can deliver high audiences. And if you don't belong to either of those groups you struggle and, increasingly… and you can also see the dangerous downside of that, for example, would be that it's not a coincidence, the number of freelance cameramen who've been injured or freelance journalists who are often getting killed at the moment, it's partly changing world events. It's also partly because they are freelance because nobody is paying for them, because they only get paid, as it were, on results, the risks that they take.'

What has been the trend in investigative journalism?

'Well, I think there has been a confusion here, in some ways. People think that there is more information available than ever before; and in one sense that is true. There is more published information, it's more easily available than before and that gives you the illusion that more information… well, more information is available but it's of a certain type, it's essentially that which has already been published.

If by investigative journalism you mean that which places in the public square something which has not been widely known before and, particularly, something that is difficult and embarrassing and so on, that has become extraordinarily difficult. On the one hand I think more things are open to public gaze. The quality of analysis by some journalists, Nick Robinson and I would say Economics and Finance editors in the BBC is very high quality. But, quite often that's the case because their contacts tell them things and they want something placed in the public area.

I think if you talk about investigative journalism in the sense of putting it into the public square, say, things which others might not want you to find out which are demonstrably in the public interest, it's taken a massive step backwards because it's this question of patrons, again. And it's a question of an understanding of what is needed.

I interviewed **Peter Taylor, BBC Panorama reporter for a BAFTA tribute** and he made it very clear that the most important thing for him was looking after his contacts. And I asked him in detail what that meant. It meant going back and back to Northern Ireland, to his contacts, not necessarily when there was… or, actually, more often when there wasn't a programme in mind, just to keep them up. And he told one extraordinary story about… the man who was the go-between, between the Government and the IRA, told him the story in confidence 10 years before he allowed Peter to tell it. So, when it comes up and when it's an exclusive, in Ireland it's not an accident. Peter Taylor has been getting on the plane, backwards and forwards, and talking to people and committing for a long time. Now, he's been able to do that in the past because he's had a broadcaster and a sponsor, who have let him do it. But, the temptation is to say now "if you've got a big story, yes, we will give you the resources to go and do it." That assumes the big story suddenly just appears. And too often it can mean when a big story appeared, go after it and get it and do it better than anybody else but, actually, it's a story that's already in the public domain.

So, those stories you can only find out by committing yourself to an area, to pursuing it, talking to people, relentlessly focusing on it for a long time. That's almost impossible to do now because you need a raft, a whole range of money before there is even a programme in prospect. The commissioning editor will not only want to know what the story is, completely, he'll also want you to guarantee you can deliver it within a limited period.

Well, the whole nature of these programmes is that they're not like that. The great advantage in the past, if you were a programme editor, and it's still possible, just, with Dispatches for example and should be possible with Panorama... is that if an editor has 40, 45 programmes then what you can do is you can let people run off for six weeks, whatever, and explore what they want to. If they can't then deliver the programme you bring them up, give them something to do which you know you want done and then let them return to the subject which means that they can keep subjects, contacts, warm for a long period and then deliver. And, if you've got the budget of 46 programmes you can always say at a certain point", it's costing us a lot, we'd better do an interview with the Prime Minister, or the Leader or the Opposition which costs us relatively little and means, and therefore we have more money available."

So, the ability to follow a story over a long period before you finally deliver it is only possible with extraordinary backing from a commissioning editor or within a programme, a series which has budgets that can be moved around.'

Chapter III
The Re-birth of the Indies and the economics of self-censorship

The 1990s proved to be a killing field for the majority of independents. The romance had gone. The dream had evaporated. Many were falling by the wayside. The original economic model was well and truly broken. The situation was accurately described in a report written by Oliver & Ohibaum and commissioned by PACT the Producers Alliance for Cinema and Television - the indies trade body. Written in July 2013, it stated:

'More than ten years ago, the UK independent sector was going in reverse as the dominant PSBs (Public Service Broadcasters) sought to increase their share of UK production activities by protecting their large in-house production units and working increasingly with tied production companies such as Granada or Freemantle. With over 90% of UK commissioning spent coming via the four main PSB groups at that time, this vertical integration squeeze in the market meant that the UK independent production sector was losing share and lacked the critical mass to invest in growth and diversification. Critically producers also lacked the opportunity to own the rights to their commissioned output meaning that companies in the sector could not build up an asset base against which to trade and raise capital.'

The political economy that dominated broadcasting before the arrival of the indies in the 1980's reasserted itself in a brutal show of power in the 1990's virtually wiping out already painfully thin margins for those independents who were lucky enough to be still making programmes. The Report continues:

'The strategies of the integrated producer/broadcasters at this time were relatively clear. For the BBC, there was a strong incentive to retain and defend the scale of its in-house production activities. As a result, its use of the independent sector was designed to meet the regulated quota for qualifying programming (which was set at 25% of qualifying hours) but not substantially exceed it. For ITV there was potentially a dual motivation as retaining a large in-house production division also benefited it in picking up 3rd party commissions from other UK broadcasters. This combination of incentives meant that independent producers were limited in their market share, had few opportunities to grow revenues beyond the mandated PSB quotas and found it difficult to grow basic production margins beyond the industry standard fees of 5% to 10%.'

The Independent Television Commission (ITC) Report at the time came to a similarly stark conclusion: ' the long-term growth of the UK independent sector had reversed between 1998 and 2001...' These were worrying days. The long-held ambition of the indies that one morning the Barbarians would be given the keys to the gates of heaven was disintegrating before their eyes. The idea that the indies would one day smash the political economy of broadcasting to pieces and end the dominance of the producer-broadcasters looked like a pipe dream.

The independent production sector went into reverse at the end of the 1990s even at the top end where the most commercial of programmes were being produced. Between 1998 and 2001 the combined profits of the top 50 independents producers declined from £8.2M to £3.5M. The PACT commissioned report:

'This shows that even the largest independent producers at that time suffered from a lack of bargaining power with commissioners and that -as a result- the sector remained highly fragmented, was generating only a small annual surplus and hence only had very limited capability to reinvest in development and production.'

With the indies on their knees, PACT mounted a very effective campaign to improve their lot. Their chance came in the run-up to the 2003 Communications Act. Instead of lobbying for an increase in the size of the independent quota they argued - successfully- for new terms of trade. The 'terms of trade' signaled a radical break with the past - a shift away from the existing commissioning model in which broadcasters generally speaking acquired the rights to the programmes they commissioned including distribution rights. Under the new system broadcasters would purchase the primary rights but the indies would control and benefit from the exploitation of all other rights. The PACT commissioned report:

'In order to grow as a truly independent commercial sector in its own right, independent producers need a few market conditions to change, including:

Limits to broadcasters' dominance in rights and their incentives to warehouse them - providing indies with the opportunity to own their own creative assets in the long-term; having a greater opportunity to compete for commissions over and above the minimum PSB quotas; and the opening up of supply relationships in other countries, driven by changes in how broadcasters source new ideas and share risks.'

The impact of the new terms of trade was quickly felt and quite dramatically. The fact that indies now owned their own IP meant that they received the benefit of owning winning formats like 'Who Wants To Be A millionaire?' and 'American Idol'. The re-birth of the sector also attracted external capital from private equity houses and venture capitalists fuelling consolidation and the arrival of Super-indies such as All Three Media and Freemantle. The PACT commissioned report notes the turn-around:

'Since the terms of trade were introduced in 2004 the UK independent production sector has grown to become a £2.8 billion industry...

The UK independent production sector today is a global leader in developing and commercialising intellectual property, doing so with broadcasters, aggregators and platform owners across the huge diversity of programme output that is commissioned each year in the UK and in every other major TV market. UK independent producers have been at the heart of some of the most iconic brands in UK TV history, whether developing some of the biggest drama and entertainment franchises (eg Idol, X-Factor) or the most popular game show formats (eg Millionaire) shown in markets around the world...'

The by-product of these changes has been to accelerate the trend towards entertainment at the cost of old style documentary and hard-hitting investigative journalism. Investors want profits. So do the indies -especially after the hardship so many endured. In the same way that the 1990 Broadcast Act handed the broadcasters over to the City, the experience of the indies as once powerless suppliers eventually led them too into the arms of the City. In the process television became just another commodity - like everything else. And there is a warning from history. The PACT commissioned report:

'Without the three main components of the UK independent production sector regulations -i.e. production quotas, ownership rules and terms of trade- in place in the market there would be considerable risk to many UK indies. The pressures which drove the adverse market conditions in the late 1990's still exist today to a large extent. The majority of original content expenditure still comes from the four main PSB network groups and the BBC and ITV still have strong incentives to maintain in-house production divisions.

'In recent years we have seen that the market forces towards broadcaster/producer vertical integration remain strong as demonstrated by News Corporation acquiring Shine, NBCU acquiring Carnival and Monkey Kingdom and ITV continuing to acquire producers internationally...'

In democratic terms the political economy of broadcasting and the ever vulnerable position of the indies within it throws the onus back onto the broadcaster. History shows that the indies are constrained by the power of the broadcaster and by the economics. The over-supply that characterised the indie market in the 1980s followed by recession crushed the plural democratic potential of the independent spirit. The indies survive today because they have morphed into the broadcaster -entering into a customer- supplier relationship, no more, no less. It is not an accident that where the indies can innovate -which they do- it is almost entirely within the wrapper of the entertainment format. As one former director general of the BBC once told me 'television is just about money'.

The Chief Executive of PACT, John McVay, played a central role in the re-birth of the indies after 2003. In the following interview specially conducted for this book he gives his account of how the revival came about and the nature of the maturation process:

What are the big successes of the independents and independent companies?

'The big successes are taking, building share of network commissioning, so the indie sector is now about 50% of all network programming; building scalable international businesses where prior to that they were small domestic, sub-scale enterprises; and, thirdly, because of that able to raise deficit finance to put into UK programming which has been to the advantage of all the broadcasters in that they no longer fully finance production. By the end of 1996, we were a service sector where we worked for an agreed fee which was managed by our buyers. By the time I started in '01 those margins were down to about 3% so we were going bust fast and being managed out of business by our buyers. Now, producers are able, because they own IP, to sell rights on to the global markets or domestic markets and to get the rewards of their success.'

And would it be true to say that in order to serve the audience, producers have moved away from documentary towards factual entertainment?

'No, no... I think the documentary skills are still very evident in a lot of the programming we see. 24 Hours in A&E, fixed camera rig, beautifully crafted as a narrative, documentary narrative; I just think what's happened is that skill set has moved into other ways of mixed genre, across genre programming.

So, one of the first formatted shows which broke out was Wife Swap. You might have done a documentary about a poor family with their kids and then another documentary about the rich family with their kids. What Wife Swap did was swap family members and create a tension in the narrative. So, I would say Steven Lambert who conceived all that, trained in documentary at the BBC, I would say documentary is still live, it's just that it's different now for mainstream prime time television. '

I wrote about "Let 1000 Flowers Bloom" in '96. Do you think that culture, '80s, '90s, the optimism, has that gone?

'I think my problem has always been with 1000 flowers blooming is that under the older model where everyone was controlled by the buyers it was all 1000 very small flowers blooming; un-investable in terms of corporate financing; un-scalable in terms of ability to grow outside of your own domestic market under the one or two people who commission you; and the buyer controlled everything.

So, I come from a tradition where I don't think creative people should be starving in a Victorian garret, I think creative people who come up with successful ideas which have commercial value should get the rewards for their creativity. So, I've never been a fan of 1000 flowers blooming, I always thought it was a mistaken policy. And when I came to Pact... thankfully I had a Board of Directors who had been one of those... some of those 1000 flowers blooming... They were thoroughly sick, fed up of it and wanted to stop being poor and not being able to control their own businesses. '

What happened to the people? Have they just gone?

'No, most of them are still in business or they've sold their companies and started new businesses. Absolutely. I have seen a… I mean, it was one of our intents in 2001 which was to create a repeat entrepreneur culture so that we didn't lose people at a certain point who just cashed out or gave up which was the big problem. People just went bust and gave up and they got lost because they couldn't have a sustainable business. We thought that was detrimental to our overall ecology so by giving people the ability to consolidate and create value and ultimately keep some of the value when they sold the business we've seen a wave of new entrepreneurs, many of the guys who were the first people to set up indies. '

How would you describe the new culture of the indies of today?

'I think the culture of today is even more ambitious. If you're an independent you don't' have to just work in the UK you can jump on a plane and be commissioned in America tomorrow. If you're a producer with good ideas and an ability to deliver them the world is wide open, there are more and more territories and networks that are desperate for good producers. So, if you're a British producer which carries a certain amount of cache in the market there's nothing to stop you getting your ideas made and that's why you got into it in the first place, was to get your ideas made.

So, I think the world we see now is full of opportunities. We don't see any barriers to companies being successful. You have to work really hard. You have to travel a lot more. The market is more competitive but being an indie was never easy. And also there's a very low barrier to entry and a very low barrier to failure in the independent sector. If you don't get a show away you're not going to survive. '

What drives the indies of today?

'They want to make their shows. They want to get their ideas on air.'

To entertain?

'Yes, all the time. They still want to do that. That's still the driver. How you do it and who you do it with is very different but all the people I know are creative producers. They have ideas that burn in their head that they want to get made and they want to go and find someone who'll give them money to go and make them. That part of the business has never changed. Who you are selling to, where you are selling, how you finance, what you own, all those bits are very different but... the driver is exactly the same as it's always been, it's you who want to get that programme made and you have to keep going until someone does say yes. That's never changed.'

What was the significance of the '03 legislation?

'The 2003 Communications Act which introduced the legislation that governs the four PSBs in terms of their ownership and control of our copyright. We own the copyright, they can't. The law requires Channel 4, ITV, 5 and the BBC to agree terms with a body representing producers, us, to have standard contracts which set out the licence they get from the money they put up for the programme but they can't own the copyright in the programme. Prior to that, since the advent of Channel 4 in the early '80s, all broadcasters, apart from ITV ironically, owned the copyright and producers' works. So, we'd make it, we'd get a fee but we wouldn't't get any of the rewards if it was successful...'

Is content king or does the power still lie with the broadcaster?

'No, content is king... because, if you look at the advent of all the new platforms, Netflix, Hulu, Amazon, they are all desperate to get the best content and our experience of the international markets which we've been very active in for the past seven or eight years is that the rest of the world is wanting great quality content and they come to the UK and the US as the first ports of call for acquiring great finished programming or acquiring formats for production in their own territory... Well basically, it's a producers market because all the broadcasters are desperate for the best ideas and the best producers. Under the four PSBs my rights are protected so I can shop to the different buyers. If they try and be very difficult to me or not give me the deal I want I can go somewhere else.

If I go to the CABSAT sector because the four PSBs are regulated there is a ripple effect in the rest of the market. So, if I go to Discovery or Nat Geo or Sky, they want the best ideas, they are going to have to cut me a deal to make it attractive for me to go and talk to them.

So, it's a lot more balanced in terms of the dialogue now. Clearly, if I'm a drama producer of a certain type of drama, say, Period, there are only going to be two buyers, ITV and BBC. So, while we've seen a readjustment between buyer and supplier power, so it's a bit more level now, there are still, it is still the case that the PSBs account for 90% of all programme commissioning and in certain genres there are only two people you can sell to. So, their dominance is still there. And if you want to work you're still going to have a conversation about what the deals are and what you're going to do for that...'

What do you think the state of investigative journalism is, in the UK?

'I think it's alive and well. I just think it's moved to other platforms in other ways. If you look at places like VICE, I think investigative journalism is thriving in a digital era. It's just not... the big mass World in Action type shows that we used to have at a time of scarce distribution... the internet is full of various sites where there are a number of journalists who are investigating various things. Some of them might just be lifestyle things; some might be punchier than that; you know, the political decisions made in other countries in the world. VICE is clearly coming up fast and causing the mainstream broadcasters concerns. I think that's just the reinvention of investigative journalism. And that's probably a good thing. It's just that not a lot of it is going to end up on mainstream television, I don't think.'

Because?

'Because I think audiences (1) mainstream television may not be as fast as some of these new internet platforms are. And (2) I think there is limited bandwidth on what people will watch now. The UK has more channels to choose from than anywhere else on the planet, more than America.'

Are the economics of terrestrial investigative journalism broken?

'No, I think the economics of any programme production are pretty robust. In fact, Ofcom just produced their next PSB review today and it shows that commercial free to air broadcasting advertising is up 4%. That's pretty good in the teeth of what's been one of the worst recessions so I would say that it's not a question of genre, it's a question of where does that sit in the schedule and how much capacity audiences have for that type of programming. If they were accessing it through other ways, through the internet, through other platforms, then they are maybe getting a lot of it already. So, I think what you see in the main networks are probably bigger, punchier pieces rather than lots of regular smaller pieces. '

Chapter IV

The near death of investigative journalism and the economics of self-censorship

In 1996 I thought that investigative journalism on terrestrial television was in Accident and Emergency. Today I believe it is close to death and desperately needs to be moved into Intensive Care. The inherent dependency of the indies on the broadcaster and the inherent inequality in the corporate structures, organisation and resources available to each leads to one singular conclusion. The democratic function of television lies squarely in the hands of the broadcasters. It is simply unrealistic and unfair to expect indies to carry the weight of this responsibility on their ultimately narrow shoulders. In this chapter, I examine the requirements needed to hold authority and individuals to account for wrong-doing through the medium of hard-hitting documentary and I look at the history and current position of the terrestrial broadcasters. I start with the commercial sector in this order: ITV, C4, C5 then turn to BBC TV to whom all roads lead in my central argument, namely, we need to understand the economic forces at work in 21st Century broadcasting and put in place an edict to overcome the current market failure. For edict by all means read the Charter so long as it is re-invented for the terrestrial space on television today.

In my 1996 study I quoted what I believe is a very good definition of exactly what investigative journalism is and why it is so important in the democratic function of television. It came from the **Editor of Granada TV: World In Action 1989 - 1992 - Nick Hayes from my LSE study**:

This is how he put it:

'... the central function of current affairs reporting is to cast a searchlight into dark areas... to lift up stones and see what's underneath them... in order to tell people what is going on in the world and how power is exercised... the best mark of a story is the one in which the people involved in that story don't want you to tell... and fight hell and high-water to stop you putting it out... it's not the only function of current affairs journalism... but it's a very important part... it's a particular discipline which needs particular resources and particular people to do it...'

Investigations fall into many categories. They include subjects such as the conduct of wars, extremism, corruption, fraud, sexual abuse... History shows that it is in these areas that freedom of speech and independence of mind are most valuable and yet always most at risk. The litmus test for the broadcasters therefore is their willingness to promote and defend a steady flow of investigations into wrong-doing. Anything less is a betrayal.

In the first instance it is important to understand the process involved in making investigative journalism for TV. Even today with light-weight technology the television process in itself is complex. It relies on a set of inter-related roles including commissioning, editorial, creative, financial, legal and administrative. Investigative journalism if it is to be turned into a watchable documentary demands a lot of resources. It also calls for a very special type of team work. Investigative programme-makers need to be very sure about themselves and about each other. It takes time to build trust. They also need to be very robust and resilient. The most common tactic used to discredit the findings of an investigation is to attack the people who made it. It matters who made the programme and why. So long as the broadcaster who commissioned the programme knows the people who made it and so long as he trusts them, he is in a much stronger position to defend it.

The vital importance of teams in the making of investigative television programmes is widely acknowledged by practitioners.

Roger James, Former Controller of Factual Programmes, Central Television from my LSE study:

'Teams are important. The team ethos is important. This building, and I say this building because in a sense people come and go but Charlotte Street has created an ethos -an atmosphere - which I think has been important and rubbed off on people. It's one of the few places where if a programme is going off the tracks... instead of celebrating someone else's misfortune... somehow there's a coming together of spirit... individuals who feel part of the Charlotte Street ethos roll up their sleeves and help people sort it out...'

Steve Haywood, Former Director, Just Television from my LSE study:

'...It's a very particular type of expertise that's required to do it... you can't just take a researcher off the street and drop them down and expect them to be able to do it... the source of the programme has to be built up... it's a matter of pride to me that prisoners in prisons... maintaining their innocence... will be much more inclined to write to us as a first port of call... that needs time to build up... '

Ray Fitzwalter, Editor World In Action, 1976-1988 from my LSE study:

'...you have to have the great strength that is to be gained from having a team of people who are highly organised, who have standards set for them, who have disciplines and know how they have to meet those disciplines in their research. It doesn't mean they won't make mistakes -they will- but when they do they will have to be responsible afterwards... they're called into the editor's office and they know there's going to be a fair examination of everything but if they're wrong, they're in trouble. They're on the line. That responsibility after the event is critical...'

While I believe that the economics of commercial television at the start of the 21st Century are such that it is very hard to see the likes of ITV ever returning to the good old days of World In

"RED by James Hogan"

Action and This Week, the history of the channel in this area is a very honourable and instructive one. In my 1996 study I examined the learnings from the making of Death On The Rock and the Birmingham Six. This is what I wrote:

'No programme demonstrates the importance of being absolutely certain about how and why an investigation was made than arguably the most controversial one of the lot, namely, 'Death On The Rock'. The fifty minutes special produced by Thames Television and transmitted on 28 April 1988, presented evidence that the three IRA terrorists shot dead by the SAS in Gibraltar - Mairaed Farrell, Daniel Mc Cann, Sean Savage- were victims of a 'Shoot To Kill' policy. This was contrary to what the Home Secretary Sir Geoffrey Howe, had told parliament, that is, the terrorists were shot after being challenged. Witnesses featured in the programme alleged that SAS soldiers opened fire without warning on two of the IRA bombers who had their hands in the air. One witness, Carmen Proetta, claimed that Sean Savage was shot in the back. The documentary which the government failed to have postponed, as it wanted, until after the inquest held in Gibraltar had taken place, provoked outrage in 10 Downing Street and in the Foreign Office. Mrs Thatcher told journalists that her reaction to the programme... 'Was not a question of being furious. It was much deeper than that.' 'Trial by television' she said or 'guilt by association is the day freedom dies.'

Sir Geoffrey Howe denounced the programme as 'a grossly and wholly improper piece of journalism'. In the face of extreme pressure on Thames Television for making the programme and on the IBA the Independent Broadcasting Authority for allowing it to be transmitted -both organisations stood full square behind the programme because they knew why it had been made, who made it, and how. As usual in the case of such a contentious programme, the IBA had viewed it before transmission and pronounced it... 'A responsibly-made documentary which assesses and analyses the role of the terrorist and the SAS in a thorough manner'. The Chairman of the IBA, Lord Thomson, refused to delay it on the grounds that to do so would simply provide the IRA with 'more oxygen of publicity'. The deliberate and ironic twist given by Lord Thomson to the famous phrase used by Mrs Thatcher to slap down the BBC Real Lives programme incensed the government and right-wing opinion which called for the abolition of the IBA which was deemed to have outlived its usefulness. The critics of the programme maintained the pressure up to and beyond the publication of the Windlesham Report, the independent enquiry into the making of the programme written by Lord Windlesham, a former Conservative Nothern Ireland and Home Office Minister and Richard Rampton QC. The Report which was published on 26 January 1989, cleared the programme of bias and of prejudicing the inquest on the three IRA terrorists shot dead in Gibraltar. The government responded by casting doubt on the integrity of the process undertaken by Lord Windlesham. Sir Geoffrey Howe said that Lord Windlesham, who was also formerly Chairman of a television company, had produced a report that was out of line with what most people believed. ' The inquiry', he said 'was conducted by the company which made the programme and it was not surprisingly'... trial of television, by television '. In the debate in parliament following the Windlesham Report, the government benches maintained the stance that Thames Television had acted irresponsibly. The Defence minister Lord Trefgarne led the charge:

"There is a place for investigative journalism but the freedom of the press is not to be treated as a licence to distort. It carries with it the duty to act with responsibility. Thames Television did not, in my judgement, live up to that duty... The report strikes me as a sad commentary on the standards now expected of the media. It is a great pity that it so regularly failed to expose the shortcomings of 'Death On The Rock'. '

Throughout the dark days of Death On the Rock, the IBA, Thames Television as the broadcaster and the production team remained steadfast and loyal to each other. You need teams to conduct investigations especially in extreme cases like Death On The Rock.

This quote from my LSE study:

Richard Dunn, The former CEO of Thames Television:

'One of the reasons I was prepared as Chief Executive to fight for 'Death On The Rock' was that we made it. I could walk down a corridor and there was Jonathan Dimbleby, Roger Bolton, Julian Manion. I pass them in the corridor... go up in the lift with them... there was a relationship there between that team of journalists and Barry Sales, David Elstein, my Chairman- Ian Trethowan -and me- we were all in it together...'

The ferocity of the attack by the Thatcher government on 'Death On The Rock' was felt by other companies in the ITV network.

In my LSE study Roger James, the former controller of factual programmes at Central television commented further:

'As a result of the aggressive stance that Margaret Thatcher's government took in terms of confronting broadcasters -to a degree the industry was, if not intimidated, it was certainly given pause for thought. I think when you've got a government that's prepared to take you on -however brave you are- you reflect how wise it is, in any given situation to do that...'

As with Thames Television so too with Granada TV of yesteryear. Some of the investigations for which the channel became famous could only have been made by keeping the same people on the payroll for several years, calling on their services as and when a new twist or turn in the story took place.

"RED by James Hogan"

The investigation into the circumstances surrounding the arrest
and imprisonment of the 'Birmingham Six' produced by the ITV
Granada Television programme World In Action over seven years
was probably the most tenacious and in-depth piece of
campaigning TV journalism ever undertaken in this country. It
was mounted step by step against the backdrop of immense
public hostility towards the alleged culprits and the implacable
opposition of the authorities directly involved. Understandably
there was a huge public outcry on 21 November 1974 when two
bombs planted by the IRA left twenty one people dead and one
hundred and sixty two people injured in a Birmingham pub.
Three days later the Birmingham Six were charged with murder.
Hugh Callaghan, Billy Power, Richard Mc Ilkenny, John Walker,
Gerald Hunter, Patrick Hill. Although they bitterly and
consistently protested their innocence, the Six were convicted in
August 1975 on twenty one counts of murder. The Court of
Appeal later refused to allow the men concerned to challenge the
convictions and stopped them being granted legal aid in order to
pursue a civil action against the police. For the next ten years they
languished in prison where they were ostracised and beaten.
There was no glimmer of light until October 1985 when World In
Action in the documentary entitled 'Who Bombed Birmingham?'
sensationally claimed that the Birmingham Six were innocent.
Several months earlier the World In Action production team had
been approached by the writer and journalist now the former
Labour MP, Chris Mullin, who was convinced someone else had
planted the Birmingham bombs. As the programme unearthed
more evidence, it produced three additional documentaries on the

story.

By January 1987 the Home Secretary felt that the volume of new material was such that the case should be referred back to the Court of Appeal. However, the Appeal was dismissed by the Court of Appeal presided over by Lord Chief Justice Lord Lane. In years to come he would be heavily criticised for the way in which he conducted proceedings. Undeterred World In Action ploughed on. Eighteen months later in July 1990, the programme declared that it knew the identity of the persons who planted the Birmingham pub bombs and transmitted an interview with one of them, in silhouette. Two months later, following the disclosure of new forensic evidence by the World In Action team that cast doubt on the confessions extracted by the police, the Home Secretary referred the case to the Court of Appeal for a second time. By then there was no turning back. On 27 March 1991, sixteen years after they had been sent to prison, the Birmingham Six were released. With the rule of law so obviously damaged, the government set up a Royal Commission into the workings of the Criminal Justice System. Three of the detectives who worked on the case were charged with perjury and conspiracy to pervert the course of justice.

The lesson for investigative TV journalism was evident. The World In Action investigation drew on the collective memory of the production team which was continually being updated as time passed and more information became available. Without that memory and the resources to be able to go on adding to it, it would have been impossible to overturn the convictions of the

"RED by James Hogan"

Birmingham Six. In my 1996 study I quote **Ray Fitzwalter the editor of World In Action in the period, 1976 to 1988**. This is what he told me:

'We would have a watching brief... We would be looking at certain developments. We poked at them. Sometimes we would discover something more and it would take a leap. At that stage we would have half a programme. We'd keep it on the shelf. Eventually it did build up and become like a roller-coaster. But if we had not had the continuity of people, of expertise, of documents, of contacts, we could never have got to the end of the tunnel.'

There is no disguising the fact that the loss of World In Action and This Week has greatly damaged ITV's journalism and made the citizenry of the UK a lot poorer. As such it is probably the best example of market failure in UK TV to the detriment of our democracy.

Unlike producer-broadcasters like ITV and the BBC, Channel 4 had to solve a riddle. As a publisher broadcaster supplied by tiny independents how it could have the best of both worlds -draw on fresh new blood to make investigations but overcome the inherent weakness of the indies? There had to be an answer. After all, the spirit of Channel 4 was inspired by plural democracy. When history came calling some years into the life of the channel, they found the answer. Channel 4 would act like a producer-broadcaster in defence of the indies when they came under intense pressure. This meant flexing institutional might under fire. To its great credit Channel 4 has kept faith with its regular investigative series, Dispatches, to this day.

Lightning is always momentous. When it hits, the TV producer - the broadcaster- you learn a lot about the animal. In the first five years of the life of Channel 4 the commissioning policy was to buy-in factual programmes from a very limited number of suppliers, no more than four or five, and to eschew almost entirely in-depth investigations. The policy then changed to what it was at the time to the 'Let A Thousand Flowers Bloom' era of the late eighties and early nineties. Three years into the life of the channel came the first test of its resolve. It was to cut its teeth on investigative journalism and what it takes to defend it when it became embroiled in a row over a documentary called 'M15's Official Secrets'. The programme was made by a small but very tenacious indie called Twenty Twenty. It featured Cathy Massiter who went on camera to tell what for many people was a deeply disturbing story of how she had been asked to sanction illegal activities in the course of the M15 surveillance operation on the Campaign For Nuclear Disarmament, CND, including the tapping of telephone conversations of trade unionists and two Labour MPs. By going public, Massiter placed herself in breach of the Official Secrets Act but she was willing to take the risk. So was Channel 4. The snag was the channel required the IBA to go along with their decision which as a statutory body it decided it could not do. To have done so the IBA believed would have been to commit a deliberate criminal offence. The programme which was due to be transmitted on 20 February 1985 did not go out. Instead it was returned to the offices of Twenty Twenty which distributed it on video cassette to MPs and other opinion formers.

"RED by James Hogan"

A furore ensued. Like a ball of string the issue began to unravel.
At first slowly. Then all in a rush, towards the end. The board of
Channel 4 which had not previously viewed the programme,
became involved. They watched it. Approved it. And asked the
IBA to think again. The IBA remained implacable. Its hands were
tied -by law.

The impasse was broken by the Attorney General who let it be
known that he had no intention of prosecuting anyone in
connection with the programme. The IBA then gave the go-ahead
for the public to view what so many people had already viewed in
private.

When I interviewed the **Executive Producer at Twenty Twenty,
Claudia Milne, for my LSE study** she was very clear about the
learnings from this episode in Channel 4's history.

She told me this:

'...the broadcaster has to be robust... I don't think it makes much
difference whether or not the programme is being made internally
or by an independent... they've got to be strong... the reason why
'M15's Official Secrets' was eventually shown on British television
was because Liz Forgan (C4's Commissioning editor of news and
current affairs at the time) insisted to the Channel 4 board that
they represent it to the IBA... she put her job on the line... she said

that now the Attorney General had said that neither Cathy Massiter nor the programme makers would be arrested... there was no longer any reason for this programme to remain banned and we should put it back to the IBA and say now it should be transmitted...'

The remit of Channel 4 and its unique funding formula allowed it to nurture a certain form of editorial defiance in its formative years.

The 1980 Broadcast Act enshrined the democratic and cultural role that the Fourth Channel as it was called initially was to play in British broadcasting. The IBA to whom it was to be answerable was to ensure that the channel contained 'a suitable proportion of matter calculated to appeal to tastes and interests not generally catered for by ITV... that a suitable proportion of the programmes were of an educational nature... and to encourage innovation and experiment in the form of content of programmes...' The new channel was to be distinctive and to complement rather than compete with ITV. The Act opened the door for the indies.

The new channel was also to be a hybrid -half public service broadcaster- half commercial broadcaster. It was on this basis that it was awarded its broadcast licence. If it failed to deliver on its remit it would simply be privatised. Under the famous Channel 4 funding formula, the channel was to be funded by the ITV contractors out of the advertising revenue generated by the channel with the safety net that if its income from advertising fell below 14 % of NAR -the total amount of advertising revenue achieved by the ITV companies would have to subsidise the new channel, giving it the equivalent of 2% of NAR. With this in mind

"RED by James Hogan"

I turn to 'The Committee'. It was to be a baptism of fire for channel 4 as a publisher broadcaster.

The Committee alleged that officers of the Royal Ulster Constabulary were amongst those involved in planning the systematic murder of Roman Catholics in Northern Ireland. According to the programme there was allegedly widespread collusion between members of the security forces, loyalist paramilitary groups and senior members of the business community, all of whom were members of a so-called Committee dedicated to the assassination of republicans in the province. The principal source of the exposé -source A- who was allegedly a member of the Committee was given a binding undertaking by the production company that made the programme, Box Productions, and by Channel 4, that he would remain anonymous. The source claimed to know the details of the murder of 19 Republicans at the hands of the Committee. He was interviewed in silhouette and his words were spoken by an actor to comply with the government ban at the time on interviews with people who were deemed to be representatives of proscribed paramilitary groups operating in Northern Ireland and to conceal his identity. The programme provoked a ferocious reaction form the authorities -especially the RUC.

Shortly after the programme was transmitted three officers from Scotland Yard visited the offices of Box Productions, served an order under the Prevention of Terrorism Act on the producer/managing director, Sean Mc Philemy, and demanded he handed over all material related to the making of The Committee. They also demanded to know the identity of source A. Channel 4 which was also served with an order under the Prevention of Terrorism Act had already voluntarily handed the RUC a dossier of material at the same time it transmitted the programme. The dossier contained the names and identities of a number of individuals whom source A claimed were members of The Committee. The document handed over by Channel 4 also described the role of different individuals as described by source A edited only slightly to protect his identity. However, while Channel 4 was prepared to make some additional information available to the authorities it resolutely refused to name the identity of source A. The channel sent some material abroad to prevent seizure.

There was no letup in the pressure. On 29 April 1992 the Director of Public Prosecutions obtained leave in the High Court to commit Box Productions and Channel 4 for contempt of court because of their refusal to name the identity of source A. The channel was warned about the dire consequences if they did not co-operate. If the case came to court these could include: an unlimited fine, sequestration of assets, even the closure of Channel 4. Faced with this prospect in August 1992 the QC acting for Channel 4, Lord Williams of Mostyn advised Lord Justice Wolf and Mr Justice Pill that the channel would not budge. He declared in a phrase that has become the mantra for many investigative journalists 'we will bow the head but we will not bend the knee'. Amid calls for the ultimate sanction to be imposed, Lord Wolf decided to take a middle course. He counselled Channel 4 and Box Productions that they should not have given unqualified undertakings to their source. This had inevitably pushed them into a breach of the law. They should have inserted an escape clause that would have allowed them to comply with the Prevention of Terrorism Act. That said, he acknowledged that the respondents were motivated by what they regarded as proper motives and stressed they found themselves in a very real dilemma. 'For genuinely held moral considerations' he said 'they felt compelled to disobey what they knew was their legal duty'. Consequently his Lordship decided that Channel 4 and Box Productions should be left off with a fine of £75,000 on this occasion. But there was a stern warning. Next time it would be different.

The outcome of the legal hearing spared everyone the absurdity of seeing only the fourth terrestrial national network being shut down. Victory for Channel 4 and Box Productions was bitter sweet. It took a heavy toll on the people involved. The lessons however were clear. Above all investigative journalism relies on the support of the broadcaster at every step of the production process and beyond transmission. In fact both Channel 4 and Box Productions had to go on defending the programme long after the legal proceedings had finished. In my 1996 study I quoted from the interviews I conducted with the editor at Channel 4 who commissioned The Committee, **David Lloyd**, and with the Chief Executive who backed it, now **Lord Grade**. This is what they told me. First, **David Lloyd from my LSE study:**

'...I recognised at an early stage of the development of 'Dispatches' that you were going to have to deny that geographical distance somehow or other. That people could not be allowed to feel that they were walking the high wire on their own account and nobody else's. They had to realise that when it came to the pressures, sometimes even the threats that others were bound to come up with in trying to forestall your journalism that they had to realise that they had the full strength of a network, terrestrial broadcaster behind them. And so I was at great pains to announce to them that they were going to have support. Now as it happens it was probably some while into the development of the strand before that was really put to the true and complete test. But I wanted people to recognise, I'm talking perhaps about 'The Committee' and one or two libel spats earlier but 'The Committee' was clearly a coming of age in some ways. I never wanted them to feel that the Channel would wave them a pleasant and cordial goodbye as they were busily engaged on defending their product in the courts...'

Lord Grade quoted in my **LSE** study:

'... investigative journalism is an important part of what we do...an important ingredient... there is a commitment from the board, a commitment from me, a commitment from the director of programmes. It goes all the way down and they -the independent production companies- provided they get it right, they'll get all the support they need. The history here has been of a very supportive board. That's the culture of the place... We are blessed that we have a board who are rigorous in their examination of whether or not you've done your homework properly but once they are satisfied they will go to the barricades...'

The impact of the row over 'The Committee' cut deep. Two quotes from my **LSE** work:

David Lloyd:

'It would be quite unreasonable to expect the board of Channel 4 not to think more carefully about it next time. Lightening doesn't often strike in the same place twice but if I was to propose the same project, with precisely the same guarantees and with precisely the same problems, I can't predict to you whether the board would say "Fine and dandy, go ahead or whether they would say "Fine, but ultimately there has to be a qualified promise of anonymity... There would be a whole range of decisions taken in the light of the experience we had...'

Sean Mc Philemy, the producer of The Committee and managing director of Box productions who made it:

'It had a severe effect on the business- because my over-riding priority has been to defend the company's reputation and my own as an investigative journalist. Until this affair is cleared up definitely and we are successful in persuading, certainly the industry at large and hopefully the wider public of the truth of our allegations, until that has happened the position will be unsatisfactory from a professional point of view and a commercial point of view. The wear and tear has been enormous. We've had contempt proceedings that lasted nine months. We've had criminal libel against myself and perjury against my researcher...'

So the political economy of Channel 4 has enabled it to promote and defend investigative journalism in peak time notably in the form of Dispatches. There is actually no reason why ITV couldn't do the same. There is nothing to stop them resurrecting World In Action or This Week. But I'll believe it when I see it. What's stopping them is economics and a lack of will power. This is a crying shame. The two most important PSB's are still ITV and BBC. What they broadcast matters most. They have the longest history. They have the biggest audiences. They have the most money. So what of the BBC?

History shows that the BBC finds it very difficult if not impossible to handle a dysfunctional relationship with the government of the day. The licence fee is the umbilical cord that tugs on the BBC's freedom of manoeuvre when it is called into question. The politicians know this. The Thatcher government knew this. The Blair government knew this. The vulnerability of the BBC in this regard is a reverse reflection of its power in society and its democratic responsibility. No other broadcaster is so defined by public service broadcasting. So if the BBC fails -or wavers under fire- the damage to our democracy is tangible. So what has been the dynamic? The history?

"RED by James Hogan"

As with people so too with institutions. Events provide the real
test of relationships. Looking back it is not readily explicable just
how successful the Thatcher government was at attacking the
nervous system of the BBC. There were layers to it. In the first
instance it was actually unique in historical terms for a
government to make such a radical attack on the BBC. Whereas
the Thatcher government was forced to declare that the NHS was
safe in its hands that same government did not feel obliged to
make the same gesture towards the BBC. In an ideal world, the
Thatcher-led government would have privatised the BBC. As a
direct result of the lobbying campaign mounted by the BBC in the
mid-80s, Mrs Thatcher accepted that privatisation would damage
commercial TV. So despite her ideology she would have to settle
for threat. Sell off this bit or that. Actually better still, terrorise.
Destabilise. The way through to this outcome was to finger not the
settlement but the principle behind the settlement that is the
licence fee. So why not ask the question in all innocence? What
exactly is public service broadcasting? Tell me. Tell us. Tell us all.
In posing this question -once in the spotlight- the Thatcher
government was to cast a long shadow over the history of the
BBC. It was pay back for two things. First I made BBC TV
programmes about the New Left and the New Right in the 1980's.
Yet I readily accept that the BBC -BBC News & Current Affairs-
was incredibly slow in coming to terms with the New Right.
Why? Because it was a dysfunctional child as far as the BBC was
concerned. Second the BBC can never be comfortable with politics
at either end of the spectrum. Its compass is set to One Nation
politics. It is not an accident that post-Thatcher, the advent of the

Major government ushered in a more settled period of BBC/government relations. The menace had evaporated.

Spin back to **Mrs Thatcher**. This is a short extract from her memoirs: **The Downing Street Years**:

'The world of the media had in common with that of the arts, a highly developed sense of its own importance to the life of the nation... So anyone who queried, as I did, whether a licence fee with non-payment subject to criminal sanctions- was the best way to pay for the BBC was likely to be pilloried as at best philistine and at worst undermining its constitutional independence.

'The notion of 'public service broadcasting' was the kernel of what the broadcasting oligopolists claimed to be defending. Unfortunately, when subjected to closer inspection that kernel began rapidly to disintegrate. 'Public service broadcasting' was extremely difficult to define.'

The Thatcher years were very difficult ones for the BBC -at times impossible. While the BBC struggled to get onto the centre ground, the Thatcher government seemed hell bent on war. Compromise was not a word that came easily to the lips of Mrs Thatcher. A few examples will suffice to sustain my thesis that the BBC cannot abide a dysfunctional relationship with the government of the day. Worse. It can't function properly in such conditions. In the 1980's the Thatcher government took violent exception to a variety of BBC TV programmes where it claimed to detect evidence of a lack of patriotism, irresponsibility, political bias.

In July 1985 the Thatcher government asked the BBC not to show a programme entitled 'Real Lives, At The Edge of the Union' in which the lives of two Ulstermen were depicted. One was Gregory Campbell, leader of the Democratic Unionist Group on Derry City Council. The other the Sinn Fein leader, Gerry Adams. Plans to screen the programme incensed the Thatcher government whose Home Secretary pronounced that to screen it would provide terrorists with 'the oxygen of publicity' they crave. In response the BBC Board of Governors over-ruled their own Board of Management and banned the programme. The decision provoked a constitutional crisis inside the BBC and beyond leading to a one-day strike by BBC journalists, including those working at Bush House and by colleagues working at ITN. The programme was eventually transmitted with just minor amendments. But the story didn't end there. As a result of the programme the Thatcher government banned all future interviews with members of Sinn Fein and the Ulster Defence Association. The ban on interviews with extremist groups in Northern Ireland was imposed on the BBC by invoking Clause 13, paragraph 4, of the Licence and Agreement governing the BBC which gives the Home Secretary the right 'to require the corporation to refrain at any specified time or at all times from sending any matter or matters of any class specified in such a notice.' The government expanded the meaning of matter which provides the Home Secretary with the right to ban a specific programme or a particular interview to include whole groups of citizens. As various observers noted at the time, in circumstances like these the BBC's independence is very fragile. Ultimately it is reliant on British public opinion and public outrage. There was no outrage against the ban. So the BBC was left powerless. Worse still, when public opinion is split, the BBC struggles. The polarised politics of the 1980's often left the BBC adrift.

The Real Lives episode drove a deep wedge between the Board of Governors and the Board of Management led by the Director-General Alasdair Milne who believed that the former had shifted significantly to the right as the result of a series of government-inspired appointments.

Two more incidents followed hard on the heels of Real Lives. First the transmission of the programme I produced about alleged far right entryism into the Tory party based on the Young Conservatives Report on the same subject entitled: "Maggies's Militant Tendency", it infuriated some elements of the government. As the programme is very close to home for me, I do not intend to rehearse the argument. What happened has been extensively covered elsewhere. In any event, I fail the Mandy Rice-Davies test:

"He would. Wouldn't He?"

Around the same time, the BBC became embroiled in a row about

one of the programme in the BBC Secret Society series
commissioned by BBC Scotland. The programme which was made
by the exceptionally hard-hitting journalist Duncan Campbell
examined the behaviour of the defence and security services. The
focus of the row centred on plans to reveal the existence of an
alleged British spy satellite code named Zircon the cost of which
had not been revealed to the Public Accounts Committee in
parliament- which it should have been. Once it became clear that
the BBC intended to transmit such a programme the Director-
General faced bitter attack from some BBC Governors and from
outside. On the 15 January 1987 the Director-General dropped the
programme. It didn't end there. Two weeks later the newly-
installed Chairman of the BBC, Duke Hussey, informed the
Director-General, Alasdair Milne, that he had been sacked. Two
days later Special Branch raided the offices of BBC Scotland and
seized the material assembled in the course of making the Secret
Society.

The legacy of the Thatcher government was a very brutal and
brittle one for the BBC. Years after Margaret Thatcher left office
there was still fragility. There were two hangovers. First the
nervosity syndrome. The desire to duck and dive to avoid
controversy -at times conscious- at times unconscious. Second
the idea that took hold in the minds of some politicians that
bullying the BBC works. Bully tactics would re-surface in the Blair
years -with devastating effect.

In the minds of many people the nervosity syndrome was evident in the case the Panorama programme entitled 'Sliding Into Slump'. The progamme was due to be transmitted the day before the budget in 1992 -close to the general election. In the programme, the BBC's Economics Editor Peter Jay, argued that if the distorting effect of the boom of the Thatcher years was taken out of account the so-called economic miracle of the 1980's disappeared. In other words the boom provoked the recession and if it had not occurred the British economy would have achieved a safer and more sustainable rate of growth in the long run -approximately 2.5 %. The programme which featured senior politicians and former chancellors from both sides of the political divide ran into trouble because of its timing. BBC management deemed that it was too retrospective to be shown on the eve of the budget -especially one that came hard on the heels of the local elections and one that would be the last before the general election which looked like being a very close run event. It appeared that there was no political intervention from the government to have the programme pulled. The postponement of Sliding Into Slump which was a matter of timing rather than content produced a public outcry as well as an internal one and led to charges of BBC self-censorship.

The effectiveness of the Thatcher government's bullying tactics towards the BBC did not go unnoticed in some Labour circles. In fact the behaviour of the Blair government in its row with the BBC over its coverage of the second Iraq war had its antecedents as far back as the late 70's and early 80's. In those days the Labour party spent a great deal of its time ripping each other apart. On an almost nightly basis left and right tore into each other on national television. As it did, so its standing in the polls slid ever lower. The country hates divided parties. So it came to hate Labour. At the 1983 general election, Labour got the lowest percentage of the popular vote in its history as a mass political party. When Neil Kinnock became leader of the Labour party in 1983 he set about introducing discipline into the party. No longer would Labour serve themselves up on a platter for the voracious hordes of TV producers and newspaper journalists at feeding time. In future, gradually, inexorably, Labour would get back in command -at least of its own voice. Once New Labour took over in the mid-90s, the drive to get a grip became iron. Over time Testosterone Man was born. In the gym BBC management had shown they crumble under weight. So make them crumble. After all Thatcher pulled it off. That was the backdrop to the biggest crisis in the history of the BBC that took the scalps of both the BBC Chairman Gavyn Davies, and the Director-General, Greg Dyke.

The ins and outs of the Today broadcast that led to the crisis have been well-rehearsed -over and over. But for the sake of completeness and context... BBC Radio 4's flagship news and current affairs programme goes on air at 6.00 am. At 6.07 am on 29 May 2003, a fateful day, the programme carried a report by Andrew Gilligan saying that the dossier that took the UK into war with Iraq with the intention of toppling Saddam Hussein, had been sexed up in 10 Downing Street. All hell let loose. Fury. Anger. Shout. On 18 July 2003, the man later revealed to be the source of the story, Dr David Kelly, an employee of the Ministry of Defence, went missing. Kelly was a biological warfare expert and former UN weapons inspector in Iraq. Two days after he went missing he was found dead in the woods near his home in Abingdon. Sadness. Guilt. More Shout. All eyes and ears fell on Lord Hutton. Appointed by the government he would hold a public enquiry into the circumstances surrounding the death of Dr Kelly. Everyone I know thought that the Hutton Report would be even-handed in its verdict on the two institutions in the dock -the government and the BBC. So did I. We were all wrong. In broad brush, the Hutton Report concluded that the government was pretty well right about everything and the BBC pretty well wrong about everything. In response first the Chairman of the BBC resigned. Then the Director-General was forced to stand down. Could there have been a better way? A different ending? Well, yes. In theory, the BBC could have issued a statement saying words to the effect 'It beggars belief that the government could be right about everything in this matter -the BBC wrong about everything.' But it couldn't do that. Why? The answer is simple. Harking back to Thatcher, the BBC simply can't be permanently at war with the government of the day. In practice it couldn't make a statement of defiance. So it didn't.

In life some numbers stick. 9/11. 7/7. 6.07. The latter cut deep into the collective memory of the BBC. Easy to remember. So always remembered. Always recalled in the lexicon of the BBC Handbook, its handle on its own history. After Hutton the BBC went into the biggest nervous breakdown imaginable. Everywhere a void. Vacuum. As you gasped for air there was none to be had. Numbness. An organisation paralysed. An ideal bereft. Hopelessly exposed. Defenceless. It would take a very long time to recover. After the deluge, the refuge. After Hutton the BBC curled itself up like a ball. Licked its wounds. Went quietly into the night. That's where it stayed by and large until Jimmy Savile came back from the grave to haunt it. That is where I turn my attention next.

In a special interview for this book I asked one of the most able and experienced broadcasters in the UK, **Peter Ibbotson**, to reflect on some of these issues. He is ideally well-placed to comment having edited Panorama in some of the Thatcher years and worked for both Channel 4 and ITV. I started by asking him about the independent production sector in the UK today:

How, in your view, has the independent production sector developed over the last 10 years?

'Well, it's obviously got bigger but in terms of factual broadcasting it suffers from two things. It suffers from the same dynamic that applies to all commercial broadcasting: it is driven by the relationship between costs and revenues. There is no guaranteed funding for factual broadcasting outside the BBC. Even inside the BBC, there can be an implicit relationship between audience size and budgets over time, but of a less aggressive nature.

The additional problem for independents is that, in order to build sustainable and lasting businesses, it requires a very good patron (such as Channel 4 from its earliest days) who help new entrants build scale with long term, repeat or rolling commissions. As those businesses get established, another dynamic comes into play. The key to maintaining scale is by successfully selling more and more programme ideas. These pitches are done by the people running the bigger companies, who pass them down to producers to execute them. This leads to two pressures. First at the pitch level, to oversell an idea to get it accepted. Second, at the execution level, to do whatever it takes to meet expectations. It leaves little room for the culture of the old BBC/ITV duopoly, in which a journalistic investigation could be reasonably generously funded without knowledge of the likely outcome. The competitive system incidentally also leads to more cloning: pitches to nervous commissioners on the basis of doing something 'similar but better' than the opposition has broadcast.

The business dynamic which has spread right through broadcasting necessarily militates against big budgets, open ended budgets and, above all, the ability to fail. Independents are now running businesses which say: "this is what we're going to make for you, and this is the price we've agreed". You must deliver to expectation if you want ongoing commissions business later. And you must come in on or under budget. '

Do you think we've seen the demise of the purely factual documentary maker in independents?

'Probably. It's not a business in the sense I've just described. It can work with an indulgent patron. An independent can operate like a sort of 16th century Italian painter if he has a Cosimo de Medici figure to bankroll him. I think that only Channel 4 ever really fulfilled that role, and chiefly in the very early days when it desperately needed to help build good independent production businesses from scratch. '

Do you think that factual documentary has morphed into factual entertainment?

'There is a much wider cultural issue. I think that television has been retreating as a serious intellectual medium for over 20 or 30 years. Not entirely, of course, and with excellent and notable landmark exceptions. But the trend is unmistakable, and there are many reasons for it. One is the changing business model in an era of expanding competition. Before Channel 4, the BBC/ITV duopoly competed both for audiences, and for the breadth and quality of the output. In ITV's case this was underpinned by the fact that it had a monopoly, and, crucially, won and kept its licences through the programme promises it made to the regulator. Channel 4 added both real viewer choice, and also the means to fund the construction of a broad and viable independent sector. Over time, with the pressure of more terrestrial and satellite channels, the 'competition by quality' mechanism for awarding commercial licences collapsed. Now, the small residual requirements in the commercial licences are the maximum that will be delivered.

In the late 1980s broadcasters like the ITV companies became public companies with shareholders. Once you've got shareholders there's enormous pressure to deliver profit, profit, profit, profit, and cut costs all the way down. You're not going to take many risks in that process. You're not going to put large amounts of money into investigative journalism whose outcome and likely audiences are unknown. What you're going to want to do is find game shows, comedies, soaps and other popular dramas, sport -genres that can indeed cost a lot, but which are certain to attract big audiences and drive an awful lot of revenue. That takes almost all commercial broadcasting, except for Channel 4 out of the picture as far as 'serious' broadcasting is concerned beyond mandated news programmes.

The BBC, of course, should be immune to these commercial pressures. Unfortunately it faces a trap which is a mirror-image of the commercial dynamic. In order to justify the licence fee, the BBC feels that it has to demonstrate that it delivers to all sections of the population, which is reasonable. Everyone has to pay, so everyone must be satisfied. So far so good. But it then faces the temptation to demonstrate its popularity by attracting audiences that are -if not quite as big as those of ITV, say -then are at least in shooting distance. Worse, there is the temptation for commissioners to prove the popularity of the BBC by copying popular formats already available on commercial television. (This may also have been exacerbated by the increasing numbers of commissioners and other managers who move between commercial television and the BBC. The old idea of a distinct 'BBC culture' is now much less strong in some areas).

The danger of all this is that the BBC starts to create for itself something very similar to the pressures which bear down on commercial broadcasters. Of course it should be popular, and of course it should be seen to give value-for-money. But it should also function as a major engine for cross subsidy between genres. It should avoid the temptation to function like its commercial competitors, and demonstrate that only the BBC can now reliably provide output at scale that adds to what is available to the public, not just replicating it. That, long-term, is real value-for-money.'

Do you think that the culture that existed, the romanticism, the optimism, that characterised the independents in the 80s has died?

'Yes. All organisations grow and get middle aged. It happened to local government in the 60s and 70s. There's always somewhere that the middle classes colonise, a new place where the ambitious young go and have fun, build careers, perhaps make some money. As organisations mature, particularly public organisations like the BBC, they become bureaucratic -and they bloat. Producer friends tell me of the daunting level of BBC commissioning staff who now come to view at a late stage in production to have their say on the programme, and of course their credits on the end of it. In addition to these committees are the focus groups advising commissioners on what to commission.

It used to be much simpler. When Bill Cotton ran BBC1, he made most commissioning decisions himself, and largely by instinct. The Head of BBC Bristol came to him with the idea of Antiques' Roadshow and took Bill through. He has thought for a while, then said: "We'll have that but just one thing I want from it. I want a big close up of the owner's face when she learns what it is worth". And that was the deal done. I don't believe that simplicity is necessarily appropriate today, but I am also certain that the committees and focus groups are a less effective way of serving the public.'

Do you think investigative journalism is dying?

'In broadcasting? It's close to dead. Could you imagine a broadcaster doing what the Guardian did on phone hacking? Could you even imagine a broadcaster buying the tapes or the discs that the Telegraph did that blew the MPs' expenses, and taking the lead with the story? For commercial television, it wouldn't be worth the expense or the fuss. Could you imagine the BBC doing it? Of course there are numerous investigations of consumer scandal, and important subjects like the Winterbourne Care Home. But they are quite cheap to produce, involve little risk, and require no courage. Putting in hidden cameras is a technical skill, no more. Such stories do nothing that goes to the guts of major corruption, or taking on powerful institutions. It's unimaginable. The BBC is always there to amplify a story once someone else has broken it, but rarely seems to have the time, resources and courage to be the initiator.

The BBC's issue in this area is political. In revenue terms, it has got just one customer, that's the Government which sets the Licence Fee. And that, at critical moments, this has a real chilling effect. It is fanciful to suppose that the BBC would itself expose the scandal of MPs expenses, and set itself against the whole House of Commons. The **Daily Telegraph** took the risk that it could use a public interest defence. '

Chapter V

Jimmy Savile and the psychology of self-censorship

The strange case of Jimmy Savile and the BBC will probably never be fully explained. The truth will probably remain hidden in the vaults of the sub-conscious mind of the BBC forever. A subject best forgotten. A subject best ignored. That said, it is highly relevant to the subject of this book because it raises questions about television in the 21st century. Specifically was the decision to self-censor the Newsnight investigation into allegations of historic sex abuse against Jimmy Savile in any way framed by the near death of investigative journalism on terrestrial television in the UK? Was the nervosity syndrome at work even though Jimmy Savile was dead? Or maybe because he had only just died?

To be clear, I use the word self-censorship to describe the BBC's handling of the Savile story. Some people object to this description. I think they are wrong. I rely on the Pollard Report discussed in the text below. Clearly the BBC had sufficient evidence on Savile. Clearly they decided to gag themselves. The position adopted by the BBC as the crisis unfolded that there was insufficient evidence is flatly denied by Pollard.

I believe that what happened in the BBC/Savile case needs to be examined through a long lens. In the post-war period the BBC

"RED by James Hogan"

positioned itself as Auntie. Through radio it accompanied us through the travails and hardship of the Second World War. Now with the advent of television and the arrival of the commercial broadcaster ITV, the BBC would once again be the guardian of the nation and its morals. A sort of midwife and cleric rolled into one. Outstretched hand. As it did during the war, it would guide us to safety through the Reconstruction and beyond.

Gradually through the 50's and 60's, a new type of broadcasting would emerge -cradle to grave. The length of time the BBC could transmit programmes was extended. So it had the capacity to accompany the public through the waking hours of the day and the lifecycle. Children's television and Youth Culture TV were born. Alongside family viewing. Against the uncertainty of a rapidly changing world you would be safe in the hands of the BBC which was to become the nation's baby-sitter.

Counsellor for adolescence. Trusted. Into the idyll stepped Jimmy Savile introduced to the nation by the BBC. Like the BBC, Savile was to become an institution. He would present the children's programme 'Jim'll Fix It' that attracted huge audiences. The format took the innocence of young children promising to make their dreams come true. 'You want to meet the Prime Minister?' 'You can'. 'You want to pilot a plane?' 'You can'. 'You want to be a TV reporter?' 'You can'. Magic. Little children would sit on Savile's lap looking up at him in awe. It didn't end there. The reassuring presence of the BBC/Savile combination would also be extended to Britain's teenagers who after all would need a helping hand to steer them through the minefield of adolescence and the Rock n' Roll era. Once again Jimmy Savile -Uncle to the Beeb's Auntie- would be on hand. Savile would be one of the regular hosts of the BBC1 smash hit Top of the Pops. With young girls wrapped around him and hanging on to his arm, Savile would greet the nation with the words 'Hi Guys and Gals. It's Top of the Pops.' And 'Goodness Gracious Me'. The peak of Savile's stardom coincided with the heyday of the BBC -70s and 80s. In those days Savile commanded audiences that would be unthinkable for similar shows today. His celebrity status also carried over to the BBC News bulletins who would praise the work he did for charity and mental homes for whom he raised many millions of pounds.

Childhood experiences seep into your bones. They provide the hard wooden frame within which you later experience life. They pre-condition your instinctive reactions -the flight from- the flight towards. You can't escape them -good or bad. So it was that a whole generation came to know Jimmy Savile. He was a family friend. He was in the family photographs. Giving out rewards. Jim'll Fix It badges. Crossing the winning line. Receiving cheques for charity. Receiving honours. As such the BBC could be forgiven for not wanting to believe bad things about Savile let alone that he was a restless, relentless peadophile. Sub-consciously. If not explicitly. Similarly it would be understandable if deep down the BBC didn't want to publicise the allegations. We will never know if this was the root of the problem. The reason for the self-censorship. But I think it is reasonable to assume that it may have been at the very least a factor. So what actually happened? On the face of it, the sequence of events and the appearance that they gave could not have been worse for the BBC. Not even the BBC's

worst enemy could have concocted a more appalling screenplay.
Just imagine. The BBC's most esteemed daily news and current
affairs programme -BBC TV Newsnight- holds centre-stage.
Newsnight is the BBC equivalent of the FT. No Newsnight. No
comment. It gets access to a world exclusive. One of the BBC's best
known, most loved, most trusted children's presenters, is
allegedly a child molester.

An independent BBC enquiry would stand the story up. Later. In
the meantime BBC management would decide to drop the
Newsnight investigation. To make matters worse BBC
management would leave various tribute programmes in the
pipeline on Savile scheduled for transmission in place. In due
course, ITV would do the BBC's job for them by running the
Newsnight material.

Jimmy Savile died on 29 October 2011. Condolences flooded in
from all over the world and from all quarters of society. Many of
them rich and famous. His funeral was a grand affair. The
headstone on his grave suitably Elaborate. Vulgar. Showbiz.
Several months prior to his death -in July 2011- the Newsnight
producer Meirion Jones and reporter Liz Mc Kean discussed
rumours that Savile had a dark side to his character. Jones took
Savile's death as the cue to begin his investigation into the
rumours in earnest. Jones and Mc Kean steadily built up a body of
evidence that Savile had abused young girls at the Dunscroft
Children's Home. In the early stages of the production of the

Newsnight report everything appears to have gone smoothly.

Jones and Mc Kean sought and got the backing of the Newsnight editorial team and wider BBC management. The programme was given a slot and was to be transmitted on 7 December 2011. Then all of a sudden the climate turned cold. Very cold. On the 1st December the Newsnight investigation was dropped. On 9 December it was formally stoned to death. Dropped entirely. Not shelved. Not drowning. Drowned. This left the various tribute programmes in place to praise a fallen BBC hero. Later the irony of the catchphrase 'Jim'll Fix It' would be lost on no one. At first the drama was confined to the corridors of the BBC. Behind the scenes. But the story started to leak   -at first drips. Stories started to appear in the press. Talk of cover-ups. Anger. Frustration. Rows. The drips turned to a steady flow. But it wasn't until the following October 2012 that the story exploded into the face of the BBC like a terrorist bomb in the middle of the night. Allegations flew in every direction. In the midst of the maelstrom, the hapless and helpless BBC management. Chaos ensued. By now the question on everybody's lips inside and outside the BBC was why had the BBC self-censored one of the biggest stories in its history? Was it that Jimmy Savile was a 'misfit' or was it 'malaise'? -A reflection of a flight away difficult, uncomfortable investigative journalism to an age of Light Entertainment? Ironically, Light Entertainment or LE is where Jimmy Savile spent most of his career. More embarrassing questions were asked. Why did the BBC stick with the tribute programmes when it was sitting on evidence of Savile's dark side? It looked terrible. Coming after Hutton it hurt. Hurt deeply. Then as if it couldn't possibly get any worse -it did. At the height of the Savile crisis -with the Director-General being strangulated on the ropes- BBC TV Newsnight falsely allowed people to believe that they had evidence that an ex-Tory grandee was a paedophile. Actually it was worse than that. The programme didn't name the falsely accused but did nothing to stop the gathering consensus over the internet that the guilty man was Lord McAlpine -the former Tory Party Treasurer in the Thatcher government. The story was completely wrong. The accuser mis-identified Lord McAlpine. At that moment crisis turned to farce. The authority of the BBC drained away. Within hours the Director-General, George Entwistle fell away. The shortest-lived Director-General in the history of the BBC.

Under siege the BBC appointed the former Sky News Editor Nick Pollard on 16 October 2012 to Chair an investigation into the BBC's handling of the Newsnight investigation. On the most serious charge the BBC was acquitted.

Pollard writes:

'The decision to drop the original investigation was flawed and the way it was taken was wrong but I believe it was done in good faith. It was not done to protect the Savile tribute programmes or for any improper reason.'

So 'Misfit'. Not 'Malaise'. I agree.

In several other ways the findings of the Pollard Report were devastating for the BBC.

Pollard:

'Newsnight's abortive Jimmy Savile of 2011 started a chain of events that was to prove disastrous for the BBC. It led to one of the worst management crises in the BBC's history and contributed to further chaos that led to the resignation of the Director-General a few weeks later over the McAlpine affair...

'When the full force of the affair broke in October 2012, the BBC's management system proved completely incapable of dealing with it. This report shows the level of chaos and confusion was even greater than was apparent at the time...

'It has to be said clearly: there is no doubt, in my mind, that Mr Jones and Ms Mc Kean were right about Savile. Their belief that Savile had a history of abusing young women was correct. They provided Newsnight with cogent evidence of this. The programme could have broken the story almost a year before the ITV documentary revealed it.'

If I am right that the sub-conscious may have played a part in the self-censorship thought process amongst BBC management I think the following observation in the report may be relevant:

"RED by James Hogan"

Pollard:

'I found it interesting that many of the people involved in this story seem to have spent all or nearly all of their working lives at the BBC...'

While I believe there was no causal link between the decision to drop the Savile exposé and the decision to stick with the various tribute programmes, I think the nervosity syndrome played a part in the decision to self-censor and the way events unfolded thereafter. Reading Pollard's excellent report you are struck by the duck and dive in various testimonies and the bad case of amnesia that spread like wild fire among the key players.

Lord Grade, former BBC chairman of the governors and chairman designate of the BBC Trust:

Why do you think the BBC decided to drop the Newsnight investigation into Jimmy Savile?

'My guess and it's entirely a guess, is that the editor of Newsnight at the time when he saw what the story was, took a rather narrow view and thought "this is really not what Newsnight should be doing", which was a kind of "it's more about the brand". He should have thought of that at the beginning when he commissioned the film, or when he told them to go and gave them the money to do the investigation. '

'But, when it transpired, when it was delivered and realised I think he felt queasy about the Newsnight brand doing that kind of investigation, which seems to me a perfectly reasonable point of view to take but at that point what he should have done is said "look, we've got a hell of a story here; can we have a Newsnight special; can we give the story to Panorama?" But, of course, the BBC doesn't work like that. It works in silos and so they made the horrendous decision not to transmit it, which was a shocking decision.

'From a distance this is only guess work but knowing how the BBC works, I suspect that editorially they didn't feel that it particularly fitted the Newsnight agenda, celebrity exposure is not something you switch on Newsnight to see. You look at world famine, you look at war zones around the world, the domestic political agenda, and corruption. Celeb exposure is not in the Newsnight can. I suspect that when the story eventually turned up at Newsnight somebody said "this is really not a Newsnight story." Who that was I've no idea but that's a perfectly legitimate judgment. There are lots of stories, I'm sure, that Newsnight, Panorama and everybody, they do and the way the story turns out they say "actually, this is not for us, this doesn't fit what this show does, the remit of this programme'.

'It's just not what they do. But, having made that decision, what they should have done, somebody should have said, Director General or whoever, I've no idea, somebody should have said, "this is too big a story to bury, we've got to find a way to get this into the public domain. There is a public interest in this story. We are here, the central purpose of the BBC is independent, impartial journalism; this is a big story". And they should have found… somebody at the BBC should have found a way to air, to transmit the story as a Newsnight Special, as a Panorama Special, as a programme on its own it would have stood up. They just kind of… I don't know, they just didn't see the wood for the trees.'

If you'd been running the BBC would you have backed the Newsnight investigation?

'What, into Savile? Absolutely, of course. Whether it was Newsnight or Panorama or the Ten o'clock News, or whoever it was that wanted to do that, wanted to make the film, absolutely, 100% yes, if they had *prima facie* evidence. You know, it's not an editorial question. The editorial decision is easy.

'It's a question of whether they've got enough information for you to invest resources for them to go and see if they could get the story. The story was certainly important, very important.'

And I think I'm right in saying that Pollard said there was enough substance to run it.

'Yes, I'm sure there was. '

And in those circumstances, had you been running the BBC...

'In what capacity? As Director General?'

Well, Director General.

'Director General, no question I would have transmitted it. Whether it's a Newsnight Special, you tell Panorama they've got to run it as a Panorama or as a special documentary, you know, it was such a big story, you clear the schedules for it. '

Do you think that it was in any way indicative of malaise, a mindset that entertainment these days is more important than hard-hitting documentary?

'No, no, no: it was human failing and classic BBC silo thinking, silo culture. And they got themselves into a shocking muddle and the lovely Director General, George Entwistle, completely failed to address the issue when the fertiliser hit the air conditioning. And he should have been on the steps of Broadcasting House saying "I have started an immediate investigation into why this film wasn't transmitted." It's the only thing the public wanted to know, the licence fee payers, "why wasn't it transmitted?" And instead, they tried to pretend, they concocted this defence that it was a film that was originally supposed to be about the shortcomings of the police investigations and it turned out to be a celebrity exposé. So what? The story is the story. They got themselves into a hopeless muddle with it. '

Roger Bolton interview, November 2014.

I'd like to ask a number of questions on self-censorship, if I may. How significant in your view is the BBC's decision to self-censor the Newsnight investigation into Jimmy Savile?

'...At the moment I think this is more cock-up than conspiracy and is a comment on the nature of leadership of the BBC at the time and the lack of courage. So, the first question is how many knew, how many people knew about Jimmy Savile? I don't think many outside of Light Entertainment. '

'I mean, I was head of the network production centre in Manchester when Stuart Hall was in the same building, though not working for me, and as we now know and I didn't think at all, committing sex crimes, some with children. Now, I didn't know about that. It's very... people say subsequently, "how could you not know?" All I can say is I did not know and I think the same when one worked in Nationwide and elsewhere, where you occasionally had contact with the Entertainment group, you thought that Rock stars and other people, you know, there were groupies around, didn't understand about paedophilia, really, or think that Jimmy Savile was involved with that. So, one didn't know.'

Should you have known?

'Well, we should have known lots of things. Then, you come up to the period of the actual investigation or, rather, the event that triggered the investigation. Did the BBC drop a Newsnight investigation into Savile because of the embarrassment and because a celebratory programme on Savile had already been commissioned? I don't think it did, from what I know. I don't think the Newsnight investigation was blocked because of the Light Entertainment celebration programme on Savile. I've seen nothing that suggests that would be the case. '

'If you're not united you can't do it. If you don't have the backing of the top you can't do it. And, to an extent, the child abuse paedophilia investigations are the equivalent of the ones we did into the IRA and into Ireland. And if the leadership doesn't back you and if you are a team who are not united then you are in real trouble. And I think they didn't sort themselves out internally for what was a very difficult investigation. '

Do you think the dropping of the Savile investigation was a case of self-censorship?

'... I don't think it was self-censorship... I think it was a failure of leadership, I would say. I quite understand why the investigation was stopped. But, it should have been stopped only to regroup and go on. That's what I think was wrong and I think the leadership of the News division did not solve that. '

Why didn't that happen?

'It's not a brave... it's not a brave organisation at various times and it wasn't a brave organisation then. And I think, ultimately, people were looking out for their own careers. This is always the case with large organisations. It's always the case with the BBC. You need a combination of people and talent to ride over that at difficult times. And it's not often available. I think it's sad because there are really good people in there. '

Do you think the BBC has been guilty of self-censorship in the past?

'Oh, yes. '

Can you give some examples?

'Well, clearly, you have... I don't know how far you want to go back but if you go back to Lord Reith, he clearly censored the coverage of the general strike when you look at the records in what he would consider the greater interests of the country and

114

the BBC. You then look at the BBC in the post-war period and the Chairman of the BBC is often a former senior figure in Government, and so on. Mind you, there, there is a general concept of the national interest and on the whole the BBC was then run by people who did see the Cold War as a continuation in some ways of World War II. And you have my generation of people coming in who are slightly naïve, perhaps, about that, but are not that same framework; and so there was a… I think rather than self-censorship you could put it this way. There was a lack of interest in examining… well, there was also respect for authority or acceptance of authority. And so what you start to see in the 60s in society generally and then percolating through into broadcasting is a questioning of authority, a greater degree of openness beginning and then seeing the reality behind that. So, I don't think you can isolate the BBC from what's happening in the rest of society. '

'Where you do get issues and problems is when the BBC thinks its existence is being threatened. For example, in 1979 when I got into a lot of trouble with a programme that never went to air about the IRA, it's no coincidence that (1) Mrs Thatcher had come into power and she had no affection or understanding of the BBC and I would say of Northern Ireland. (2) The BBC also was in danger of exceeding its borrowing powers; was desperate at a time of high inflation to have an increase in the licence fee. At that moment the last thing the governors wanted was anything that would cause any problem with the Government. '

"RED by James Hogan"

So, what you have to say is when the BBC thinks its vital interests and future is involved it is sensitive...

'I think when the BBC thinks its own interests, its future and its own existence is threatened and it self-censors.

I think once you get into an election period it pulls back. I sometimes despair that, you know, if a Conservative politician says "it's dark outside" and a Labour politician said "It's light" the presenter wouldn't have the nerve to look out the window. I think it's a bit better than that now but I think that's when the dangers happen. '

Let's be absolutely clear... if you'd been Newsnight editor you would have backed the programme?

'If I'd been Newsnight editor I would have done a programme... But, it might have been transmitted two months' later, it might have been different three months later... Then there is the McAlpine programme... the one that the BBC allowed people to believe that they were referring to Lord McAlpine... It was such a collection of errors... It was a perfect storm. It was a mistake I wouldn't have made.'

'I mean, I would have checked that this is your witness. You show the photographs. I mean, there was actually competence questions in that second one and lines of command problems.'

What would you say to the defenders of the BBC who say the follow up programmes conducted by the Today programme and Panorama went along way to limiting the damage done by Newsnight?

'Well, what I would say is that the whole incident caused great damage to the BBC. It will have inhibited it from doing a lot of journalism. It will have damaged its reputation in the public mind. It will have reinforced with the second programme some politicians' views of the BBC. I think the damage was mitigated by the Panorama and Today interviews, although you can always rely such is the competitive nature of individual programmes and interviewers who like nothing better than sticking it to the boss, they will obviously prove their reputations, which is a good thing that they do. '

'But, overall, it was a tragedy for the BBC. It was a tragedy for the journalists. It was a tragedy for the Director General, George Entwistle and I think it was sad that the absence of leadership or the failure of leadership more widely in the BBC at that time is a cause of sadness and some wonder. '

In your view, is it the greatest crisis of trust in the history of the BBC?

'BBC has always had those occasions of trust. I think it comes with the job. It was the greatest crisis of trust in the last, what, five years… I don't know. It will always happen. If you have something called the BBC which is financed by the licence fee and which… I mean, the BBC has freedom under licence but it doesn't have absolute freedom and the licence terms are something quite hard. There is always going to be a tension, usually when it's over the BBC's existence.

It's a very tough gig. On the other hand you've got guaranteed income! You're paid very well. It's a fabulous job to do, to be involved in any of that. And so it is tough but I think that instance severely damaged the BBC's credibility and is to be regretted. '

To Round Up this chapter. Economics are the single and singular driving force of the new television: enabling and disabling. The PSB's need to fill the void. It's their moral and constitutional duty. Despite events like Savile, the BBC's role in defending our democracy is more vital than ever before. It has the ability and resources to act as a counter-weight to the unfettered commercialisation of television and the endangered species status of investigative journalism on TV.

#

Chapter VI

Invisible TV

Part II: "RED by James Hogan" Screenplay

Written by Nick Peterson with the following participants:

James Hogan, Dawn Airey, Lord Grade, Peter Ibbotson, Roger Bolton, Richard Horwood Greg Dyke,Chris Carter, Rob Woodward, Jean Seaton, Sir Peter Bazalgette, Sir Trevor McDonald, Adam Boulton, David Montgomery and Virtual Alien.

Storyline

Red was King George the Third's most favorite and powerful color: red for anger, red for love and red for madness. Is the madness floating over the court of King George the Third the same insanity guiding a country with the highest amount of TV channels in the world? Is broadcasting and communication in the 21st century enthralled with the same madness raging at the court of King George the Third? Some of the leading broadcasters in TV, web and communication strategists are arguing and commenting about broadcasting in the 21st century.

The film opens at the court of King George the Third. Broadcasting is just like a painting being fed to a court or a nation;

120

it tells a story and this story is "RED by James Hogan" a documentary about 21st century broadcasting within a 21st century background in its setting and design where the past meets the present and the future.

The interviews are in monochromatic red and the animated foreground in colour. The total running time is 6 hours long.

Prologue

The year is 1780.

At the Court of King George the Third fourteen paintings in red are being presented to the King. Amongst a chaotic crowd shaping the King's court the King responds by blasting the Royal Cannons.

At the beginning of the 21st century...

Chapter I

Dawn Airey

CEO of Getty Images, former Senior Vice-President of Yahoo Europe, Africa and the Middle East. In July 2015 the British government appointed Dawn Airey to join the board of the newly formed committee that will decide on the future of the BBC. Chairman of the British National Youth Theatre. Formerly a Senior Executive with C4, C5, SKY TV.

Interviewer: James Hogan

Q   Dawn, many thanks for taking part. Hugely grateful. What's happened to television?

A   I think television's in a great place. Television I think has had a complete lease of life because suddenly the barriers to distribution have gone down, and that means that if you've got production and you've got content you can distribute it very, very widely at very, very, very nominal costs.

I think that the death knell of television has been sounded on too many occasions. The truth is, is that the world that we're now in, the digital world that we're now in, means that there are infinite possibilities for distribution, infinite possibilities for viewers to interact with your content and if you liberate that content, the ability to monetize that interaction has never, ever, ever been higher.

So I think the business model for television has suddenly got a whole host more rosy. There are challenges around advertising because clearly the digital players, the pure digital players, are also going after the digital pounds. But the reality is, in terms of content, original production I think is in an amazing place at the moment. It is sort of like another tsunami of golden age of television. You're just seeing unbelievable breadth and richness of content.

Q   Do you think that the internet will eventually kill off television?

A   I don't think the internet will kill of television at all. No, what the internet does it provides a means of distribution for long form content if television wants that as a means of distribution. I think the online players interestingly are brilliant at curation, are brilliant at aggregation and the publishing. But in terms of creating original content, there's still a degree of nervousness around that.

I work for Yahoo!. We produce some original content. We actually produce quite a lot of original content, but we're a technology company that facilitates the access of content and that's where I think you'll find that sort of the internet companies will continue to be most comfortable which is around the technical liberation and curation of content which, like I said, exists very, very well with content producers.

That doesn't mean to say because we're in a world where many executives, including myself, have a crystal ball on your desk because the truth is you don't quite know what's going to happen. I never thought I would see in my lifetime that the younger audience, and this is in the States, so the under 25s spend more time online than they do watching television. They still watch television content, but they don't necessarily watch it on a large screen in a single room in the home. They're watching it on mobiles, on tablets, and they're also creating their own content because that's the other thing that the internet has done is allowed everybody to be a creator of content because the barriers to creation have come crashing down.

Q   What do you think the future holds for the BBC?

A   Well, I think the BBC—I'm British and I think that part of being British is having a really strong BBC. I think it's a quintessential part of society in the United Kingdom, and I think it's a really, really important broadcaster.

What will happen? I think that the BBC has proved itself once again—Darwin's theory—that it's not the strongest, it's not the most powerful. It's the most adaptable. And I think the BBC has demonstrated particularly over the last, I would say, ten years but particularly the last five years that it can become very adaptable to the demands of the digital world. So whether it's through the iPlayer or many of the new initiatives that it's doing in terms of accessing, allowing its content to be accessed not only online but actually launching things online, having a two-way interaction with the population online is all a good thing.

But, the truth is that the license fee does stick out as a rather unusual anomaly, this tax on everybody with a television set and yet increasingly families are not accessing BBC services through the set. So, I think there will continue to be a challenge and a questioning of the level in funding of the BBC. I think the BBC has to continue to demonstrate real value for money, and with an organisation of, what, £3.5 billion or whatever guaranteed income it has each year, I think it has to just be very transparent; it has to be operationally incredibly efficient; I think it has to continue to produce content that not only the market doesn't naturally provide but also has to continue to provide really mainstream, high quality content that unifies the nation.

I would like to think that in my lifetime and indeed in my children's lifetime there will be a place for the BBC. You only have to go abroad, and I travel a lot abroad, and see state broadcasters to just value the breadth and depth and quality of what we get for that 140 quid or whatever it is we pay a year for the BBC.

Q   Do you think the licence fee should be scrapped?

A   Absolutely not. No, I don't think it should be scrapped.

Q   Do you think it should be cut?

A   Well, I think it's cut insofar as it doesn't go up because it hasn't gone up for, what, the last five years and so in real terms that's a cut. I think the BBC's licence fee standing still will be the new going forward. I don't see it going up, but equally by virtue it not going up it goes down.

Q   Do you think the BBC's too big?

A   Well, that's an interesting debate. Quintessentially, a lot of people say the BBC is too big. It's a lot smaller than it used to be. I think it's got to find smarter ways of working with partners. I think that it needs to in the constant search for efficiency look very, very hard at itself at its overhead. But it has to do a huge amount of things. You could argue does the BBC do too much? Should it actually do everything that it does or should it concentrate on fewer things and continue to do those at an exceptionally high standard? And one assumes that the license renewal and the charter renewal period that we're now entering, those are going to be some of the quintessential debates about what does it do? What does it continue to do? What does it stop doing? What does it do differently? Because it's going to have to justify that rather sizeable amount of money that it takes off every family that's got a television set.

Q   What do you think the future holds for ITV?

A   Again, the obituaries for ITV have been written on many occasions. I think ITV has proved, again over the last five years under the guidance of the new leadership, itself to be again adaptable and it's been clever. It has finally been able to do what I think it should've done a long time ago but partly hasn't had to and hasn't been able to which is to extend its reach into owning original content.

So the big spending spree that happened under Adam Crozier of acquiring production companies really does future proof the company going forward and sort of makes it a little bit immune to the highs and the lows of broadcasting revenues because it's going to be getting revenues from the productions it makes and the formats that go with those productions internationally. So I think ITV has done well.

I think the question is and it's always the on-going question which is who ends up owning it? Will somebody take over ITV? Are there synergies to be made if ITV's acquired? It's always been said acquired by a US company. So I don't know. ITV has been—it's taken, what was it? Fifteen years ago that it became a single PLC and, gosh, when I started my career there were 15 regional ITV companies. Now there's a single ITV PLC, and over the course of the last five years it's done well. Look at the share price. It's gone from sort of 60p, I think it's £2.75. It's doing well for shareholders, but it's doing so well it's quite expensive in terms of acquisition.

But I think a good, strong, free-to-air, commercial broadcaster that's mainstream as a rival particularly to BBC 1 is really important and actually is going to continue to have a good, long sort of life ahead of it.

Q   Do you think Channel 4 should be privatised?

A   It's an interesting question, isn't it? Because as the government is short of money, Channel 4 sits there as an asset you could probably get a billion for. There's been a huge range in terms of the value potentially associated with it. I think that Channel 4 still fulfils a really important part in the ecology of British broadcasting which is to provide different voices in the broadcasting world, to try and do things that are different. I think it's done that actually incredibly well. I think if Channel 4 was to be privatised I think then the tendency would be for maybe it to lose some of its USP, to go a little bit more mainstream than it has, maybe dilute the amount of money that you spend in the schedule. So I think if Channel 4 was to be privatised, and it's not necessarily the end of the world if it was privatised, I think it would be terrific if it was privatised but under some form of remit where it always had to, it's hard to mandate that it absolutely had to adhere to. But the Channel 4 privatisation debate has been alive and kicking for the last ten years.

Q   What do you think about Channel 5 these days?

A   Well, I have to be honest and say I rarely watch it apart from *Celebrity Big Brother*. I think it's got a really good and careful owner under Viacom, and I was really, really thrilled when they bought the business because I thought, "Ha ha! Here's a company that is in it for the long term." Richard Desmond was in, he turned it round very quickly and made a lot of money, and all credit to him for doing that. He bought it at the right time.

But I think to be sold and now to be part of a bigger and an American broadcasting production powerhouse that has an absolute commitment to the medium is really, really good for 5. So I've got high hopes that it will find its voice again and will go back to being what it was right in the beginning which was this modern, mainstream channel that was a cheeky upstart, that was younger, that gave an awful lot of talent and incredibly established their first break.

So I'm really pleased it's in the ownership that it is at the moment, and I want to see it thrive and flourish and I want to see myself going to it more often than I currently do.

Q Can you explain the power of Yahoo! in the new world?

A Well, Yahoo! is—it's an indispensable guide to the digital world, sort of yours and the digital world. It's an extraordinary company. We've got 1.2 billion users. That's one of the reasons I'm here. We've got a worldwide audience, 1.2 billion users. We're a mobile first company. Everything we think about is how do we deliver our users a very superior mobile experience. And we've got a multiplicity of products. So we have communications tools. So we have a massive number of our users who use us for email. We've got the fastest growing social site in the world in the form of Tumblr, a very, very creative social site. We have a lot of our own video, both owned and operated exclusive content and content that we make ourselves. Whether that's Yahoo! news, whether that's fantasy football, whether that's Community which was a series that came off one of the US broadcasters that we picked up as a comedy, whether it's the just announced deal with Simon Cowell, so he's producing the show for us in search of the world's best electronic DJ. We're into long form content, but we do a lot of short form content as well.

And we are a portal of content, and everything's very, very highly personalised, so we're an unusual business. We curate. We're the biggest publisher in the world, but we also provide a very, very, very personalised content experience to our users because we know them so well. And we're different to the existing—to the monoliths. So Google is search; Facebook is social. Yahoo! has been around 20 years. We started off—it was Dave and Jerry's Guide to the Web. Now we still have a very sophisticated search product, but we do a whole raft of other things as well.

There are very few businesses that have over 1.2 billion users. We have over 1.2 billion users. We take more than 5 billion in revenue a year from digital advertising. There are only three other businesses in the world, two other businesses in the world that do that. So, we occupy a unique and very special place.

Q   What challenges does Yahoo! face?

A   I think the challenges that Yahoo! faces are the same really as everybody in the digital world which is how do you continue to surprise, delight, and engage your users with products that they find indispensable and that's what we're relentlessly focused on, delivering a really superior product and user experience, and if we do that then the users keep coming back. The users come back, then we sell those users to advertisers. It becomes a beautiful, virtual circle.

But we're in a world where new ideas pop up all the time. You look at WhatsApp; now WhatsApp Facebook bought but there are—just a statistic. A couple of years ago—no, last year, there were 7.3 trillion text messages sent. WhatsApp which didn't exist three years ago, 7.3 trillion texts were sent just on WhatsApp. The size and scale of what can come sort of tomorrow really very quickly, what can become scalable very quickly is quite extraordinary, but we're just beginning to see the revolution in apps which is where we all tend to go.

We all sort of thought on mobiles everyone would go to mobile web. It's all about apps and so everyone's creating the most sophisticated app experience you possibly can that has a high degree of utility that solves a need. But there's so much iteration going on at the moment because the world is just exploding in terms of digital opportunity, particularly in commerce. And so that is the thing that we relentlessly focus on which is product, product, product.

Q   Dawn, huge thanks.

A   You're welcome. Is that all right?

Q   Very, very good indeed.

A   Good. Thank you.

End of recording

Chapter II

Lord Grade

Former BBC chairman of the governors and chairman designate of the BBC Trust, ex-Chief Executive of ITV and Channel 4.

Interviewer: James Hogan

Q   With me is Lord Grade, formerly head of the BBC, ITV, and Channel 4. Michael, thank you for taking part. What do you think has happened to television?

A   Well, more competition has made life a lot tougher. That's competition—there are more channels. Competition from the internet and so on, so life is a lot harder today for traditional broadcasters. And I think they've got to work a lot harder which is the lesson from America about creating distinction on their channel with their content. You see the new Netflix and people in America doing these amazingly brilliant, quite adventurous, quite innovative drama series. We've got to work harder. The old formulas aren't good enough anymore to distinguish your service.

Q   Do you think the internet will eventually kill off television?

A   No, because the internet is just the delivery system. It needs content; and whoever can provide content and the leaders of content provision are essentially the Hollywood studios and the traditional broadcasters, and the internet needs that stuff in order to attract users.

Q   And what's happened to the indies in the UK?

A   Well, the independent sector is one of the huge success stories of the UK of the last 20 years. It's grown. It's consolidating now which is just a sign that the market's maturing, but it's been a huge success story to the extent that if the indies disappeared tomorrow I think ITV, Channel 4, and the BBC would struggle, really struggle.

Q   And what's happened to investigative journalism on terrestrial television in the UK?

A   It's less prevalent than it used to be, but that's for good commercial reasons. There's still more investigative journalism on British television than most free world networks, but there isn't as much as there used to be and I'm afraid that's economics.

Q   Is it dying?

A   I don't think it's dying because as long as there are journalists there are people who want to break stories and investigate. The BBC is in the vanguard of that. I don't think a great deal of their investigative journalism at the moment, but that's just a phase thing. I think it will no doubt improve.

Q   Does the standing army that made the *Birmingham Six* investigation exist anywhere in today's television?

"RED by James Hogan"

A   I don't think it does. I don't think the kind of investment that Granada and that Thames Television and London Weekend and others used to put into keeping a regular team of investigative journalists working around the clock, 52 weeks a year, with no certainty that they were going to get a story at the end of it or film at the end of it, I think those days have gone. The economics are just against it.

Q   Should the BBC have exposed the MPs' expenses scandal?

A   No, I think you've got to give credit. Stories fall where they fall. It depends on contacts and so on. What would've been wrong is if the BBC had had the story and sat on it which they did with the Jimmy Savile film or they tried to.

Q   Would it have been politically possible for the BBC to do the MPs' expenses scandal?

A   Absolutely possible. Yes, I have no doubt. If the BBC had got those tapes, that data, I have no doubt they would've published.

Q   Could the BBC have broken the phone hacking scandal at News International?

A   Again, I think if the BBC had got the story, they absolutely would've published. Yes.

Q   It would've been politically possible?

A   Oh, absolutely. Yes. Yes. I've never known a case in 30 or

40 years in broadcasting where the BBC has been leaned on and not published a story. You just can't get away with that at the BBC. The public wouldn't stand for it, and the news would leak that the story had been killed by those upstairs, whoever they are. It just would never happen. It couldn't possibly happen.

Q   Why were these stories broken by the newspapers do you think and not television?

A   Well, the television breaks stories. It's just the luck of where the story falls: who's got the contacts, who's got the information. No organisation, no newspaper, no broadcaster has got an exclusive on exclusives. They fall where they fall, and that's luck really.

Q   Do you think that the whole of UK television has let down the victims of historic sex abuse over 50 years?

A   This is such a complex story. I don't think there's anyone singularly to blame because I don't believe, but we'll see what the BBC independent report says about who knew what. If they knew and they hushed it up, then that is a very serious matter. If they didn't know, then you have to ask why didn't they know. Why didn't the victims come forward and complain? It's a very complex story. Very complex story. But we'll see what the Janet Smith report reveals, which I think is going to be published very shortly and that will help us.

Q   Why do you think the BBC self-censored its own Jimmy Savile investigation?

A   I think it was a complete cock-up. Total cock-up from the

beginning. Most scandals at the BBC of an editorial nature
are a cock-up. I think that the *Newsnight*, and I don't know
for sure. I've read the report, the Horrock's report. It
seemed to me that the editor of *Newsnight* thought
"actually *Newsnight* is not the place to be running celebrity
exposés. It's not really a *Newsnight* story. I've somehow got
myself into this, probably not right". But what he
should've done then was say, "Well, this is such an
important film. We have to get this into the public interest.
I must give it to *Panorama* or we'll just have a *Newsnight*
special or we must do something". You can't sit on a film
like that. You know what the departments at the BBC are
like. They're very, very protective of their own stories, and
they just got it wrong.

Q   A lot of people are asking what's the BBC for in today's
      internet age. Do you think that the BBC has a unique
      responsibility to mount major investigations and that
      that's an answer?

A   Journalism—no, I think it's more complex than that.
      Journalism, impartial journalism and investigative
      journalism is at the heart of the BBC's mission certainly,
      but also at the heart of the BBC's mission is to take the
      public's money and create wonderful programmes for
      radio and television made by British producers for British
      audiences with nothing on its mind other than to delight,
      to inform, to entertain, to educate. That's what the BBC
      stands for, and it is a huge engine for the creative

industries in the UK.

Q   Do you think the licence fee should be scrapped?

A   No, I don't. No.

Q   Do you think it will be scrapped?

A   No, I don't. Not in my lifetime. I think that it's too big. I
       think the BBC is too big, but we need to wait and see what
       the devolution settlement is; if we end up with a federal
       United Kingdom how the BBC fits into that, how much
       resource is needed to sustain an independent BBC
       Scotland, BBC Wales, BBC Northern Ireland, BBC England.
       The economics of that I don't know yet, but, given the
       status quo, I think the licence fee is far too high. The BBC
       does too many things.

Q   The license fee is far too high?

A   Much too high, yes.

Q   What would you do about it? Would you freeze it?

A   No. I wouldn't do anything other than start to look at the
       BBC from the bottom up, look at every single line of its
       total budget. "Why are we doing that? Is that nice to have
       or is it essential to our mission?" There are lots of things
       that the BBC does that they don't need to do anymore.

Q   So if the licence fee is far too high, what do you do? Do
       you cut it?

A   No, you work out what the BBC essentially has to have in
       order to maintain its role at the heart of British

broadcasting, radio, and television, and what it doesn't need to be doing. Does it still need studios? Does it still need to produce entertainment and drama? Can we leave that to the independent sector? Do we need all these people in strategy, all these people in HR, all this post production, all these studios? It's massive—all this property. It's a giant organisation. It's much too big in the current world.

Q   If the answer today's points is, "no, they don't", what then happens to the licence fee?

A   Well, you've got to work out what the core of the BBC needs to provide. Do they need four digital networks? Spectrum—even though Spectrum is more plentiful than it used to be in an analogue world, it's still very precious. There's a frequency debate going on inside Ofcom at the moment. Everybody's clamouring for more bandwidth and more frequency: the phone companies, everybody is. The BBC's sitting on a lot of that. Does it need four digital channels? Why?

Q   Would it satisfy your position if the government said, "Okay, well, we hear all that, Michael, and we agree with you, so we're going to freeze the licence fee for this parliament"? Would that be sufficient or would you want to cut?

A   I think you're coming at it the wrong way. You've got to look, you've got to build the BBC up. There's a phrase we use in business which is zero budgeting. You start the year; you don't start at the top and say, "We're going to cut 10%." You start at the bottom and say, "What is it we absolutely have to do and we absolutely need to do?" And then you work out how much do we need to fund that core mission of the BBC.

Q   Do you think Channel 4 should be privatised?

A   I'm not sufficiently up to speed on the economics of Channel 4 and the performance of Channel 4 and how threatened it is. I think it's a risk.

Q   To privatise it.

A   To privatise it. It may well be a risk not to privatise it. It's been a very successful and unique experiment anywhere in the world where you have a fully commercial channel, a public service channel, funded out of advertising revenue. It's done an amazing job over the years. How threatened it is—I worry about it long term, and I would imagine the Treasury worries about it long term.

Q   Say more about that?

A   Advertising revenue for free-to-air broadcasting is enjoying a bit of a bounce at the moment. Free-to-air television can still deliver impact, immediate impact for advertisers which the web can't do. But nevertheless, lots of money is moving onto the web in a more addressable, you can address individual consumers in a way you can't on television. So that's the big threat, the overall threat. At the moment, the economy's growing. Advertising spend is growing. I noticed this morning that Channel 4's revenue was only 2% up; whereas, that's well below where the market is, and that's due to their falling share. So the balance with Channel 4 of this innovative public service 'be different' remit is struggling a little bit in the face of commercial competition, both from other channels—and ITV's got its act together over the last five or six years—and the internet. There are serious challenges facing Channel 4.

Q   And would privatisation help that?

A   Well, it would sink or swim then on the basis of the market. It would have to pay shareholders, but it would have to be freed of its remit to be different and do the things that it does. I think British broadcasting would lose something in that. I have little doubt that every year the treasury runs the rule over whether to privatise Channel 4 or not.

Q   Michael, many thanks.

A   Pleasure. Is that all right?

Q   Perfect. Is there anything I haven't asked you that you'd like me to ask you?

A   No. You're fine.

Q   One of the problems with Channel 4 is its falling value because it doesn't own the rights. **End of recording**

Chapter III

Peter Ibbotson

The Editor of BBC TV Panorama programme at the height of Mrs Thatcher's power. Formerly BBC, ITV, C4 Executive.

Interviewer: James Hogan

Q   I'm joined now by Peter Ibbotson who edited *Panorama* during the Thatcher years and who was a senior figure at the BBC, Channel 4, and indeed ITV. Peter, welcome.

A   Thank you.

Q   What do you think has happened to television?

A   It has grown up. It has got bigger and it has changed due to an onslaught of technical, cultural, and economic forces.

Q   Do you think the internet will eventually kill off television?

A   No, it will extend it. Television is only one means of getting pictures and sound from people to people, starting off from the very few to the very many and increasingly from rather more people still to the many, but in so doing it is beginning to overturn. It's in the middle of overturning all the models that appeared to work in the earlier stages.

Q   What do you think has happened to the indies?

"RED by James Hogan"

A   Well, I think there was enormous hope and expectation in the late 70s, early 80s, when the indie movement finally lobbied and got Channel 4 that it would break the economic monopoly and the transmission monopoly of the existing channels and allow a thousand flowers to bloom. What it failed to recognise, and we probably all fail to recognise, was that the gatekeepers remained the broadcasters, so as you yourself have noted what happened was in the end to be successful, the indies had to accommodate themselves to the broadcasters and not the other way around.

Q   What has happened to investigative television on terrestrial TV?

A   Well, it's dying a—I'd like to say a slow, lingering death. It seems to be rather quick, lingering death because it's very expensive, because in commercial television you don't have licence conditions which require it as part of your right to broadcast, and because in a world of hundreds and hundreds of available channels, outlets, blogs, whatever, right across the scale, the ratio of paying viewers one way or another through a licence fee or through advertising subscription, the number of paying customers for the cost of making those hundred programmes just becomes less and less economic.

Q   Do the investigative teams exist anywhere in television today that could make the *Birmingham Six* or *Death on the*

Rock?

A   I would never say absolutely not but what they don't have is the continuity of outlets that used to exist like *World in Action, This Week, Panorama*. I think *Panorama* has the potential for that, but the pressure is now on for journalism to be as entertaining as it is investigative. For any programme editor with a set number of slots to fill a year and a limited budget, putting large chunks of that budget into investigations which may not bear fruit for months and years, if indeed at all, becomes a very, very serious risk.

Q   What's happened to the BBC?

A   Well, the BBC, like all big public institutions, is going through its middle age and its late middle age, and what happens is—to put it crudely—nice middle class people, health administrators, education administrators, local government, for all I know the MoD, but certainly the BBC, good, well-minded people go into these organisations, but they get bigger and bigger. The management structures get bigger and bigger and, in the end, the interests of the institution begin to drive out the creative needs for which the organisation was founded. Now I don't mean to be overly critical about that, but this is a process which is inexorable in all big institutions and it is clearly happening within the BBC.

Q   Should the BBC have exposed the MPs' expenses scandal?

A   Of course.

Q   Why didn't it?

"RED by James Hogan"

A I think the problem for the BBC is an innate caution because in the end it only has one customer.

Q The government.

A The government is the body, the customer, who decides what the income shall be; and that puts the BBC into two traps. The first trap is one of political caution that one sees is over the long view. You remember back in the '70s when the kind of ideas of Keith Joseph, the precursors of Thatcher, were first bubbling up, making programmes about that was thought to be slightly eccentric, and you remember we did make programmes about things like that. Move on into the kind of post-Thatcher era, and suddenly there's a new orthodoxy and the BBC will move with it, partly just to move with the times and where the debate has gone to but also with an eye to what the customer wants.

Q Do you think it was politically impossible for the BBC to do the MPs' expenses scandal?

A No. It would've caused enormous ructions, and I think that it's not unreasonable—sorry, it's an understandable - calculation that if your customer is parliament as a whole and the government in power then to offend that customer mightily. I mean the *Telegraph* did it. It didn't cost the *Telegraph*, apart from buying the CDs, a great deal. It wasn't an investment of huge investigative effort when it came to it but very good for the *Telegraph* for publishing.

Q   Do you think that the BBC's failure to do the MPs' expenses scandal was a case of self-censorship?

A   I don't know the detail. I don't know whether those CDs were offered to the BBC. I don't know whether anyone saw what was on them, took a view, whether it was debated.

Q   Should the BBC have exposed phone hacking at News International?

A   Well, that's the other great—well, there are two great stories that print press has done. One is the *Guardian*'s pursuit on that story and then the *Sunday Times* now very topical on FIFA. That requires dogged diligence and the *Sunday Times* case, being rebuffed time and time again, coming up with evidence of what was going on in the Qatar bid, etc., etc., and continuing to publish, continuing to tease away at it. I don't think the BBC is now constructed in a way in which it could allow individual reporters the time, the leeway to run for months and years pursuing something like that. The nearest is probably the stuff Peter Taylor's done on Northern Ireland, but I don't see many successors to that.

Q   It's notable, isn't it, that the two examples you've just given were both broken by newspapers and not by the BBC. Why is it that an organisation that's got an income of between £3-4 billion and has got at its core a public service remit, why is it the BBC can't organise itself to do those programmes?

A   Well, because a lot of television journalism has now

become derivative. I see in your book you give due praise to the *Today* programme for being thoughtful and intelligent. Nonetheless, when you listen to it, you are aware that a lot of it has happened at three in the morning, looking at the cuttings, looking at the diary. What are the stories of the day? And it does brilliantly a sort of exegesis on stories which are being broken elsewhere. I'm not aware, and I may be wrong, that the *Today* programme does a whole lot of primary investigative journalism.

Q   So television focuses on the visible, not the invisible.

A   And also the immediate. There are two things there. The picture is too often the driver. The example of there's a great flood in Mexico, a child is rescued from a car in a swollen river, and you'll get a minute of it at the top of the news because it's absolutely dramatic; it's gripping. And then a very dull economic story will be second or third in the bulletin. Now those are not in global terms or even national terms the right news values.

Q   They're picture values.

A   They are picture values, and I think a lot of news becomes derivative, becomes cyclical. Also, before the technology took a grip, before satellite news exchange, it was possible, say on *Panorama*, to send out a team on a Tuesday to Israel to interview the prime minister, to do a round-up of whatever, and bring back a new story. News reporters would go to places around the world and spend three or four days putting together a report on something that hadn't been broken. Because all stories are now available as they break 24 hours a day, most of what happens in news is reacting to something someone else has reported.

Now, this is not to say that television doesn't have incredible uses. It is a dramatic medium. It is very good at the interview. It's very good at the confrontation. *Question Time* will run forever because it's got the immediacy and it also speaks directly to people.

Q   Has the whole of UK television let down the victims of child sex abuse over 50 years?

A   Gosh, that's a very big and difficult question. Let's look at it. The word Kincora has been kicking around for, to my knowledge, 30 or 40 years. Did anyone do anything about it? No. Why? Impossible to penetrate, too difficult, and again it's the waiting for someone else to blow the whistle. As for the Savile stuff, most of the people at the BBC even hadn't got an inkling of what was going on.

Q   Just on the failure to expose child sex abuse over 50 years. Was one of the reasons do you think or maybe even the major reason why it wasn't done by television that you need a very specialist team of producers and researchers and so on dealing with very damaged people and that those teams have simply disappeared from British broadcasting?

A   I'm not sure they actually existed in that way. Just thinking back to the *Guardian* and phone hacking and television.

Yes, it should be possible for a broadcaster to allow a very good reporter to be following and investigating a story of that sort whilst doing other things. The problem is with broadcasting you've got from time to time to go and shoot an interview. It's not just putting something in a notebook and coming back to it. There is actually an expense of the physical process of maintaining the information you're gathering as you go along. I don't know.

Q   Why do you think the BBC self-censored its own investigation into Jimmy Savile?

A   I think partly because *Newsnight* saw itself as a Westminster-based political programme and this was sort of off its radar. It's something, well, had been commissioned by the programme but came in and they didn't really have a sense of how to handle it because it was outside its sense of its remit. But also because the BBC works in silos and the night entertainment silo—call it what you will—very important audience driver and the rest of it were seen as a force in the debate. Should you force the Savile Christmas tributes off air?

Now, what would've happened in an ideal world is that that decision would've been taken above the silo, someone saying, "Referred up. This is the issue. Should we transmit this?" Corporate lawyer comes to see it. Someone advises the DG. The DG takes a view, and in a sane world it would've gone out.

Q   Do you think that subconsciously the BBC didn't want to believe it [the Savile story] and so, therefore, they didn't want to publish it?

A   I think there were probably huge legal risks involved or perceived legal risks. I can't see inside other people's heads. There may have been a feeling that this was a can of worms which was too dangerous to open. I don't know. But the decisions I think should've been taken at the top and should've been taken. If it were legally transmittable, it should've been transmitted.

Q   Do you think that the BBC licence fee should be scrapped?

A   The problem with the licence fee, as I said earlier, is that there is one customer. The customer is the government. The great strength of the licence fee is that it allows for cross subsidy, that you can take the great pot of money, three billion or whatever, and do not only the most entertaining and fun programmes that commercial broadcasters also do but a fair amount of it also goes into more challenging stuff: music, arts, news, current affairs, whatever. That is not true forever of course. One of the traps that the BBC falls into is that in order to please its customer, the government, it's inclined to say, "Look. We are doing programmes for the whole nation. We're not just elitist." But in doing so, it then starts to look at ratings too hard to prove it is popular. It creates for itself the same, not economic straightjacket, but economic environment quite often that commercial television is working in. So that's why it has to be seen to beat ITV on this, that, and the other or to be within shouting distance in this genre or that genre.

So instead of having the freedom of cross subsidy, I think it sometimes wastes it. Now whether the licence fee should continue, for some time I thought it would be interesting to look at subscription models that if the BBC is so valuable to the public, news and whatever, presumably it could be market tested. A very large number of people will continue to pay it. Technology would allow it to be a subscription model. Keep out people who don't pay. In order to get the things they want. The danger then of course would be you would exacerbate the mimicking of the full market that in order to drive more and more subscriptions you'd do more and more popular and less and less demanding programmes. I mean you'd have to be very, very careful what mix of programmes you thought was going to maximise your income.

Q   Last question from me and then we'll go to other points you may wish to make. Tell me why you think that television is in long term decline as a serious intellectual medium.

A   I haven't said that television's in decline as much as it is mutating very fast, and a lot of it is obviously through the internet and through the ability of millions more people to have their say. No one can say that is a bad thing. Instead of three channel controllers in the land deciding what people should watch on a screen in their house, there is now amazing intellectual freedom, as well as all the bad things on the internet, of people to say things to each other and to do some of them very cheaply, ideas in particular.

Television has to change. I think if you look at the overarching view, if you could stand back two centuries, we are probably going through something as fundamental as the invention of print in the 15th century which led to everything. It led to the Reformation, the Wars of Religion. It led to the Enlightenment. It led to the scientific world we know now. The knock-ons of 15th century technology are absolutely colossal. I think that the technology which has grown in pace since the '70s in terms of electronic communication are still, despite the huge changes already in their infancy, will radically change the way we think about things, look at things, talk about things, and I suppose one has to be optimistic about that. The ways we did things must decline. New things you hope will be some of them positive and enlightening.

Q   I argue in the book, as you know, that because of what I describe as the economics of self-censorship and the decline of investigative journalism that really it is incumbent on the BBC more than ever to ensure that it properly resources.

A   But it fails, you see.

Q   Yeah, I know. So shall I ask you this other question?

A   Yeah.

Q   Ok. So a question in the context that we've been talking about the BBC. Do you believe that the BBC has a special role, more than ever actually over the coming years, to ensure that the democratic deficit is closed, that it delivers hard-hitting, investigative journalism that it properly resources?

A   Yeah, I think in terms of its contribution to democracy the BBC does an awful with the air time it gives to national politics and indeed local politics. That is a shop window which everyone has access to which very good teams, parliamentary and around the country, who do that. I have no worries on that account per se. I think the BBC handled the Leaders' Debate conundrum very maladroitly and may pay a price for that.

When you talk about investigative journalism, I think it completely fails at a local level even or perhaps even especially, and I think ITV does too. You turn on regional news programmes and you're looking at a police report. There's been a murder here. There's been a fire there. There's been a big pile-up on the motorway here. I can count on the fingers of one hand in the last year when I've seen a good report on a council scandal, some planning issue where corruption might've been alleged or whatever. That bit of kind of digging into—and local newspapers are as bad too because they have economic interests which they have to protect locally. But I would like to think that the BBC could be sufficiently resourced to do local journalism which did much more credit to local democracy.

Q   Obviously, it's a very hot topic about the future of the BBC
        and its future role and the licence fee in the new world of
        television and media. Do you think that the answer or one
        of the most important answers to what should the role of
        the BBC be in the future is that it really embraces and
        accepts that a key part of what it should be doing is
        holding authority to account and making major series of
        programmes which are teamed with very well resourced
        and very specialist people who can do these major
        investigations?

A   In an ideal world, yes.

Q   And will it happen?

A   I have my doubts.

Q   Why?

A   Well, because of the government as customer. I think
        there's a cosy relationship because in terms of formal
        Westminster politics the ding-dong is understood and
        sharp questions are asked, *Newsnight*, wherever. But
        spending a lot of time looking into let's say a scandal
        within a Ministry or something, I think it's much more
        likely still that it's going to be print journalists who fly the
        flag there.

Q   Just to go back to the whole question of the licence fee and
        subscription because you played a major part in the
        thinking around Peacock in the '80s when you were
        looking at this question of subscription. What's your
        reflection?

"RED by James Hogan"

A First, I think Peacock got one thing wrong. They quite rightly said that you have to open up the market in terms of television and they were great champions of the independents in that. The mistake they made was thinking that television channels could be, and they often use this analogy, like magazines, that you could have just as you have an angling magazine or an opera magazine you could have channels dedicated to these interests. That missed some essential points. First of all that people's viewing is finite. You can buy an angling magazine you can buy an opera magazine as long as you pay the cover price. It doesn't matter whether you flip through it for 30 seconds or spend the evening watching it. People have their own time budget for television, and even if you're a keen opera buff, the amount of time you're going to spend of an evening watching opera programmes is not going to be great because you want, like everyone else, to be watching other things.

The other point of course is that the magazine analogy breaks down because of production costs. To produce even six hours of television a day, most are even bought in, on angling or opera costs a hell of a lot more than putting a magazine out. So the sort of model they had in mind was slightly curious.

But when it comes to people paying directly for television, we now have some sophisticated models. Netflix is a superb example of how a commercial business has been made out of top-end drama. Now, how much of television can independently do that? I'm not sure. We obviously use sport and films as pay operations. News—unlikely. Game shows actually quite unlikely. So if you look at the BBC, you're looking about having a pay basis for the whole package. I think there are some political attractions in that because it would make the customer the public very directly and not the government and that will be a great escape for the BBC.

The problem, as I said before, is it would depend on the then managers of the BBC as to how they would use that income. Would they then skew the output to become sort of another ITV just to get that highest number of possible subscriptions in? Because that would not, in old-fashioned public service terms, serve everyone well because people might not say, "Well, I'll pay for news even though they want it." A lot of them would say, "Well, we don't want any opera or drama of a difficult sort," which traditionally would be something the BBC would do from time to time. So to give it commercial freedom in a market relationship with willing purchasers would have its downsides too.

Q   Could you replace the BBC licence fee with a tax or a licence on internet?

A   You could, but that's just rejigging the licence fee, isn't it? It gets the BBC out of the problem of it being a licence to have a television set which is clearly rather quaint now since there are so many other ways you could receive BBC programmes without having a machine in the corner of your sitting room. It just kicks the problem further down the road.

Q   Peter, many, many thanks.

A   Ok.

Q   Excellent.

End of Recording

Chapter IV

Roger Bolton

The presenter of BBC Radio 4 Feedback programme. Formerly Editor of BBC TV Panorama and the ITV flagship investigative series "This week".

Interviewer: James Hogan

Q   I'd be very interested to know what you think about the structure of the argument, yes? Okay, first of all I'm delighted to have with me Roger Bolton who's a contributor to the LSE study and also now to the latest study. Roger, good afternoon.

You have the book in front of you, in proof form there, would you like to pick out two or three ideas to comment on?

A   Well, it's certainly Red isn't it so congratulations on that. I think that the danger of books like this, I think, is that they get out of date very quickly and too many people who you talk to with these things have glorious pasts and inglorious futures. I think I'm one of them. Maybe I didn't have such a glorious past. So, there is a danger of looking at the past in terms of a golden age and I don't believe golden ages ever existed.

What I do believe, however, in this book is that there are some very perceptive analyses of what seems to be about to happen to British broadcasting and it's very unpleasant reading in that sense. I think Peter Ibbotson's interview is particularly good in looking at the state of the independent sector. Most indies lie. They lie about their profitability; they lie about their success and they lie to commissioning editors about what they can do because they are involved – most of them – outside of entertainment in a desperate struggle to survive with very low margins.

As a result, they don't have the self-confidence and they don't have the financial backing, often. And, therefore, don't have the courage to stand in front of commissioning editors and others and tell them they're wrong, their assumptions are wrong and they can't deliver. And all the pressures are on you to promise to deliver more than you can and, above all, to cater to the prejudices, well informed or not and the commissioning editor.

So, I think Peter's got that spot on. He says here, in particular, there are two pressures, these financial pressures. First at the pitch level to oversell and idea to get it accepted; second, at the execution level to do whatever it takes to meet expectations. The expectations are, of course, the commissioning editor.

The thing about the programme that you make as an independent is that you make a good programme, perhaps, there is no guarantee of getting another commission. The person who controls the power and future of your company is a commissioning editor. Unless you have such a successful programme with such large audiences that the commissioning editor just has to commission it whatever happens, unless you are like that and that doesn't apply in the factual area and doesn't apply in the investigative area, then in the end you are a suitor at the court of the commissioning editor.

Q   Do you think that today's indies could ever have produced *Death on the Rock*?

A   The problem about doing something like *Death on the Rock* is first of all that you have to commit massive resources without knowing what the result is. Secondly, when you've made that programme you have to face the onslaught of the government – Mrs Thatcher's Government in that case – and associated newspapers and other hangers on who want to curry favour with her. You have to have enough people prepared to stand up for that.

In the end, Thames did but they Thames lost its franchise; perhaps, as a result of that, perhaps not. But, it's not an encouraging precedent in terms of the BBC, that's very vulnerable, does it wish to end the government?

The investigative programmes that cause most trouble are those about government, the existing authorities, and about those areas which go to the heart of the nature of our democracy. So, in Northern Ireland where the argument was about was Northern Ireland part of the UK or not, the very existence of the UK was at stake, or thought to be; that's where the tensions came.

With the BBC, it has the money, it has the resources, it has the stated commitment but it has the vulnerability of needing the government to pay the licence fee; needing the government to renew its charter.

When you come to ITV in those days, in those days there were dependent upon the government allocating the right to broadcast.

Now, it's essentially in the hands of independents who have virtually no significant financial security; who, if they take risks and offend government, may well be cut loose by the broadcasters. It's much more difficult to do it. It depends crucially not so much on the programme makers but on the commissioners. If you have nothing, you still have a Channel 4. Some people are prepared to stand up for this sort of programming. It will survive, to a degree.

Whether it will survive in the BBC is a very, very big question. And I don't see it at all existing in ITV.

Q   Do you think that specialist teams of investigative journalists like the one that produced *Death on the Rock* and the *Birmingham Six*, still exist in British broadcasting?

A   The teams don't exist but the people who could make up those teams do. In other words, the talent is there; the commitment of individual journalists is there; their expertise is there; but, what is required to meld them into a team apart from leadership is money and a commitment to support such teams without knowing that they are going to

162

be productive.

It's crucial, if you think of the *Newsnight* problem, the problems they've got into each other… sorry, think of the *Newsnight* problems they got into over child abuse and the incorrect allegations that were made about a former Tory Peer in particular, that story, well, they tried to do that in a week. They did it with a team that wasn't that well balanced or had a great deal of expertise. You can't do really difficult investigations like that in a week, it takes a lot of time.

You need, for example, in terms of child abuse, people who understand about those who've been abused and the way in which they will have been affected, and their testimony will have been affected subsequently. So, it may well be the case that somebody has been abused horribly but whether they are telling the truth is another matter; they may no longer know what the truth is such is the nature of the disturbance that occurred.

So, in just making the assessments there you have to have people who have dealt with that before, let alone people who have the common sense to show photographs of the people who are alleged, the leading figures who are alleged to have caused that abuse to the people involved in the first place. So, the whole lot of journalistic things you need to know about.

But, in areas of real difficulty you need to know, you need to have specialisms. If you are dealing with Northern Ireland you make judgments at a certain stage which are very difficult if you don't know Ireland very well, Northern Ireland very well, if you don't have contacts you can go to who will talk to you off the record, who you have built up over a long period.

When we look at what Peter Taylor still does for the BBC, and Peter is now in his 70s, he got on the plane back to Northern Ireland when there were not programmes being made just to keep his contacts going and the BBC were prepared to fund that. They aren't now. It also meant that people would tell him, for example, the person who was the key link between the government and the IRA was prepared to speak to Peter but tell Peter the story 10 years before he was prepared to allow Peter to tell it.

That level of trust between a source for a reporter is built up over a long period. It leads to scoops. But, you can't sort of say "oh, we've got a week here; can you do this story and deliver me a scoop at the same time". So, there has to be a commitment ahead of knowing what the programmes are and there have to be specialist teams which are built up with specialist knowledge. That's almost, that is impossible for an independent to do unless a commissioner takes a long term view and backs them over a long period.

So, it means the BBC is best placed, still, to do that sort of programming in principle but the courage required in a hostile political environment is great.

Q   Do you accept that the near death of investigative journalism has created a serious democratic deficit in British broadcasting?

A   Well, I think we're in a paradoxical position here which is that due to the internet and due to the way in which communications have gone we know more about politics and politicians than we ever did. So, we are better informed. The public is better informed. So, to that extent political reporting, I think, is better just because there is more information out there. However, in terms of things we don't know about that we should know about which is what investigative journalism should be about, we are worse placed. So, overall, we know more and, yet, in certain areas we know less. And we will know in 20-30 years' time what it is we didn't know. And that is what investigative journalists are supposed to tell you, what you don't know now and you think afterwards "how could we not have known?"

I used to see on Panorama, perhaps rather pompously because I was quite pompous when I was running Panorama, I keep thinking "what are the important stories in 20 years' time when we look back that we didn't spot or do?" You can see what's on the surface, what's going on underneath that really matters far more than what's on the surface and that the public ought to know about? That's the job of investigative journalism and that job, largely, is not now being done because the … I don't know if it's courage or whatever, but the economics of the business make it very difficult and also the political will to do that stuff is lacking.

I'll give you an example. And I'm not sure how many, how much people are aware of it. I sat on a jury for the Royal

Television Society, and we looked for investigative journalists and there were one or two outstanding examples, including the BBC one by John Ware which won which was about army death squads in Northern Ireland; brilliant piece of journalism but it took him probably, 20 years to make really.

We were judging that against a superb, two superb observational documentaries from Channel 4. They were excellent. They took us into communities that we'd not been. We saw things that we didn't know, we'd never seen before. They were superb. But, they weren't journalism; they weren't investigative journalism because they never interrogated what they were being shown. They never asked questions about what was happening; they never followed up about whether what people said was true, false or whatever. So, those documentaries took you to mind-boggling places but there was no interrogation of the facts or the evidence. And you didn't know, for example, the terms on which access had been gained.

But, Channel 4 was trying to tell us this was investigative documentaries. No, it's not. And the other thing, of course, is that the thing about that observational documentary is that costs are containable. Once you've got access, which is very difficult and takes some time, you're in and then you film nearly everything; it's containable; then you edit. So, you can cost. So, you know before you are embarking on the project, if you are any good, what it will cost. When you start an investigative documentary, you don't even know if you've got the documentary let alone what it will cost. You try; you have a rough idea. But, if you get to the lawyers and they say "that's very interesting but, hold on, you need more evidence about this, more evidence about that", you have to go back, you don't know how long it takes you to get the evidence. Or, something changes, a witness comes forward who you didn't know about who can tell you something but can't do it for another month, you know, what do you do? You can't say "we'll stop filming, we'll stop editing, we'll put the programme out when the investigation is complete."

So, whereas, in terms of access documentary and also because of part of the technology we have better, more interesting documentaries, they are, in the end, showing you what's on the surface. Investigative journalism and documentaries should show you what's beneath the surface. So, more is above the surface, more is visible but there's a lot under there that we're not touching. And, of course, there are a lot of very happy people in this country that we are touching, mainly, the powerful, as usual.

Q   Now, as ever, very topical indeed is the future role of the BBC. Do you accept that if there is a democratic deficit in British broadcasting that the BBC is really the only one, the only institution that can fill the void?

A   BBC is a means to an end. In the past it's been the only way of achieving public service broadcasting. I now think it's deeply flawed. I think there are lots of things wrong with it but I do not see a convincing picture of the future which involves public service broadcasting that does not have the BBC in some form, at its heart. It needs reform in many areas but what's the alternative?

There is a national newspaper. We've just finished the election. There's a national newspaper that has just rewarded certain of its journalists because the right party won the election and the journalists played their part in that. In other words, the journalists are not being rewarded for their journalism, they are being rewarded for their propaganda which assisted one party in the election, got the right result, that the owners wanted.

Now, at least the BBC isn't involved in that sort of game!

Q   Finally, if we accept that we need to protect and defend specialist teams working on investigative journalism, and that that costs money and broad shoulders, does that not suggest that the BBC has a very particular role in years to come?

A   I think it does because you've got to have an organisation that, first of all, knows what its income is, isn't living hand to mouth, can say "we've got a guaranteed income; we know we can allocate these resources for a year because we know where the money is". So, you need guaranteed income. You can't be living hand to mouth as most organisations are and can't do it. Secondly, you have to assemble a body of specialists, legal as well as anything else, that can back up productions.

It does mean you are very tough on the producers, doesn't mean that you have to stop, lay off some investigations and say "come back in three or four months' time and we'll look at it again", and whatever. But, it does mean there has to be a fundamental commitment to that sort of journalism and the resourcing of it, not just in money but in terms of editorial time, back-up, legal assistance and so on. But, I would say that if the BBC wasn't prepared to do that then one of the major planks, one of the major reasons for having it goes by the wayside.

Channel 4? Well, I think that one of the things that helps Channel 4 is the BBC. Michael Grade used to say "the BBC keeps us all straight". And it was certainly when I was in ITV having Granada competing with Thames Television, *World in Action* against *This Week*, that element of competition was very healthy and when *World in Action* was taking the heat we'd do something on *This Week* that was adventurous, and so on. And at one stage when *This Week* was taking particular heat over Ireland they passed stuff to me in the BBC a *Nationwide* programme which I ran.

If Channel 4 was left by itself I think independent journalism would whither because it would be picked upon, it would be the only organisation doing it. So, Channel 4, in order for Channel 4 to be brave, in a way, it also needs the BBC. These things are very much related and you pick off one and the second is much easier to pick off.

There may be a proper reason to look at the way its run but one of its primary public purposes ought to be investigative journalism. And if it doesn't do that I'm not sure we should be supporting it.

Q   Many thanks.

End of interview

Chapter V

Richard Horwood

Richard has been an entrepreneurial innovator in British media for some 20 years, after careers in law and investment banking. Chief Executive of Blink TV, a TV production and distribution company specializing in live music content and on stage screen visuals, he is also Chairman of The Local Digital Company, a joint venture with local press groups developing interactive native advertising videos for brands and local advertisers.

He is best known for his resolutely commercial approach to local television, which started in the early nineties with his founding and running the Mirror Group's cable network of affiliated local TV stations opting out of a national programming spine. As well as a successful broadcaster, the business included a substantial TV production company, a premium rate telephone service provider, and an airtime sales house.

Richard bought technology company Vio from BT and Scitex in 2001, and AdSEND from the Associated Press in America in 2005, turning them into a world market leader in print advertising online delivery solutions. Living in America for two years, he was instrumental in merging competing European and American technology standards for print advertising processes.

Returning to British local television in 2010, Richard formed the Channel 6 Consortium, one of the main players in the

"RED by James Hogan"

Government's local TV initiative, and led its bid for the London Public Service Broadcaster TV franchise.

Interviewer: James Hogan

Q   With me today is Richard Horwood. Richard, many thanks for taking part. Could you just identify your job title please?

A   Yes, I'm Chairman of a company called The Local Digital Company, and I'm also Chief Executive of Blink TV.

Q   What do you think has happened to television?

A   I actually think it's gone from strength to strength, but one of the issues about television is defining it now. You know, when you say television, I assume you mean linear broadcast television, and maybe the catch up services, so we're talking about channels. So scheduled television. But of course television appears in lots of different ways now, because the way that you get it is so different. You know, it doesn't have to be over the air, it can be by satellite or cable, it can be over the Internet, it can be on your phone. This is all television, broadcast in these ways, and yet you're consuming it, the people who-, the consumer is receiving it in a variety of different ways and for different purposes.

So one of the other key things here is that we've got to look at the supply side as well as the demand side of it. So on the supply side you've got lots of different ways of doing the same thing, and so it's been sliced and diced, so you have a really fragmented marketplace, although it's dominated by a few big players. On the consumer side, you've got confusion. You've got really an amazing array of things that you can actually consume that are television. The problem is when you're trying to find commercial ways of actually making it pay, and from the advertising point of view, it's just got very complicated. So they end up doing the same thing but in lots of different ways. So you've got targeted television, you've got broadcast television, you've got on demand type television, and all that kind of stuff will mean that the advertiser or whoever it is that ends up paying for it will deal with it, and you, in a different way.

Q   What's been happening to local television?

A   It's got a bit confused. I mean, local television is actually a great idea, and it's a very important idea, especially when you're talking about lots of local devolution going on, because television puts a spotlight on things, and again here we're talking about broadcast television, essentially. Broadcast television is the only thing that can really show up, in a very meaningful and direct way, what's going on right now. On demand stuff requires people to want to actually get it. They need to know that they want to know whatever the information is, and then they have to go and get it. Broadcast is pushing it out all the time, and that's really important to democracy, and, well, in terms of local television, as we're devolving more and more to local politicians and to local businesses and so on, local television actually ought to play a very big part. What's happened is that an initiative which was, in principle, a political initiative which was, 'We ought to do local television,' which was five years ago, has turned itself into more of an initiative about being there, as opposed to achieving, I think, the political goals that were set for it, and the problem we've got is that the way it's been set up is not commercial.

Q   Explain the democratic potential of local TV.

A   We've just-, today we're having the elections for the Tower Hamlets mayor following the ousting of a corrupt mayor who was banned and then kicked out. There is a London TV station. It should be all over this, and it can be all over this, and I'm sure it is actually on London Live, because they are, I've seen a piece on it, but local television could really get to grips with this and go through all the issues in a very detailed way. In a way that national television with regional opt outs is just not going to happen. The issues that are going on in Tower Hamlets are fascinating, as well as being quite serious.

The election's happening today, we were doing some hustings just a couple of days ago, and I was wandering around trying to get people interested in coming. Very few people even knew the elections were happening, despite this being a one off and being such a dramatic thing with a mayor actually thrown out by an electoral court. So local television could have really focused on that so much more, along with print, because the Standard owns the local television station, and the Standard has covered the story

174

really quite well, but local television could have really brought it alive, and that, I don't think, has happened, and that's a shame.

Q   And why is it not doing that?

A   It's expensive to do it. You need to put the resources in, and you need to set it up properly, commercially, so that the money can be raised to fund these things. I actually have a lot of time for the people behind London Live, because they've put their heart and soul into it. It was just structured wrongly from day one, in my opinion. What they promised to do was 100% local programming all day, every day, for 12 years. That's what their licence says they have to do, and unfortunately, and most-, an awful lot of it has to be first run, as well, which is really tough and you know that. So they've given themselves a herculean task which simply cannot be done. The BBC wouldn't even begin to try and do that.

So that's the issue, it's structured wrongly, and that's why they can't do it. They need to actually do programming that generates a lot of viewing to get commercial revenues, and then really focus their resources, their own resources, into doing things like investigative journalism, which you can do on television just as well as you can do in the newspapers, but they work with the newspaper. They're owned by the newspaper. They could put that together and they could do a really good service if it was focused and they didn't have to spread themselves so thinly. That's the problem.

Q   Can local TV deliver hard hitting investigative journalism?

"RED by James Hogan"

A   It's difficult, because it's very hard to monetise it. If that's all you're doing, you probably won't actually get a return. Why? Because advertisers don't want to advertise around news. News is highly valued, but it's actually not watched by large numbers in the way that entertainment is. So you've got two forces there, where the advertisers don't really want to advertise around it, because people are watching bad news and not in a good mood and, therefore, they don't want to buy the product, so advertisers tend to shy away from it; and at the same time, you've got the cost of making it is really quite high, unless you're going to do it in a very thin way. So it tends to frustrate itself, which is why you've got to combine a focused attention on news and current affairs and put resource into it, but fund it from something that is of a completely different character, which is probably entertainment-led, which is what gets the viewers, and then strong marketing around that. Now that's not the structure that they were allowed to do. They had a licence that says they can't do that, and they volunteered that licence in order to win the licence, and that was a mistake.

Q   What do you think the future holds for the BBC?

A   I have a huge amount of time for the BBC, because it does stuff that wouldn't otherwise be done. It does set a standard, and British-, I mean, I've lived in America and been all over the world. The quality of television we have here, we take it for granted and we shouldn't, and it's really driven by the fact that the BBC is up there as a competitor to commercial idols as far as audience is concerned, and so the commercial broadcasters have to step up to the same sort of standards. They can't not, otherwise they'd get no viewing at all. So the BBC is hugely valuable for that.

The other thing that the BBC must do, and does look for, is areas where there isn't an obvious commercial market for what would otherwise still be a very valuable programme, and kinds of programme, whether it's children's programming, whether it's doing documentaries about things that are important but may not affect a huge number of people, that sort of thing. The BBC can step up and do that.

Q   Is it too big?

A   It is huge, and any huge organisation tends to get lazy, tends to get bureaucratic, because you need the systems to communicate within the organisation, and it makes it harder for the organisation to work. So it's almost inevitable that it's too big because it's very big. So there is an argument that you could strip it down to do focused things, without having to have all that massive bureaucracy around it. The trouble is if you take the bureaucracy out of it, the management out, as in the NHS, as in any other large organisation, that's when errors start to happen, and that's when you get South Staffs, that's when you get other things, because the managers are being stripped back and so people aren't keeping control of things, but the bureaucracy, kind of, ends up taking control of itself, and it, sort of, feeds on itself, and that's part of the problem with a huge organisation.

Q   Is the BBC damaging local journalism?

A   The BBC has an interesting symbiosis with local journalism
     because where do you think-, and again you know this, but
     where do you think the BBC reporters get their stories? The
     first thing they do is read the local press. It's the local press
     who do the local journalism, for the most part. If it weren't
     for the local press, the BBC would have a really tough time
     actually filling their local programmes or their regional
     programme. So there is this symbiotic relationship that's
     really important for the BBC. If the BBC steps up its
     activities in the local market in terms of online, for example,
     and really beefs up its online presence for the local market
     with online news, which no other commercial broadcaster
     could possibly do, because it would be too expensive to do it
     in terms of the return you might get, that could damage the
     local press, which is clearly migrating, as well, to digital and
     to online services, and has to.

     So the local press has to get a commercial return. Its USP is
     that it gives you the local news. If the local news is available
     for free, and of very high quality, from the BBC as an
     alternative, people will go to the BBC. They won't go to the
     local press. So the local press then will fail, but that will
     damage the BBC because it won't be able to do its job
     properly because it relies on the local press. So there is an
     absolute crying need, and it's something that I think the

charter renewal should look at, for the BBC to look at ways where it can help support local journalism in-, I know it's going to be very difficult, because it's commercial local journalism, that has to be paid for, and the BBC should find a way to work with the local press. Now at the moment, inevitably and for as long as you and I can remember, they've been at war, because they feel that the BBC's got its tanks on their lawn. That war has to be over. That war has to stop.

When-, you may remember, the BBC, when ITV first started saying that it wanted to cut back on its regional coverage because it wasn't worth the PSB licence, which was probably about 10 years ago now, the BBC stepped up and said, 'Oh, well we'll do local television,' and they did an experiment and it was actually very good. The BBC then-, the people who did it, wanted to roll it out. The BBC Trust, on the back of, or in response to the local press, already getting very upset about this, banned itself, banned the BBC from actually doing local television, because they knew it would destroy the local press. So the BBC has done a self-denying ordinance.

I think we may be at an interesting point here, a crossroads, where the local press, because it's had such a tough time anyway, with circulations falling, with-, it's much harder to monetise online than it is to monetise print. Rough rule of thumb, for every £1 of print advertising, you get maybe 10p on digital advertising. So that's a very difficult thing to deal with if you're migrating your business online. So I think this may be a moment where the BBC could actually step up and help save the local press, and help save local journalism that way.

Q   Should the licence fee be scrapped?

A   No.

Q   Should it be cut?

A   I think it needs to be examined closely. It's a huge amount of money. What the-, the tradition over the last few years has been to get the BBC to pay for more things, whether it's the BBC World Service, or whether it's dealing with funding the pensioners' free licences and that sort of thing, there is an argument that the BBC should take more of that on, out of the licence fee, but that's effectively cutting the licence fee. I do think there is an argument that says that it should be more targeted so that we know that the licence fee is being paid to the BBC to do specific things, not just as a great big blank cheque.

Do I think it's too much? Well, the BBC is competing in a world of very, very powerful and very well financed media companies where, once upon a time, the BBC with billions of revenue from the licence fee was the biggest beast in the jungle. Now they're, you know, quite a modest beast, in terms of broadcasters. So they're big, but I'm not sure that cutting the licence fee would actually enhance the offering that the BBC can do, where it's valuable, and we just have to do this very careful analysis of what, you know, what the value is. What do we want the BBC to do? Where is it achieving most? What shouldn't it be doing is another question.

I do have to ask myself whether it should be competing for Saturday night entertainment viewing. It's very hard for it not to, because that's such an important part of people's lives and culture and so on, but when they go down the 'me too' talent show type competitions, which are done brilliantly by commercial broadcasters, does the BBC actually need to do that as well? The trouble is, if you say they can't, then they kind of hand over Saturday night entertainment, or Saturday night viewing to commercial broadcasters.

Q   Are there other things you don't think they should be doing?

A   No. I don't think I could put my finger on any broad category that the BBC touches that I don't think they should do at all. As I said, I think the one area where personally I feel there's a question mark is this populist television. The audience grabbing stuff, the pure ratings rush. I think the BBC-, I mean, Channel 4 has, sort of, faced the same sort of issues, and Channel 4 I think has had a more creative solution to it.

Q   Do you think Channel 4 should be privatised?

A   There's a case for it. I think it's quite difficult, because Channel 4 does have a mission to do things that are not necessarily compatible with living in a commercial world, but it is commercially financed through advertising, so it has to get the ratings to get the advertising, so it's kind of half there already. It could distort the market a bit, if it were genuinely commercial, and-, because it would have to be allowed to compete in the real world. So I think there's a real issue there that-, can you privatise Channel 4 and at the same time force it to do things that aren't really commercial, which is kind of where it is at the moment, but are culturally really valuable. So I don't think it's a clean cut answer, that one.

Q   What do you think the future for local television in London is?

A   I think we've got it wrong. The right answer was probably not politically the most acceptable answer which was to allow the London television station, the London franchise, which is so different to any other franchise, because it's-, London is so different to any other city in the country. I think it had to be allowed to be a different kind of commercial beast in order to really do its job properly. I would say that, because I ran a bid that was based on a much more commercial structure.

I have absolutely no doubt that if our bid had won, then we would now have a very successful business. I would say that, wouldn't I? But the logic is there, and I don't think anyone actually really argues with that, because what we said was, 'You've got to have a lot of commercial programming, and behave like a grown up broadcaster.' If you've got prominent listing, if you're cheek by jowl with the big PSBs, with ITV1, ITV2 and so on, you've got to actually look like you belong there; if you don't look like you belong there, you're going to actually fail worse than if you were buried further down in the listings.

So London could have had, I don't know whether the world can change, but London certainly could have had a station that would have looked like it belonged at the top of the listings and would have got the viewing as a result, but to do that you had to allow it to be a much more commercial beast than politically was acceptable, and that was the problem. It went to the party that said, 'We will do all local, all the time,' and that was the main factor that won them the bid. They bid what they had to bid to win the licence. They didn't bid what would be a commercial success, and I think that was a mistake. I think it was a mistake of Ofcom, though they were forced into a particular way of analysing and assessing these bids, but I think Ofcom-, clearly I think Ofcom made a mistake in going for the bid that gave them the biggest political success, lots and lots of local television, rather than the one that was most clearly commercially viable.

There was an interesting subtlety in the way the bids were run, which was that Ofcom didn't actually look at commercial viability. It looked at what it called 'commercial sustainability', and there's a very interesting difference between the two. It may not be obvious. Commercial viability means it can sustain itself, commercially. Commercial sustainability says someone will write a cheque to support it. It doesn't have to sustain itself; it could be sustained by something else. It could be part of a larger organisation, it could be a loss leader; it could be something like that. And they went for commercial sustainability, not commercial viability, and I think that was a mistake.

Q   What does London Live need to do, in your view, to meet the challenge in front of it?

A   I think it needs a lot more investment and I think it needs a re-launch, to be honest. I think it needs to be a different thing to what it was launched to be. The people who are doing the work for it are actually doing a pretty good job. They've just got the wrong remit, and it's very hard to change that. One of the things that we discussed when the bids were being put together and I was actually talking to the Standard, was one of the things that I was saying to them, in my view, is you can't sort of start with a broadcast television channel-, you can't easily start small and then gradually grow and hope people will get to like you. The way with a TV channel is if you start small, you stay small.

If you-, you have to really go for it at the start, do something that is really going to be attention grabbing, audience grabbing, advertiser grabbing, people are going to be talking about, marquee programmes, that sort of thing. Make your mark on the world. And then once you've got yourself to a level that can work, then you can look at driving it towards profitability in a host of different ways.

But if you look, for example, at what they're doing online,

there was meant to be a huge online offering, as well, around the broadcast station, as part of what won them the bid. That hasn't really happened. Why hasn't it happened? Because they've had to put all their efforts into trying to make the broadcast station work and they haven't really put the resources, or had the resources, to make the rest of it work. So the whole thing is kind of drifting along a little bit.

Now I wish them well. The last thing I want is for London Live to fail. There's been a lot of discussion about that, and it would be fantastic if the current owners, for whatever reason, if they don't want to fund it and really launch it and push it properly, then if somebody else came along and did that, I think that would be great, but I think it's got-, personally, I think the only way that will work is if the licence is completely changed, and that's rather difficult, because it was a competitive auction, and they won because of what they promised to do in the licence.

So it's a Catch 22. So it's a very, very difficult situation. It's not getting significant viewing, which is public knowledge, and as I said earlier, I don't think that the election coverage for the local-, for the Tower Hamlets mayor, let alone for the General Election, when London had a completely different story to the rest of the country. The London TV channel had an opportunity, really to take ownership of what was going on in London politics, because it was so different to what we saw in the whole of the rest of the country, and it was a really quite exciting election, in the end. London Live didn't do that, and that's a shame. They didn't do it not because they didn't want to do it, but they just haven't got the resources to do it.

"RED by James Hogan"

Q   Richard, many thanks.

A   My pleasure. **End of interview**

Chapter VI

Greg Dyke

Chairman of the Football Association and the British Film Institute. Formerly Director-General of the BBC. He resigned as Director-General when the BBC was criticised by the Hutton enquiry over its handling of the story that the British government "sexed up" the argument for going to war in Iraq.

Interviewer: James Hogan

Q   Many thanks for taking part. Please tell me how you came into television.

A   I got a job at London Weekend as a researcher. I've been a journalist in my early life, I then went onto university, I then went and did other things. And I then wanted to go somewhere where I could do serious... some serious work, and so I went... I was very lucky to get a job as a researcher at London Weekend Television.

Q   How tough was it to do that?

A   What, to get the job?

Q   Yes.

A   I had a mate who worked there who made sure I got onto the shortlist, and then it was a strange interviewing process, but I mean, I was 30 at the time, and I applied for a job on a programmed called *Weekend World* and eventually got a job on a programme called *The London Programme*.

Q   What were your earliest observations of the television industry?

A   Well, I joined London Weekend Television at a time when its Current Affairs Department was growing pretty rapidly. It did a particular sort of current affairs, which I still believe was very valid, which was try to understand what the subject is about, and if you see a problem, try to explain what could be done about it, as opposed to just that style of current affairs that says, 'Isn't everything terrible? See you next week.'

Q   What were the biggest changes that took place in the 1980s that you experienced?

A   Well, the period say... the '60s changed television quite dramatically, because the BBC invented what I would call quality popular programming. You know, from *Z-Cars* to *Steptoe* to all that sort of thing, that sort of programming, and turned around... I mean, if you go back to 1960, you know, ITV was the dominant broadcaster, in popular terms. By 10 years later, they weren't. The BBC had changed the whole landscape of television, by creating British popular programming, and what it meant for the next 20 years was the amount of American material on British television went into a pretty sharp decline. The '80s was a different period, because the '80s came with Channel 4, breakfast television, and then of course Sky and multichannel television, and that was... it didn't seem it at the time, but actually it was a pretty dramatic change, and had an impact on what came afterwards.

Q   What do you think the impact of satellite television has been?

A   Well the coming of satellite with multichannel television has had an enormous impact, particularly on ITV. It's changed... we should have seen it coming. We should have known what impact it had, because you could see that impact it's had with cable in America, but those of us who were working, say, in ITV at the time, thought we could see it off; and instead of changing our whole strategy to embrace it, and be part of it, we thought we could see it off, which was a big mistake.

Q   What was the impact of the 1990 Broadcast Act and the auctioning of ITV licences?

A   Well, the auctioning of the licences was the sort of... it really was, you know, shutting the stable door after the horse had bolted. So it only ever happened that one time; some quite good companies lost, some pretty average companies won, but of course not soon after that you got the whole change in the ownership rules and everything else so you know, ITV... You were still hanging onto this idea that there were 15 regions and that was only possible because of the monopoly that ITV had had.

The monopoly was going, and the franchise auction was a

sort of throwback to the past, really, and was irrelevant by the time it happened, but it didn't help ITV. It helped some of us, I mean, you know, I was running London Weekend at the time. We did very well. We won London Weekend, we won breakfast television and we won... we bought a chunk of Yorkshire Television at a later stage, because we'd been one of the successful ones, but if I tell you we bid £11 million and won, and the people bidding against us bid £32 million and lost, it was a rather strange process.

Q   What do you think about breakfast television these days?

A   I think breakfast television today is pretty dull. I don't think it's... when it started, of course there were very few people watching, and the first people there were women and children, mothers with children, often, and it was quite interesting and quite innovative. I think today it's pretty dull. I don't think it's very exciting. I think the BBC show is aimed at over 65s, and the ITV show is lost. It doesn't know what it is.

Q   What's been the impact of 24 hour news?

A   I think there is a problem with 24 hour news. I think it was inevitable, but I think there is a problem and that is every story has to be exciting, every story has to be breaking news, and often nothing's happening. Every so often you watch... I mean, I'll never forget the one where the ticker tape said, 'Prime Minister leaves Downing Street.' You know, the ticker across the bottom of the... he'd got in his car and gone out of Downing Street. I mean that's not news, that's just... and 24 hour news is brilliant when there's a really good story, but for a lot of the time it's tedious.

Q   What has happened to the coverage of sport in the last 20 years, on TV?

A   Well sport has become... well, I'll say again. When people ask, 'Why have we not got home box office in this country? Why are we not making that, sort of, brilliant drama paid for by paid television?' the answer is because we gave all that money to footballers, and with the coming of Sky and the coming of paid television, they chose the business model of football, which has been enormously successful for Sky and for football, but it does mean millions, billions, really, that came in through paid television, was not spent on drama. It was handed over to footballers.

Q   Do you think too much money is being spent on sports coverage?

A   Well it's a market. Sky couldn't live without football, which is why now enormous sums are paid. If anyone had told you when they set up the Premier League that 20-odd years later they'd be getting the sort of sums they get, no one would have believed it. So it's been... for sport overall, well there are certain sports that television really wants and the rest have got left behind, but I mean it has put a lot of money into sport. But you see things like cricket where a lot of money is spent, and cricket needs that money, but it's damaging cricket because it's not on terrestrial television. It's only on satellite television, and your audiences for sport are much lower on satellite television than terrestrial television. I always remember when the England Wales rugby match, one year was obviously in Cardiff, one year in Twickenham. The year it was in Twickenham, it was on Sky and got audiences of about a million, then the following year it was on the BBC and got audiences of six and seven million. So sport on television has become a business. The BBC, which always had a reputation for great sport on television has struggled to keep up, because it just hasn't got enough money.

Q   What's your view about the state of ITV today?

A   I think ITV today... I think ITV has had a very difficult period. I think ITV in the first decade of this century was not particularly well run. I think they failed to respond to competition, but I think in recent years it's done better because it's worked out what its position is in this market. But if you think of... go back to when I first worked in ITV, which was, sort of, the dominant commercial broadcaster, it's nothing like that now.

Q   What's your view about the state of Channel 4 today?

A   Well Channel 4 has gone the same way as most... as all broadcasters. You know, they've all lost audience. Now if you're the BBC and you managed to keep the licence fee, that's fine. If you're Channel 4, ITV, you've just lost... losing audience means you're losing revenue, and I think as a result, Channel 4 is not what you'd say was the radical, interesting, racy channel it was, but that was probably inevitable in a world of much greater competition.

Q Do you think it should be privatised?

A I don't think it makes much difference. I think if you did privatise Channel 4, I would turn it into a trust. I think it should be a public trust or something like that. I don't think it would make much difference to what Channel 4 is.

Q And if it was turned into a trust, it would have to retain its remit, would you say?

A Well yes, it would be silly to lose its remit, because its remit is very commercial. I mean, what people didn't understand when Channel 4 first started was that if you could get the young, as they did, early on, then that was commercially very attractive. As opposed to, you know... you've got to look at television, commercial television, as it was, I mean, advertisers would pay large sums of money to get the right sort of audience. Channel 4 delivered that sort of audience, so once they started selling their own advertising it became immensely successful for a period.

Q What's your view about the state of Channel 5 today?

A I mean, Channel 5 came into existence at a very difficult time and it had to cope with that. It had to cope with much, much greater competition. It's survived, I don't think it's something that you could be particularly proud of, but it's survived.

Q What's happened to the indies?

"RED by James Hogan"

A   Well I think the coming of the independent sector changed television dramatically; some of it to the benefit of television and some of it not. To the benefit of television, suddenly a lot more people are working on new ideas, thinking up new ideas and trying to sell them in, and that's been to the benefit of television.

I think many successful Channel 4 programmes are being sold overseas by the independent producers, whereas they wouldn't have been if they'd belonged to Channel 4 or BBC International, those sorts of things, and I think that's to the good of television, but I do think it has meant that money has come to dominate television in a way that it wouldn't have done 30 years ago.

When I first got a job in television, if you had a good idea, you got a buzz that it was on the television. Today if you've got a good idea, your major aim is, 'How do I maximise my income from it?' I'm not sure that's to the benefit of television.

I think with the independents, and with Channel 4, also came the commissioning editor system, which I think has been quite damaging to television. I think too many people are now involved in a decision of whether a programme hits the air or not, and I think that has... I think often there's a lack of trust, that actually what... I made a television programme one time about HBO, and why HBO in America had been so successful. How did they turn HBO from a channel that did old movies and boxing into something that did some of the best drama in the world? In the end you routed it down, they trusted the creatives. So if someone went in with an idea for a series, they said, 'Yes,' they let it go, they then trusted the creatives. I think the commissioning editor system we've got in this country means there's a double guessing of creatives all the time, and my view is television would be far better to say, 'Look, you just made a great series. Make us another one. Tell us what you want it to be about and make it, and if it doesn't work then we'll move on to someone else.' But this idea that you've got, often... often the commissioning editors, in creative terms, are less talented then the producers and directors who are making the shows, and that can't be in anybody's interest.

Q   Do you think the 'let a thousand flowers bloom' philosophy of the '80s is dead?

A   Well there are many more channels, so there are many more outlets. But of course they haven't really got the money, a lot of them haven't got the money, so I mean programming is much cheaper than it was, because of technological changes, so it's cheaper to make, but I think it was probably inevitable that television would hit a stage where maybe it wasn't novel anymore, it wasn't new anymore and people were less interested.

Q   It's got middle aged.

A   Yes. It's got middle aged, I think that's right, and I think when I look now, what do I watch on television? Not a lot. News, events, sport. Middle range programming has got lost. So if you look at what's happened, say, to Saturday nights. *Strictly, X-Factor, X-Factor* I think is now gradually going, but *Strictly*, big success, massive budget, big event, live, and I think that's what's happened. You know, I don't think... I think those big live shows, like big sports events, like big event shows, work. I don't think the average show from the... what was the average in the '70s and '80s, it would work now.

Q   What do you think about the state of investigative journalism on TV? Is it dead?

A   No, there's still some good investigative journalism but most of it... a bit of it's on Channel 4 and the rest of it's on the BBC.

Q   Is it dying?

A   Well, as budgets got tighter, so it became, investigative journalism became more difficult, but you still see some brilliant pieces. I watched, oh I don't know, probably a year ago, Peter Taylor's piece on Iraq, and it was, you know, where he found the original sources of all sorts of information and discovered that they'd all lied. It was brilliant, and I still thing that happens, but it's like so much on television. There's so much of it now, that actually it's harder to have an impact.

Q   Do you think that economics are causing a form in self-censorship on British television? Let me give you an example. If you're an indie these days, you know what the broadcaster wants. He wants one type of product, entertainment, at a price they're willing to pay, so the indies give it to them, little or nothing else. Do you recognise that syndrome?

A   Well I've met indies who complain that they had a great idea, they went in to sell one of three ideas, and the broadcaster chose the worst one. Now that's their view. I'm a great believer in letting creatives, if they've got a good idea, make it and see what happens, and I think the commissioning editor system has been quite damaging in that regard. I think there's a lack of trust between the creatives and the commissioning editors.

Q   Why is that?

A   I suspect because failure... it's quite difficult to fail now. There are many more people looking at you, there are many more people sitting on top of you trying to understand, 'Why did that fail?' and commissioning editors are often not as talented as the producers and the directors.

Q   Is there a fear, as well, where the indies are concerned that their ideas are going to just be stolen?

A   Well there was always that idea. I mean, when I was first in television if you were interviewing for a job, you'd ask people their ideas and you'd quite regularly say, 'Well he wasn't very good, was he? But that was a great idea, we'll pinch that.' Now today people are much more protective of their ideas, because they think, 'I can make money out of this,' you know. I always remember the girl who had the original, just a gleam of an idea for *Strictly*, was given a £5,000 bonus. If she'd done it for an indie, she would have made millions.

Q   Investigative journalism and the economics of self-censorship. Do you recognise this syndrome? It's expensive, it causes trouble, it gets low audiences, so don't do it. Not dead, but dying.

A   Well, when I was first in television, you know, causing trouble was what we were there for. You know, I think, you know, we were there to find programmes that caused... had a bit of an impact and caused a bit of trouble.

Q   Is that dying?

A   Well you've got to remember there was a battle between news and current affairs, and it's been won by news, so the money got shifted to news, and news isn't really brave, most of the time. It just churns it out.

Q   The BBC. What were your impressions when you joined the BBC as Director General?

A   I thought what was quite a simple idea had been made desperately complicated, and therefore a lot of my time as Director General we were trying to simplify it back. You know, that's why I did a... in my MacTaggart Lecture that year, I said it's about... I pinched Bill Clinton's line. You know, 'It's the programme, stupid.' That in the end you can run a wonderful organisation, but if the programmes are rubbish, what's the point? And it's about the programmes, and the more you could... I banged on about that, which I thought gave... you know, my predecessor didn't have that sort of credibility because they didn't think he was a programme maker, although actually he was a very good programme maker. So when I got there, I decided we had to talk about the programmes.

Q   When you say it got too complicated, what were they doing if they weren't making programmes, at your time?

A   Well someone said to me... I remember very early on, someone said to me, 'It's a very complicated place, you know. It will take you a long time to understand how this works and how it operates,' and I said, 'It doesn't seem very complicated to me. Someone gives me £3.5 billion per year and I spend it.' You know, most places I'd been it was getting the £3.5 billion that was the difficult bit. So I thought they'd made... I'm a great believer in the BBC, I'm a great believer and always have been, you know, even when I was working for commercial television. I was a great believer that, in the famous Michael Grade words, you know, it kept us all honest. That actually, spending a lot of money on original, British television, meant the commercial sector had to do the same, which is why we've got a much bigger television industry than we have film industry, because say in France, they spent the money on film. Here, we spent it on television, and that led to the growth of a big television industry. Initially in the broadcasters, but since then, outside.

"RED by James Hogan"

Q   When you were Director General, did you think the BBC
     was too big?

A   When I first got there, someone, again, said to me, 'How do
     you want it to feel?' I said, 'I'd like it to feel smaller.' I
     certainly took out layers of management, but I didn't feel it
     wasn't manageable. I didn't feel... but you did have to spend
     a lot more time getting people on side, than, say, in a small
     ITV company when you were based in one building. I mean,
     the BBC was harder than that. It meant a lot of your time, if
     you're the leader, had to be spent out there talking to people
     and getting to know them. Finding out what they wanted.
     But I didn't think it was too big, no.

Q   Do you think it's too big today?

A   No.

Q   Did you think it was inefficient?

A   All big organisations are inefficient. In the end, there was
     bound to be a degree of inefficiency, but if you looked at
     IBM at that time, or if you'd looked at Marks and Spencer at
     that time, all organisations, all big organisations are
     comparatively inefficient, which is why they always get
     beaten, in the end, by small organisations coming round the
     back. But I didn't think it was grossly inefficient, no.

Q   What view did you form about the licence fee?

A   Well, when I was at the BBC, we invented *Freeview*. I mean, it was the classic case where two of us sat in an office, myself and Carolyn Fairbairn who was my Head of Strategy, invented *Freeview*. We saw the opportunity, we grabbed it and we got it going, but of course what *Freeview* could have meant was that you could have switched BBC from the licence fee to paid television because you could have put a chip in every one of those boxes. I came to the conclusion that actually the single most important thing about the BBC is universality; that it's available to everyone. It's even available to the people who don't pay the licence fee. I mean, they can get in trouble for it, but they can still see it, and I think a universal service, in a world where fragmentation was happening amongst broadcasters on a major scale, I thought a universal service was very important, and I think the BBC is more important now than at any time in its history, because of that fragmentation of a marketplace. The BBC is still the dominant player.

Q   Do you have any regrets about your handling of the *Today* programme report by Andrew Gilligan on the dodgy dossier?

A   Well, there are always a few regrets, but by and large I think history has shown we were right. I think... I don't... it's very hard to meet anybody today who doesn't think that Blair and Co. didn't sex up the dossier, and didn't sex up the case for war, but you could have... could we have dealt with it differently? Yes. Would it have made much difference? Probably not. If Dr Kelly hadn't killed himself, the story would have just died like all stories die, in the end. It was only Dr Kelly's suicide, or alleged suicide, that changed the whole game, and really after that happened it was out of our control.

What I do think we made a mistake with was when Lord Hutton was appointed, we should have said, 'No, that's not fair. You've got to have more than one judge, and you can't have a judge who's been very close over the years to the Security Services,' because in the end the whole thing was about the Security Services and their relationship with the government of the day.

Q   When the Hutton Report was published, couldn't the BBC have slapped it down saying it beggars believe that the government was right about everything, the BBC wrong about everything?

A   We did say that a bit, but we didn't need to, because the media said that. I mean, Hutton was... Hutton... I mean, I remember talking to Labour government ministers that weekend, and they were saying, 'We don't know what to do. Hutton came out and completely absolved us of all blame, and we're still getting the blame.' Well they're getting the blame because they deserved it. You know, there is no doubt now when you look back, Tony Blair didn't tell the truth. Now you could argue he didn't tell the truth on all sorts of things, but he certainly didn't tell the truth when he said he wasn't the man who had allowed Dr Kelly's name to be released to the press, because he was, and that's now conclusively proved.

Q   What do you think the future holds for the BBC?

A   I think that the BBC itself needs to be a bit more on the front
      foot. It needs to be braver, but I think the BBC will be fine. I
      think there's a bunch of us who will get together and fight
      for it. The Conservatives haven't got a very large majority.
      Why did Mrs Thatcher never really take on the BBC? The
      answer: because most of the people who loved the BBC were
      her supporters. Now look at the strength of the BBC in the
      south of England, outside London, where they're virtually
      all Conservative seats.

      I mean, I was Director of Programmes at Television South at
      one time, which covered the whole of, you know, Dorset,
      Hampshire, Sussex, Surrey. All that area. We didn't have a...
      for one period, we didn't have a single Labour MP;
      everybody was Conservative and yet the ratings for the BBC
      there were enormous. I think if this government thinks
      they're going to take on the BBC, and destroy it, they're in
      for a big, big shock, and they'll back off.

Q   What do you think the future of the BBC should be... sorry,
      what do you think the future of the BBC should be, in terms
      of its size, scope and role?

A   Well I'll come back to your earlier question, because I didn't
      really answer it, about the licence fee. I think it's... I think the
      thing about the licence fee is it doesn't belong to the
      politicians, it belongs to the public, and I think one of the
      things the BBC has failed to stand up and say enough in
      recent years is, 'Excuse me, we're not paid for by you, we're
      paid for by the public,' to the government of the day.

I mean, it is inevitable. If you go back and read Grace Wyndham Goldie, who saw the BBC through the Suez Crisis, and ever since, it is inevitable that there is going to be conflict between the BBC and the government of the day, Labour or Tory, it makes no difference, because they want only their view of the world to be seen. I remember writing to Tony Blair who wrote and complained to me about our coverage leading up to the Iraq War, and I wrote back just saying, 'I'm sorry, Prime Minister, but you cannot be the arbiter of impartiality, because you're not impartial.'

And the BBC's major aim is to be impartial. We have gone to enormous lengths during the run up to the Iraq War to try to be impartial, which was very difficult, because on phone in programmes and things like that, people in favour of the war didn't phone in, so we'd extended the number, we'd done all sorts of things, but still, Blair, pushed by Alastair Campbell, believed we hadn't been impartial. I wrote to him and I said, 'You can't be the judge. You've got thousands of your people, millions of people on the streets protesting. You've got half your party voting against you. You cannot be the judge,' and of course, as it's turned out, the Iraq War is one of the great disasters of post-war Britain.

Q   I'd like to ask you some questions now about the Savile affair. How damaging was the decision to drop the Savile investigation conducted by *Newsnight* into allegations of historical sex abuse?

A   Well it was clearly a mistake. I don't think it's the most devastating decision. In the end, I don't believe it was taken by anybody up there. That's the good conspiracy theory, you know, someone up there said, 'Oh, Jimmy Savile, we've got another programme about him. He was a much loved figure at the BBC, God, we mustn't let this go out.' I just don't believe that would happen.

When I was Director General, if that had been around, and it wasn't, but if that had been around, the one thing you would know is if you in any way tried to interfere, it would have been all over the newspapers tomorrow, and quite rightly. So I just don't believe the conspiracy theories that a decision was taken at the top to stop this.

I think the decision was taken by the editor of *Newsnight*. I think it would have been a very difficult programme. I don't think *Newsnight* is equipped to do that sort of programme. It hasn't got the resources. What should have happened was that they should have handed it all over to *Panorama* and said, 'Look, here's some interesting material, why don't you go and do it?' but of course as you know only too well, you know, the people at *Newsnight* and the people on *Panorama*, by and large, hate each other, because that's the rival and, therefore, they would never do it, but that's what they should have done.

Q   So why didn't they shelve it? Why did they drop it?

A   I don't know. You'd have to ask the editor. You'd have to ask the editor of *Newsnight*. I suspect he didn't have the resource to do it, the police didn't take it up, didn't take up the complaints, and I suspect he thought, wrongly, that it was too difficult to do.

Q   With the benefit of hindsight, do you think it should have been delayed but they should have continued to make investigations, and then, when they were ready, to publish?

A   No, I think they should have handed it over to *Panorama*, but I think what the... the issue of Savile is much, much bigger than whether or not *Newsnight* should have run the programme.

Q   Do you think that the subconscious was at work? That somehow or other, it just felt deeply uncomfortable to who knows whom, but various people in the BBC, to the point where they just didn't want to pursue it?

A   No, I think that's the conspiracy theory that I just don't believe. I think it might have been difficult for the editor of *Newsnight*, but in the end, it would have been his decision. Seriously. The BBC didn't... the power in the BBC is well down, as it should be in an organisation as big as the BBC. The power of what goes on and what doesn't go on is well down. I mean, for instance, I'll give you an example.

At the time of Dr Kelly's performances before the Foreign Affairs Committee, and things like that, *Newsnight* had a tape which they'd made the same day of an interview with Dr Kelly, which by and large supported everything Gilligan said. They didn't tell us. They said, 'This is ours. This belongs to *Newsnight*, it doesn't belong to you,' and as you can imagine I was quite annoyed when I found out; but that shows you, they did not regard themselves as subservient to someone up there in the BBC, up at the top of the BBC.

Q Would you have expected, had you been Director General, at the time of the *Newsnight* investigation, to have been informed about its progress and the decision to drop it?

A No. No, that wouldn't have been at the level of the Director General, at any stage, I don't think. The number of times a programme came to me as Director General was quite small.

Q Knowing what you now know, and having read the Pollard Report, as I have, would you like to think that as Director General you would have run it? Had that material been presented to you.

A Well, it's a hypothetical position because it wasn't presented to the Director General, but if it had been, I'd have said, 'Can you stand this up? Are you content with it? Is it good enough? Do the lawyers agree it?' If you've got all those things, then you'd run it, but I suspect you wouldn't have got all those things. I mean, I don't think the editor of *Newsnight* was content with it. I think he had doubts.

Q Do you think that the Director General, George Entwistle, was right to resign?

A My view was that George Entwistle had been appointed, he was the chairman's candidate, Chris Patten; he had been appointed by Chris Patten, and I think he was then hung out to dry by Chris Patten.

Q Because?

A   Well, I don't... the job of a... in organisations, when the going gets rough, the job of the chairman is either to support and be close to the chief executive, or to decide he has to go. In this case, I don't... having appointed Entwistle [the former Director General George Entwistle who resigned at the time of the Saville affair], it was Patten's job was to be in with him every day, talking to him, supporting him, seeing how to get him through, giving him some advice, and that's not what happened. He was fundamentally a politician, and politicians, at times of difficulty, run for the hills, and that's what he did. Therefore, I think Entwistle was hung out to dry, but I think he probably found the pressure intolerable.

Q   One last question. When we spoke on the phone yesterday, you made a point that you wanted to make about American television in relation to the UK. Would you like to...

A   What was I saying?

Q   I think you were saying something to the effect of, that it seems strange that the UK has allowed itself to have so much American ownership of its media assets.

A   Oh yes, well it always struck me as interesting that... well, there's... start again. There's something interesting about the independent sector, that as they get to a certain stage and size in this country, instead of building up to an enormous size, they sell out to Americans, and that's not only to be found in the television industry, but it is an interesting question.

Q   And why is it, do you think?

A   I don't know. Why is it when someone's made, can make
     £10 or £15 million they say, 'Fine, I'll sell out now, I'll have a
     comfortable life,' instead of saying, 'I want to build this into
     the biggest independent production company in the world'?
     I don't know why it happens. It doesn't only happen in
     television, it happens in the games industry, it happens in
     film, it happens, I suspect, in many industries in this
     country, but it is a fundamental problem for Britain.

Q   There's one more question I should ask you, which is about
     the Internet.

A   Yes.

Q   Bearing in mind your comments about the nature and fabric
     of the television of today, what is the impact of the Internet?
     Do you think the Internet will kill television? What do you
     think?

A   I don't think television will be killed. I think television has
     got quite a good future, but it certainly changes. I don't
     think the Internet kills it, because I don't think the Internet
     will ever give the investment into British production that the
     British broadcasters can and will. I don't think it will... the
     hardest problem about the Internet is about marketing. How
     does anyone know what it is, where it is, how do they find
     it? So I do think television still has quite a healthy future,
     but it has changed. I mean, it'll be...

     The middle road programme doesn't work anymore. You've

got to be up there. It's got to be top rank. It's got to be...
that's why live programming works if it's special. It's why
good drama still works, but the days when you could make
cheap drama have gone, that works. Soap... it's very hard to
launch a new soap now. Gradually, the audience declines,
but I don't think we are living through the death of
television which is what some people think. I think they're
premature. I think it's got a long run yet.

Q   Great. Many, many thanks.

A   Thank you.

Q   Excellent. Brilliant.

End of interview

Chapter VII

Chris Carter

Professor of Strategy and Organization at the Edinburgh University Business School in Scotland. He has co-authored two best-selling books on strategy. Away from research and teaching, he started the 'Business School at the Fringe: the Media Series' at the 2014 Edinburgh Fringe Festival.

Interviewer: James Hogan

Q   I am delighted that with me today is Professor Christopher Carter of the Edinburgh University Business School. Chris, welcome. What do you think has happened to television?

A   That's a good question. I mean over the course of three decades, we have seen television go from four channels, four terrestrial channels to hundreds of channels and the dawn of the digital age and, of course, the rise of Sky.

I mean broadly, television, there's much more of it; it's much more internationalised. There are three major players, the BBC, Sky and ITV and content has gone global.

Q   And what's the biggest change?

A   The biggest change? I think it would have to be the rise of digital, the move away from terrestrial television.

Q   Do you think the internet will eventually kill off television?

"RED by James Hogan"

A   I think as we know, the death of linear television has been long prophesised, long predicted and yet it's proved to be a remarkably durable phenomenon and medium and people get together and watch things on television and it's not just event television, a cup final, something of that nature; it's other things as well. I think will the future generation watch linear television in the way in which we did as children? Almost certainly not but I'm not sure television will die but it will be complemented by other things. But I think content will remain very important and become more important.

Q   What's happened to the indies?

A   Okay, what's happened to the indies? The indies, from fledgling beginnings in the 1980s with the foundation of Channel 4 and then the flourishing of the indies post 1990 Broadcasting Act really created the indies sector in the UK. I think the big change with the indies came in 2003 when in the UK, at least, the IP, intellectual property, remained with the indies rather than big broadcasters. I think it's difficult to overemphasise how important that was.

Q   What has happened to investigative journalism on terrestrial television?

A   I think investigative journalism is expensive. It takes a long time and it quite possibly will get a broadcaster into trouble and it only takes a small part of the story to be wrong for the broadcaster to be in trouble. So it's something that I think broadcasters are wary of but that would have always been the case. I think when the duopoly of ITV and BBC started to become more accountable, more financialized and when costs started to attach to programmes, I think the senior executives in television just thought, "This is a very, very expensive medium," and I think in terms of the economic arguments against investigative journalism started to play out.

Of course, the broader arguments around the public good, what investigative journalism does in terms of civil society are profoundly important but that wouldn't particularly be in the interests of television executives looking to save money on their schedule.

Q   Is it dying?

A   That's a good question; is it dying? I think that it bears little relation to the investigative journalism of the '70s and '80s and that goes for print journalism as well as broadcast if we think of the *Insight* team of Sunday Times or *Panorama* team, which you were part of or *World in Action* with Ray Fitzwalter and so forth.

I think it's transformed or some might say transmogrified. I think it's different. So what's *Newsnight*? It's not news as traditionally produced. It's not current affairs as traditionally produced; it's a hybrid. And I would imagine that investigative journalism, serious current affairs, if it's to have a future, it will be through some kind of hybrid bringing together different things.

Q   Do you think the BBC is too big?

"RED by James Hogan"

A   No.

Q   Why not?

A   I think to fully appreciate the BBC, one needs to be outside of Britain for a bit and the BBC is probably a British organisation that has done most for British soft power and influence around the world in the post Empire era and I think the BBC has its detractors and it's criticised for editorial bias, profligacy, management cock ups, all sorts of things but this is the stuff of a large organisation.

But if we look at a media environment where there are a few giant players, the BBC is one of those players and I think in broadcasting it's an important mechanism for Britain being a leader in broadcasting.

Q   Do you think the licence fee should be scrapped?

A   The licence fee is really vital for the BBC. It's the umbilical cord that connects the BBC with British state. Now, it's also very, very unpopular. It's been very, very unpopular for a very long time. Mrs Thatcher described it as a poll tax backed up by criminal sanctions, which was kind of ironic with the policy she then brought out later in her term as premier. I think the BBC licence fee is highly idiosyncratic. The question is whether it's anachronistic.

Q   Do you think the licence fee should be frozen?

A   I think the licence fee should be linked to inflation, which I think was a policy recommendation in the Peacock Committee. I think the thing is if you were to remove the licence fee and then if the BBC was to take advertising, what would that do?

Q   What would it do?

A   It would decimate advertising for other channels in the UK, which, interestingly, when this was mooted 30 years ago, why the then ITV companies were so against it. What it also does, it's a fundamental of a mixed economy of broadcasting. If we were to look at British broadcasting, I think it has been a great success. I think it is a great export earner and it is a generator of soft power and then if we look at the ecosystem of broadcasting, well, what do we have? We have a very robust subscription model through Sky, we have a very robust commercial advertising through Channel 3, primarily and we have the national broadcaster in the form of the BBC that's funded through the licence fee.

So we have three different mechanisms for funding and that, I think, helps produce a vibrant ecosystem.

Q   Do you think that Channel 4 should be privatised?

A   No, I think… interestingly, I'm sure many of your viewers would be surprised that it is a publicly run company, that it is a public organisation because I think that's a bit of a secret. And I think Channel 4 has been one of the great success stories of the last 30 years in broadcasting and we've seen from the high minded risk taking of Jeremy Isaacs, through to the sure commercial cool hand of Lord Grade and then subsequent chief executives, each putting their stamp on it. I think it's been great for British broadcasting.

We have to remember Channel 4 was essential to giving life to the indies and it came out of a need to do something different. The Annan Committee reported in the late '70s and they were saying the duopoly that serves particular markets would do well, particular parts of the population very well but it doesn't serve youth, it doesn't serve minorities, it doesn't really take risks and at different stages of its life, I think Channel 4 has done that very, very well.

So I guess the… what would Channel 4 raise for the Treasury? A £1 billion, possibly not that? To take that out of a rich ecosystem I think would be a mistake.

Q   Do you think that television is in decline as a serious intellectual medium?

A   I think every generation of television professionals, television executives, there's always the harking back to an era that was, a golden age, a nostalgia for that. I think every serious television station, there are always competing logics between populism, commercialism and then serious, serious television made to make serious points.

I actually think there's a great appetite for rich, interesting and challenging content, whether that will be produced by broadcasters or whether it will appear on YouTube channels, I'm not so sure… or other platforms.

Q   A lot of people are asking, "What's the BBC for in today's internet age?" Do you think the BBC has a unique responsibility to mount major investigations into wrongdoing and that that's an answer?

A   I mean, I think the BBC has a wide role. I mean, in a sense, it's a broadcaster of record in UK; it's an important cultural export around the world. Its news and current affairs, it's very important to report accurately, to inform, to educate as well as entertain. I think the BBC needs to be at the forefront of news stories, current affairs issues and it needs to do that well. But that's part of what it's about.

I once did an interview with an American consultant who had spent a lot of time inviting the BBC and reflecting on it, he said, "You know what? The BBC, the closest American equivalent is NASA and really, the BBC is a guardian of British culture." Now, of course, the BBC would like to see itself in that way but it struck me as quite a good way of thinking about the BBC and its unique role within British public life.

But it is right that people challenge it, criticise it but I think that's one part of the story. The other part is it's an organisation that has this huge footprint, huge respect across the world.

Q   Do you think the BBC could have broken the MPs' expenses scandal?

A   I think it would have been a very brave decision on the part of the director general and the head of news and current affairs. But clearly, the BBC is there to break stories. It is there to challenge. It is there, ultimately, to render major institutions accountable, to hold them to account. But it would have been a big call. But what I would be very sure of is the coverage would have been really quite different from what was served up in the press.

Q   It would have been a big call because they would be seen to be attacking their paymasters?

A   Yes, I mean, ultimately, you know, the BBC is governed, really, through two mechanisms, the Charter, which gets renewed every 10 years and the licence fee, which is reviewed periodically. It would have been a huge call; much easier for the Fourth Estate, much easier for Fleet Street to do that, I would imagine.

But I guess it would be interesting to think would *Panorama* have of old or, indeed, on Channel 3, would *World in Action* of old, would they have broken it? How would they have framed the story? And the story was sensationalist and pulled out the most egregious acts by MPs. It didn't place it into a broader context for a very, very long time; these expenses were, in effect, seen as part of the pay package by MPs.

Q   And a last question, politically, could the BBC have broken the phone hacking scandal at News International?

A   Difficult one; I would imagine there would be some

journalists at the BBC who would have loved to have done so and whilst they didn't break the story, I mean, certainly it was well covered on the BBC. I mean, clearly, News International, particularly through Sky and the BBC are two of the big giants of contemporary broadcasting and it would have been a big coup for BBC to do that. But I don't see them as ducking away from major stories.

Q   Chris, huge thanks.

A   Okay, so this is on the indies now. I think if we think about the history of indies in British television, it's a remarkable story from the fledgling industry post Channel 4, growing in the '90s but then absolutely booming during the noughties to the present day. And why is that? I think if you look at the 2003 Communications Act, which shifted intellectual property to the indies, away from the broadcaster, it's difficult to overstate how important that was.

So what kind of effects did it have? Well, first of all, it meant that the indies became very, very attractive commercially and what we've seen over the last few years is the acquisition of British indies by American corporates. You also see the particular types of television emerging, particularly reality television, factual entertainment.

But I think one of the remarkable stories is the rise of formats and I think I have it right when I say that British indies basically produce about 50 per cent of the world television's formats from a place that's basically six per cent of the global television market. That's an absolutely phenomenal statistic and, I guess, an advert and a testament to how successful the super indies have been within the UK.

I think what we can see more generally, though, is the margins are really falling within British television. So the margins on independent productions are down to five or six per cent, which isn't so much better than having your money in gilts or whatever. So I think it's an area that has been lucrative but will be increasingly economically challenged.

Chapter VIII

Rob Woodward

The Chief Executive of STV Plc. the Scottish broadcaster
equivalent to ITV in Scotland. Under Rob's leadership STV has
made a dramatic improvement creatively and financially by
serving its audience and exploiting the strength of its brand as a
trusted host. Prior to STV Rob was Commercial Director of
Channel 4 where he built a set of successful new media and digital
business. A banker by background, he was a Managing Director at
UBS Warburg an a Managing partner at Deloitte where in both
cases he specialised in media and communications. In addition to
his STV role he is also pro-chancellor of City University and a
Trustee at Nesta.

Interviewer: James Hogan

Q   Why don't we start off by just asking Rob to introduce
      himself on camera? So-,

M   We could.

Q   Yes.

A   I'm Rob Woodward, I'm the chief executive of STV Group
      Plc.

Q   Rob, please describe STV's coverage of the Scottish
      Referendum.

"RED by James Hogan"

A   Well, comprehensive, in one word. So as soon as the referendum was announced, we decided as an organisation that we could play a unique role through the referendum, reflecting the voices of Scotland, and we saw it as the most significant political event in Scotland for some 300 years. And we could use the connection, the unique connection, that we have with the millions of consumers across Scotland, but rather than just think of it as a broadcast opportunity, we very much wanted to work with other platforms and other organisations to amplify our existing voice.

So for example, we were the first broadcaster in Europe to work with Facebook, and we actually hosted a joint debate with Facebook, which was extremely successful. We worked with Twitter, we worked-, and we were, again, the first in the UK to use a piece of technology which Twitter have, which is called Twitter Reverb, which enabled us to-, real time, to analyse during one of our debates, you know, how many people were tweeting, where they were tweeting from, geographically, whether they were tweeting yes, no or don't know. Then we were able to look at what they called the 'reverb', so how many times are those tweets then subsequently retweeted?

Then our first readers debate with Alex Salmond and Alistair Darling where we had-, it was a record TV audience. It was the largest TV audience for a political event in Scotland for over 10 years, but through working with

Twitter then we were able to magnify that by an absolute order of magnitude, literally reaching millions of people, not just in the UK but around the world.

Q   And tell us a bit more about the relationship, the working relationship with Facebook.

A   I mean, it's all about innovation and it's all about us using the power of what we have, and our existing platform, combining it with the power of what Facebook has and, in particular, we were very keen on connecting with younger audiences, and that's exactly what Facebook enabled us to do.

Q   Was it a unique television event?

A   I would say that the whole referendum experience was unique. I think that we had a number of landmark components of it, so we were the first broadcaster to secure and produced the leaders' debate, which was with Alex Salmond and Alistair Darling. In the run up to that, we used our very popular *Scotland Tonight* programme, and we had various political head to head debates in the run up to that event. We worked with an organisation called Debating Matters, where we organised a debating competition for high schools across the country, so every-, we had 32 schools participate, representing every one of the local authority areas, and it culminated with an event that took place at Glasgow University. So it was a very diverse series of events that were specifically aimed at ensuring that we reached the most representative audience as possible.

Q   And what was the response of the audience to the coverage?

"RED by James Hogan"

A   Well, the press and other media commentators would say that we had a very good referendum, and I think we were seen as representative of the voices of Scotland, which is exactly what we set out to do, and from a reputational standpoint, then, it did us absolutely the power of good, paving the way for our role as an important provider of public service delivery in the post-referendum Scotland.

Q   And what, as a broadcaster, did you learn from the experience?

A   The key learning points were the level of interest that we could encourage in a genre which is kind of seen as pretty dry. I think that working with others, absolutely was key for us, so, using the power of other platforms. I was particularly pleased with the result that we had connecting with a younger audience, for example through *Debating Matters*, as I just described. I think that-, we also ran a daily blog which got not only a lot of publicity, kind of, through our own channel, but it was the kind of thing that the press picked up on pretty much on a daily basis, to see what our blog was actually saying.

Q   How would you sum up the state of broadcasting at the start of the 21st century?

A   Well I think broadcasting has reinvented itself, and will continue to reinvent itself. A lot of people, for a long time, have been kind of saying that broadcasting is essentially an old media, and I actually don't buy that at all. We are at the heart of digital delivery. Everything that we do is digital, and I think that certainly as an organisation, but I think as an industry, we are working very quickly to work out, in the world of the future, how people are going to be conceiving content because, ultimately, it's all about access to unique content, and when I describe, kind of, our own company, then we are a content company, and it's all about content that we either acquire through our relationship with ITV, content that we produce ourselves, or content that we buy in, and it doesn't matter what platform it is, it's all about curation and delivery of that content across multiple platforms.

Q   How do you think broadcasting will look in 10 years' time?

A   I think that-, I think pretty positive. I think the industry will continue to redefine, kind of, who it is, what it is, what it delivers, but I think, you know, as I just said, if you always focus on the fact that you're there to curate content, then that's actually what our industry is all about. So it's back to the old adage of you're there to inform and entertain. That's absolutely what we're doing. The thing that's changing are the distribution platforms, and it's up to us to keep ahead of the game, to experiment, and don't be afraid to stop doing things if they look like they're not working, and accelerate things that are working.

Q   What do you think the future holds for the BBC?

A   I'm a huge fan of the BBC, and everything that it has done, and I think it's such an important part, if not the kingpin of the broadcasting ecology in the UK, so what I want to see is, kind of, a continuing, strong BBC, and from a commercial standpoint, having a strong BBC is actually-, perversely, it's actually good news for the industry as a whole. I think what worries me is the scope of activity. I think you have seen, kind of, a continued creep. I think you also need to look at the impact that the BBC can have on the commercial sector, and I think that needs to be looked at, not just through its broadcasting footprint, but through, particularly its non-broadcast activities. I welcome the idea that's just been endorsed by the BBC Trust of taking BBC3 off air, and essentially, kind of, giving it a completely fresh lease of life as an Internet only based channel, but I think there's more that could be done just to, kind of, redefine, kind of, what we actually want the BBC to do, and also think through the consequences that the BBC will then have on other organisations and other parts of the sector.

Q   Do you think the BBC's too big?

A   I think that goes to my point about scope. I think that there is an opportunity to cut back on the scope, refocus the BBC on what's, kind of, essentially its core everything that it stands for. It would still be-, in the UK it would still be a massive organisation, even if it was kind of-, even if it was-, even if it was cut back. I believe that their BBC Worldwide is an absolute necessity, a lifeline, and I think that it's a great flag carrier for Britain and British content.

Q   Do you think the licence fee should be scrapped?

A I think it's right that we debate whether the licence fee is scrapped. I think-, personally I don't think now is the right time to really, to think about scrapping it. I think that we need to find a way to ensure that everybody that consumes BBC's content actually pays for that content, and I think it can't be right that if you don't own a, what we used to describe as a television, in your household, but you consume off other devices, then you avoid paying the licence fee. That just doesn't seem fair. So I would much prefer to see a system where, you know, everybody that consumes BBC content has to pay for that content, and the licence fee, or a derivative of the current licence fee, would seem to me to be a pretty strong place to start.

Q What do you think the future holds for Channel 4?

A Well Channel 4 has also played a really important role in British broadcasting and the media industry. I think that the-, where I would start is what is the remit for Channel 4? And it seems to me that over the years it's, kind of-, or we've lost sight of what the remit for the organisation should be. Because when it was set up, it was always very clear, and it was there, absolutely to kind of support the independent production sector, and it's done that absolutely brilliantly. It was also there to focus very much on the younger, 16-34 year old audience. It delivered that for many years, brilliantly. It has also developed a great reputation in the delivery of American series, but I think over the last few years, I know it is now recovering, but it's difficult to actually determine quite what it stands for. So I would start with, kind of, let's define a new remit and a new role for Channel 4.

Q   What might that new remit look like?

A   I would, kind of-, maybe a bit like the BBC. Like, kind of take it away from just being a broadcasting remit. I would very much focus-, if it is to continue to focus on younger audiences, then work and develop, maybe slightly different services that are, again, non-broadcast services, to enable it to particularly reach that hard to find younger audience.

Q   Do you think that Channel 4 should be privatised?

A   I don't think that privatisation is a solution. It's probably just a way for the government to generate umpteen hundred million pounds of income, and it's a one off event. I think I'd go back to, let's work out what the remit is, and then ensure that the corporation then has an appropriate ownership structure in order to deliver that remit, whether it's going to privatise it or not. I would say that the majority of people in the UK already think that Channel 4 is a commercial organisation and is actually in private hands. But I don't think to privatise or not to privatise is actually the question. It's all about the remit.

Q   Okay. Might a new remit for Channel 4 make it more public service oriented and less entertainment oriented?

A   I'm not sure. I'm not absolutely sure about that. I think that clearly it depends what the remit is. I mean, one of the things that I would take a careful look at is the future status of Channel 4. So at the moment it's a not-for-profit. It carries not-for-profit status. It might be time to take a fresh look at that, and, you know, they have no problem in the corporation, acting in an even more commercial way than it currently is. I think it would remove the slight, kind of, schism of the, kind of, the public service side and the commercial side. It would maybe help the two sit more closely together, and kind of unify around a new totemic remit.

Q   Finally, do you think the Internet will eventually kill off television?

A   I don't believe that. I think that-, I think television is here to stay. I think that television will rely on the Internet. It will rely on the growth of social media, it will rely on other platforms to ensure that it reaches the widest possible audience and has the biggest impact, but there are some things that just cannot be replicated. So, you know, that's why you've seen the resurgence of live events, event based TV. That's why you've seen such a focus around sport, around news, around current affairs. All these events are-, you have to watch them live, because there's a kind of a-, you want to watch at the same time as the impact is being made, and I think that-, so in answer to your question, no, I think the future for TV is a good one.

Q   Rob, many, many thanks.

A   Thank you.

End of interview

Chapter IX

Jean Seaton

Professor of Media History at the University of Westminster and the Official Historian of the BBC. She is the Director of the Orwell Prize and on the editorial board of Political Quarterly. Her volume of the official history of the BBC, Pinkoes and Traitors: the BBC and the Nation 1974-1987, was published by Profile Books in February 2015.

Interviewer: James Hogan

Q   Jean, many thanks for taking part. Maybe, if you just start off by identifying yourself?

A   Do you want my name as well?

Q   I'm Jean Seaton and I wrote the last volume of the official history of the BBC but before that, I'd spent 30 years writing about media history and politics in the media and I'm the director of the Orwell Prize.

Q   And how did you become an academic?

A   How did I become an academic?

Q   Yes, has it been your whole life?

A   Yes! How did I become an academic? I was a revolting student and then I went to what was seen as the absolutely best sociology department in the country, which was Essex in those days and my parents, who are absolutely lovely, my father was a butcher, it had long been my observation that the only thing they really talked about was what was on telly and the house was always littered with newspapers, with the night's programmes circled on them. And so I just thought that was a very interesting thing so I started to do work on the media. So I've always worked on the media, really and then, really, in an odd kind of way...

And then I started a book which is called *Power Without Responsibility* with James Curran, which, in its day, was fantastically innovative because we went back to the history of the media in order to situate policy issues about the media. So James went back to the 17th Century of the press and that book, which is about to come out in another edition, has never been out of print for 30 years, translated into a dozen languages. I suppose that got me into how, if you look at the past of institutions, they don't tell you what's going to happen in the future but there's no other evidence that's half as good about the problems you may face.

Q   And how did you become the official historian of the BBC?

A   I have no idea, really. Well, in a technical way, two gentlemen from the BBC arrived at my office door and I think I thought they were coming about something to do about the BBC; I'd already written quite a lot about the BBC. In particular, there was a nasty...

"RED by James Hogan"

Q   So how did you become the official historian of the BBC?

A   I have no idea, is one answer but two gentlemen from the
     BBC arrived at my office door. I thought it might have
     something to do with the BBC but I didn't know... I mean, I
     knew that but I didn't know what and they asked me to do
     it. And to say you could have knocked me over with a
     feather and picked me off the floor afterwards...

     I've now looked at the papers around the appointment of
     Lord Briggs, which was completely riveting and quite a
     complicated process and it's very interesting because the
     official history emerged out of a political crisis; and the
     political crisis was, really, Suez and during Suez, lots of
     people stood up in parliament and said all sorts of things
     about the control of the BBC during the war, which weren't
     true. And so the BBC wanted the history as an aid to record,
     I think particularly how it had behaved during the Second
     World War and secondly in a sense as a kind of bulwark
     against that political misappropriation of the history.

     So that's how they set up Lord Briggs. Lord Briggs was
     closed, for all sorts of reasons, you know, came to the end of
     his contract. He was closed quite brutally in a way and then
     by some mysterious process, which, certainly... I mean, I
     know Asa quite well but his list of possible people certainly
     didn't include me. So some internal process goes on and
     these people arrive at my door and they ask me to write the
     official history.

I now realise, really, at that point I should have put my foot down.

Q   In what way?

A   Oh, I think… well, you know how the BBC is? I couldn't put my foot down partly because I hadn't finished a book I was already writing on; I was doing something else because the BBC thinks you can just drop everything and I had a full time job and they somehow thought they were commissioning me, perhaps like an independent television maker to make something, as if, somehow, I'd bid for it. I think I should have thought through the processes that Lord Briggs had and I should have understood those and demanded more of those.

Lord Briggs had a large internal team of people, most of whom were sort of, as it were, BBC saints like Frank Gillard and Leonard Miall, I mean really important players. And I was offered a fee but I wasn't offered the money, really, to do it, although it always takes involvement… the archive always takes a lot of money… getting archives ready for somebody to use takes a lot of money.

So I think I should have been a bit more demanding, I think, all the way through but I just don't think I understood the process. But then again…

So they asked me and I went away and raised an Arts and Humanities research grant, which then had a completely different set of drivers, which I think is absolutely appropriate in the modern world. They had young scholars, PhD scholars, people who had to own bits of work themselves who work on it.

And then later, I was very alarmed because none of that paid for me to have time off. I mean, that's how academic grants, are they mad? You get them to do something called research but you can't get them for yourself. So I went back to Mark Thompson and we got a bit more money and then I put in for a Leverhulme which got me some time off. So it was quite a complicated process of recruiting but it was obviously a fantastic honour.

Q   What was your brief?

A   Oh, to write the next volume. And I chose the time span because it seemed to me that we could have gone to the end of Mike Checkland and in a way, that might have been a good thing to do because Mike Checkland's a very underestimated director general. But it seemed to me that in a way, a lot of Checkland's reforms really lead into, however contested they are, some of the Birt reforms; indeed that's the interesting side where I decided to go at a rather traumatic moment of high Maoist Thatcherism, which is how I put it, when Alasdair Milne gets sacked because that all, it seemed to me, had a drama to it. I mean, you're looking for a story, at least I am, not just a sort of conveyor belt… I was looking for some narrative drive to it, I suppose.

Q   Why did you call it *Pinkoes and Traitors*?

A   Oh, because lots of other names got thrown out on the way, much more anodyne names...

Q   What kinds of names?

A   Oh, '*The BBC Under Siege*'; '*Breaking Waves*'; I can't remember... they were sort of anodyne names and right at the last moment, there's this very... "*Pinkoes and traitors*," is a quote from a spoof Denis Thatcher letter to Bill Deedes in *Private Eye* in which he says, "That nest of pinkoes and traitors down at Shepherd's Bush – the BBC." We know that those views in those letters are pretty close to what Denis Thatcher actually thought. I just thought, in my head, actually, the whole book had been an answer... an interrogation, really, of the Conservative attack on the BBC and, indeed, the Labour attack on the BBC. So it had been an interrogation.

So I came up with that and everybody said, "Oh, you can't possibly have that; it's far too provocative," and some people have misunderstood it so perhaps it was. And then the BBC decided that that was good. And, in a way, it's got a kind of joke in it. Now, if people don't get the joke, there's not much I can do about it.

Q   Do you think the BBC is full of Pinkoes and Traitors?

A   I absolutely show in the book that the BBC certainly was not full of Pinkoes and Traitors, it just wasn't. I mean, you can have arguments about liberalism. But I don't. But that's one of the views that bits of the Conservative government certainly had.

Q   Do you regret using the title?

"RED by James Hogan"

A   No, I think it's a wonderful title. It's got a joke in it. It's got ebullience in it. But, quite a lot of elderly BBC people have beaten me up and said, "But we weren't Pinkoes and Traitors." "You just have to go onto the…inside flap of the book and I tell you it's a joke." So, you know…

Q   Tell us about the reaction to your book.

A   Well, one reaction by, as it were, non-partisan public reviewers like Bonnie Greer, I suppose Chris Patten was a bit… or Chris Patten and the FT… The reviews in the papers were unequivocally great, beyond that, you know, sort of praised the writing, praised the attempt to describe the BBC, found it very readable and that's without exception.

And then there were two other responses, one of which is… the book was a surprise. I mean, Asa Briggs is very big, you know, 300,000 or 400,000 words a volume. I struggled, absolutely, I can't tell you how I struggled with not only how I would be responsible to the standard that I thought that the BBC required of me, which was to try to be impartial which, actually, mostly when people write books, they're not. The academic, particularly does, maybe, have an argument… and I'd struggled, again, very painfully, actually, with what I was supposed to be as the successor to Lord Briggs. Was I supposed to knit another stripe on the bottom of the great Briggs histories?

But there were lots of issues that felt to me absolutely core to the BBC that the public needed to understand and academics needed to understand. I used to put programmes at the centre, not at the periphery of the issue and try and put programmes and structures out of which programmes get made and the structures of response to that into a much bigger picture. Asa Briggs never looked at 'news values'. The word 'news values' never occurs in five volumes or a really newsroom culture.

And secondly, I thought that the BBC abutted important arguments in the world, not just within the BBC so that when you were looking at something like Live Aid and the Ethiopian story, which is regarded as iconic, nevertheless, it had this extraordinary impact on charities, which perhaps it's going to happen anyway but it's the moment when charities stop being small and start being very big. It has an extraordinary impact on the bar, which is set, really, I think, for famine stories. Nobody can ever replicate the very particular conditions of those stories in Ethiopia. And, for instance, in that chapter, I demonstrate all of my colleagues, sociologists know that the media did have effect.

I trace the impact of those programmes right the way through to Cabinet. You can see Cabinet for the first time – because I did the work on the papers – responding to a programme, responding in terms of the aid it gives Ethiopia. That helps you to understand why politicians get aerated but also it makes a bigger case about when you're talking about the effects that the media might have. It's not just down; it's also up.

So, I was trying always to make an argument, which I don't

think I overdid and I was trying to put programmes at the centre and I think it wasn't what people expected.

Q What kind of pressures have you come under as a result of writing the book and the reaction to the book?

A I think one of the reactions that has been very interesting, which again I completely understand actually, is that there's a very interesting issue of where authorial voice comes, where you put the voice in and I think in official histories, people expected to see… they expect it to be bigger. They expected – this is going to be slightly rude – they expected all sausages that were made well to have "Well-made sausages" labels attached, whereas, in a sense, I thought I was arguing.

Of course, I've not worked for the BBC. I watched it from the outside so I'm an outsider. I don't know why… well, I may be far worse than Peter Hennessy or Christopher Andrews, official historians of, you know, MI5 or Kevin Jeffrey's [Keith Jeffrey] of MI6. Subsequently, I've understood that nearly all people writing official histories come under the most immense pressure and I would say…

So, when I was writing it, I didn't come under pressure from the BBC to include that or not include that. There was fantastic anxiety around Northern Ireland, real anxiety and I had to negotiate that quite carefully and get access to state papers, which took a lot of time.

Afterwards, I've come in for a hammering. Now, I understand why people's achievements that they hope to find there, that were real, they find that upsetting. I understand that I've made judgments about really important things in people's lives. I understand all of that. I understand that I made mistakes.

Asa made 1,800 mistakes; nobody has ever complained of one of them, not one because I think they didn't… you know, I don't really want to dwell on that but, you know, Lord Asa Briggs on the Labour benches, a great historian, Vice Chancellor of Sussex, Worcester College, the Open University, a great radical historian but a great man. I'm just very evidently not a great woman; I'm just not. I'm a person who has done my best and I don't have any of those defences that make people kowtow to me. So I think that's not made it easy. And they've made a decision that they now won't do another volume of the history until everybody is dead because I think they feel that…

Q   The BBC?

A   Yes. So I think they think… somebody at the BBC said if they'd have known about it, they'd have sent me on a… they think all historians ought to be sent on a hostile environments course.

So I'm sure I have made mistakes but I have come in for… the only thing that really upsets me about that is that the book was, as it were, perfectly honed for this moment. I didn't know that it would be but by looking at the Conservative attacks around the licence fee, round the charter and the war in the Falklands and the conflict in

"RED by James Hogan"

Northern Ireland, the fact that the BBC was accused of being a traitor, that it was under fantastic political pressure, that the press was on its way to becoming where it is now, fantastically hostile for commercial reasons, in lots of ways, I've produced a book in which I was trying to balance – it's very interesting – I think I was trying to balance three things which weren't natural for me to balance, one of which was to take the Conservative attack seriously because I think the BBC failed to take it seriously in the period I'm looking at. But also, it seemed to me that was a… I have very clear, very, very clear political engagements and I was married to a leading Labour historian, you know, my own views, it seemed to me, I had to put aside and that my job was to interrogate that Conservative attack on its own terms, to understand it, not to dismiss it but to understand it because only if you understand it can you go forward.

I think my second thing I was trying to balance, which is odd, really, was knowing that the period afterwards was even more contested, my period, the sort of John Birt period. It was fantastically contested. And one of its things that it did was "say that this period was awful". So I've tried to balance, "Were they right? Was this period right? Who was right?" Out of which, actually, Mike Checkland comes as a kind of… John Birt says he's the Gorbachev; I don't think that's quite right. I think he was…

And, of course, Mike Checkland is also sacked by the government but do we have lament and wailing? We don't.

So I'm trying to balance things that didn't necessarily come naturally to me because it seemed to me... so I'm very critical of the BBC. So I've been accused of being too pro BBC but I mean, you know, actually, I'm very critical of it but, of course, I believe that the BBC is an incredibly important impartial bit of our national understanding of ourselves and I'm in favour of the BBC. But I wasn't always in favour of the decisions it made but I always tried to understand them. I've got passion to understand why people do things, not actually to condemn.

Q   Has the experience of writing the book taken a very heavy toll on you?

A   That's not fair. That's not fair...

[weeping]

Q   Are you okay?

A   Yes.

Q   Do you want to stop?

A   I'm sorry. Sorry, I'll just gather myself and I'll be absolutely fine. I do apologise. I'm so sorry. How pathetic, how weedy! How dreadful.

Q   No, not at all.

A   Has it taken a toll? Yes! It's taken a toll because it's become... of course I've made mistakes and I've owned them. I mean, I think I've just absolutely gone out and owned mistakes and some of those mistakes were absolutely mine and some of them were because it was cut and edited and I didn't know and I should have had another process at the end.

I think the attack… I'm very alone. I'm just… there is a really interesting – which I kind of relish, I absolutely relish – I've always worked not in posh institutions. I evangelically believe in the capacity of teaching to inspire and elevate people. I've worked in non-posh institutions; I've worked in polys… I've worked in a wonderful department, which was the founding media department. But there is a kind of contempt; I don't come from the same teams as some of the people and… you know, some people have great access to the media and they've used that against the book and I found that – sorry, I can't really articulate what I – but I found it very… I find it quite difficult to find within myself, if you go on, say, our Beeb, the answer to it because it felt relentless and I've had nine months when I thought I would be starting to write the biography of Hugh Greene or, perhaps, making cakes or, perhaps, talking to my children or, perhaps, actually having a holiday. And I've found myself defending up hill and down dale.

Q   Let's turn now to what you've learned about the BBC. Do you think the BBC is independent?

A   I absolutely think that the BBC has a really important independence but that independence, like nearly all independences, has a sort of number of… it's like the Lilliputians and Gulliver. There are ties and those ties are proper ties. So the BBC has a relationship to the state. Of course it has a relationship to the state; that's not a bad thing. But I really worry about the way in which some of those conventions are being eroded. But if you look at my book, I suppose people are always trying to erode them. One of the big discoveries was that the Labour government, the late '70s Labour government actually sort of, for financial reasons because inflation - which we can't remember - was spiralling out of control, considered basically making the BBC part of general expenditure and they knew that that was so toxic. They had that in papers which had 'Secret'.

So I think the BBC's independence, which is... the three bits to the BBC's independence, one of which is it gets the money and it's allowed to spend it as it wants; secondly, that the politicians take their tanks off its lawn and thirdly, that it's essentially an editorial independence are under threat at the moment. They've always been under threat but it varies.

Q   Do you think the BBC can ever be permanently at war with the government of the day?

A   No... well... one of the problems about now is the BBC, like all impartial institutions, like the monarchy and the church and, indeed, the civil service, is really stuck when there isn't a strong opposition, when the opposition is very weak or doesn't have purchase, it doesn't come anywhere because then, when the BBC put the alternative case to the government, it looks as if it is being the opposition. That was absolutely true in the early '80s. It seems to me it's a dangerous potential now because the BBC then looks at being at the opposition. And the BBC, if it can hide behind a sensible opposition, then it isn't so exposed.

Q   So would you say that because of the licence fee it's only ever pseudo independent?

A   No. I would say that as one of those great fudges of the British constitutional way, the license fee has given it more independence than any other broadcaster and longer survival than any other broadcaster and more capacity to innovate, though it would be very interesting to ask what have government stopped the BBC doing in the last, say, 15 years that it would have been very much in the national interest for us to do? Is the civil service independent? These are all things that we have to obsess about and worry about and be concerned about and you have to say that too many appearances, even before the magnificent Margaret – chair of the...

Q   Hodge.

A   Too many appearances, even before the magnificent Margaret Hodge, are really damaging. The BBC should not be held to account by politicians like that. You need them to move off. But independence, rather like democracy, is always a work in the making. It always has to be remade. You never get there, you never get to it. So it's a much more political nuanced thing. And that's good.

Q   Do you think the BBC licence fee imprisons BBC journalism in times of crisis?

A   I see no sign of that. I mean, if you looked at... well, okay, let me start from another end. The world is full of news outlets at the moment but it is the journalism that supports that news is in radical, dramatic and terrifying decline. So there's lots more news outlets; you can get news from everywhere but the actual journalism, which is what I'm interested in, which is the investigative, holding to account, finding stories, both locally, in most of Britain, is in dramatic decline, really no proper professional journalists in great swathes of Britain now and also internationally, for all sorts of reasons, not least the threats to journalists.

So the BBC journalism remains a world class bit of journalism, which we would lose at our peril because we won't understand the world, let alone the nation. I think in times of crisis... actually, again, you need a bit of history. In Suez, the BBC stood up to the government. The government thumped it. The next director general, wonderful, wonderful man, Hugh Greene, comes in knowing that's he's got to protect the BBC. Cuban missile crisis, BBC triumphant, doesn't have a row with the government, does independent reporting, manages not to... managed our way through the crisis. I've just written about that really interestingly.

Northern Ireland is more like a cancer than a crisis. It's a long running, sulphurous, difficult to manage, very, very illuminating for our present circumstances, Fifth Column at home, divided nation, difficult things on the ground. I think the BBC basically temporised sometimes and in the end, rather triumphantly, just believed it had to tell the story.

So, my answer would be it depends on the crisis and it depends on the government and it depends on… but public information and an accurate testing of things… again, if you go back to the Falklands, quite an illuminating war, BBC gets called a traitor. It does brilliant reporting on the ground in as far as is possible, Brian Hanrahan, Robert Fox, Jenny Abramsky ran the news, Newsnight does wonderful reporting. At the centre, I think, they lose – partly because of the government – they lose a proper judgment of the battles that are going on in Whitehall and they get terribly done over and that damages them all.

Q   How important is it to defend the licence fee at this stage of the BBC's history?

A   I would want to defend the principles embodied within it, which is that it's universal so it produces a universal obligation within the BBC. The BBC has an obligation, again, never perfectly done, to represent and bring into the national conversation weaker minority voices. It's a pure John Stuart Mill, pure John Stuart Mill, you know, not just majoritarian views but also minority views, oppositional views, weaker views, views from the not sexy, older, younger people. Universality is very important. That the BBC gets to spend it more or less on the things it thinks it should spend it on, that's also very, very important because that's related to editorial independence.

But it also has to be fair and at the moment, young people, my sons access the BBC website all the time, BBC Radio One, Two, Three, Four, Five and the World Service and Six the whole time. They watch stuff on Catch Up. They don't pay licence fees because they watch it on their computers. They're not trying to avoid paying licence fee; that's just how their lives work and, indeed, the middle son has gone out of his way to pay the licence fee even though he doesn't have a telly.

So that's no longer fair. So you have to have something that when people are watching it, that doesn't mean that... that it's fair but also because that calls the BBC to represent those voices. There's another bit.

Q   Do you think the BBC is too big?

A   No! I'm really worried that the BBC has been stopped doing some things that would have been in our national interest. The most obvious of that would be supposing it had launched a public service search engine in about 2001, what a different world we would live in. Would we be under the monopoly of Google? No. Would the values that that could have gone into a public service search engine have directed people in a really interesting way? What a brilliant Utopia that would have been. Perhaps it could do public service Twitter.

So I think that as a piece of... it's very fitted in its shape and institutional form, oddly, for the contemporary world because it both does abroad in the World Service but also, it has that fantastic reporting from abroad that comes back in. Last year, I was in India, Kabul and Pakistan, about to run a big conference, South Asia Conference for journalists and the sense of the BBC as a reliable voice in those countries is amazing. That, of course, does us the most extraordinary amount of good. And yet, that foreign is brought right the way back to domestic.

Most institutions we have don't fit the style of the communications of the modern world. Crime doesn't come from another nation; it's international. Problems can only be solved, as it were, globally. So the BBC fits that. So why don't we go with it. And I worry about where news is going and how it's being reconstituted at the moment but I don't think those are things that we need smaller.

Q   Do you think the BBC is inefficient?

A   Oh, I'm sure it is. But I mean, it's just had a report… but only in the sense that you should try universities. I mean, institutions always have bits of inefficiency. There's just been a report that says it delivers very, very good value for money. I think there's another problem, actually. I think younger members of staff who are on short term contracts – actually, particularly women I worry about because of the particular career that women need in order to have families – may not have BBC values in their DNA in the same way. That worries me.

248

I'm sure that there are inefficiencies but I'm not sure that those… for instance, does The Daily Mail have inefficiencies? Does The Daily Mail website have inefficiencies? So I think we need to keep an eye on that but I don't think that the BBC is peculiarly inefficient and, indeed, all of the recent scandals, oddly, emerged from, for instance, Chris Patten, when he became chairman, trying to bear down on top salaries and then that got out of hand.

Q   Why do you think the BBC found Margaret Thatcher almost impossible to deal with?

A   Well, in the BBC's defence, so did lots of other institutions. Lots of senior civil servants found her very difficult to deal with. She's a very, very powerful, fierce personality who takes no hostages. Douglas Hurd said Margaret didn't like the BBC because she thought they didn't like her. That was the feeling she got from them. I mean, she could be incredibly… I mean, they had a real problem and it's really interesting. It's like the stepmother problem. Mrs Thatcher motored herself on aggression and she liked to have enemies; most of us like to have friends but it's part of her extraordinariness. She kind of liked to have enemies. And the trick was not to be an enemy and the BBC, I think at the top, frankly, never managed not to be an enemy.

Now, would that have been… could she have held principle? I completely understand your holding principle on the inside that she's impossible to woo. There's a wonderful BBC memo, actually said she's a very, very difficult woman to woo and they do try and woo her.

It's a good 'what if?' Could another set of personalities

perhaps a little less hostile to her have brought her round? I think one of the things is Douglas Hurd said, who did lots to defend the BBC, actually – so where is the Douglas Hurd now – that you had to always sort of stand up to her, that you had to listen to her. But she was very, very, very difficult to manage so I don't know that they could have done but I know that they failed to do so.

Q   Would you like to put on record your assessment of the BBC director general Alasdair Milne who was sacked at the height of Mrs Thatcher's power?

A   Alasdair, who I saw lots of times, interviewed lots of times, was a complex man who'd been formed… one argument is that he'd been formed, really, by Grace Wyndham Goldie, that the BBC was run in this period by two sets of people. One lot had been formed by Grace Wyndham Goldie, the other had been formed by Huw Wheldon and that Grace Wyndham Goldie, who was the most extraordinary and formidable female inventor of political television around and one of the many august women married to the BBC in a funny kind of way, a very, very terrifying and magnificent and important person who I also, as a young woman, interviewed – absolutely scary – that she set people off to glow in her eyes and that was a quite competitive glowing.

I think Alasdair was an amazingly gifted programme maker with a real eye for really great programmes which he edited and kept an eye on and he knew actually how to nurture those relationships and protect those relationships.

A friend of mine, one of the people that worked on the project, actually, was on a plane as a young *Newsnight* producer, sitting next to Hugh Greene accidentally, to America on the day that Alasdair's appointment was announced and Hugh is completely ecstatic and says it's the first proper programme maker who has really controlled the BBC.

I think he was a brilliant programme maker. I think he was an honourable man and I think he was… he wasn't interested in the other side of the BBC, which was the structures and relating to government. I think he was enormously damaged by confrontation with baying Tories at the beginning of the Falklands War. I think if Trethowan had taken that hit, he would have started off in a better mood. So he was bullied by these ghastly, ghastly Conservatives at the beginning of the Falklands War, really bullied. And somehow he gets bullied. I mean, that sort of sets him into a tone in which he'd get bullied. He's no left-wing person. I mean, he's absolutely behind getting rid of the unions. He doesn't do much about it but he empowers other people to deal with the BBC unions.

Everybody who worked closely with him attests to a kind of boredom or frustration or misery at running the thing and he very, very quickly loses the confidence of the governors. Now, he's got difficult governors to deal with. I can understand that. But they're the only governors he's got; there's no alternative because the BBC has also lost with Mrs Thatcher and doesn't regain until after he's gone, really, the capacity to talk to government properly about who will be a governor, what kind of form.

So, of course, he inherits Mrs Thatcher's belief that boards are to do things, not to represent things. But he loses that capacity to have that really key conversation so he gets... I mean, he's right; he gets governors he doesn't want but... I mean, obviously I wasn't there. But a couple of the most sympathetic to him governors, including Alwyn Roberts, the Welsh governor, who was very, very sympathetic, very warm about Alasdair, you know, just goes through the times when Alasdair could have won the Board round and doesn't.

And when he, for instance, goes to the Peacock Report, which looks like a big tank, going to look at the licence fee, look at advertising, behind the scenes, Alasdair's been rather good. He said, "Go on and do some proper research," and he gives it to Brian Wenham. He says, "Really investigate the problems."

When he goes to see them, they ask him, "What is public service broadcasting?" He says, "Everything the BBC does," rather abruptly. I mean, he's a shy... you would know better, some odd mixture of shy, bulliable, abrupt, arrogant... some very odd chemical combination in him led him to be sometimes very charming but quite often rather abrupt and dismissive and not plastic enough in the places he needed to be plastic in.

Now, he said to me, "I was always polite to the governors." That's not the issue. Being polite to the governors is… so by the end of him, I think the whole place is toxic. I think everything is toxic. The governors are conspiring but not talking to him. He's blighted by chairmen who are ill and die on him, actually and have got other problems, really, until he gets to Hussey and Hussey is there to appoint him. Nobody's talking to him about what's going wrong. He and Wenham and various people are plotting against the governors; I understand why.

The entire structure of referral – this is such a BBC thing – the entire structure of referral happens in the wrong place. It happens after programmes are made. The BBC's always moving to defend programmes as opposed to own them as they get taken. So programme makers, understandably, feel done over by the outside world and betrayed by the BBC and they feel they're being censored. And that's a structural problem and he doesn't really quite have that mind for the structural, where it is you've got to have referral, where you've got to own programmes.

So in that period all power is, in a sense, delegated to programme makers and all responsibility for problems is held at the centre. Later, it turns round; all responsibility is at the bottom and all power is at the centre. Both of those are wrong. You have to get the structure, the whole power and responsibility in the right kind of order.

Q   As a student of BBC directors general, do you think Greg Dyke had to resign over the BBC's handling of the so-called 'dodgy dossier' that took the UK into the second Iraq war?

"RED by James Hogan"

A   Yes, I think he… okay, that's another of those great blizzards that go through the BBC, great fires, great firestorms. So Greg arrives and he feels very warmly… he's just what the staff wants; he cheers the staff up and he spends a lot of money. He has a new chairman, Gavyn Davies who is less of an acute brute from Christopher Bland and not new to… so you've got two new people – quite dangerous.

Most BBC rows – in fact I've written about this – most BBC rows are not really about whether the story in the programme is right or wrong. Indeed, most BBC rows, it turns out that mostly the story in the programme was right. And the programme makers think, "These people were shits," or, "It was a dodgy dossier." They think that the story, understandably, because they're story owners, constructors, finders. Most BBC rows, absolutely historically, look as if they're about the story but they're not about how the story is handled up. And if you are going to accuse the prime minister of lying, which I'm completely happy with, you have to do it in a fairly orderly way because you shouldn't do it casually because, somehow, we've got a very degraded public life, I think, at the moment, in which we assume a politician would lie all of the time and blah, blah, blah. But I don't think they do and I think that sometimes, opacity is sometimes absolutely what you need, you know. I understand secrecy.

So I think it was a combination of how that story went out and then the handling of it upwards. And the fact that

254

Gavyn, who is a lovely man and Greg, who is a very charismatic, good sort of demotic, very demotic voice for the BBC were both new to that position and what they did is they defended the journalism.

And, of course, the journalism by then – that's the other interesting thing – in Mrs Thatcher's period, the Exocets come in at the top of the BBC. They go right to the top, you know, Ingham phones up, it's go to the top. New Labour learns that something else could be done and they send their Exocets right the way down the feeding chain to poor damned producers who are making programmes, who get very resentful because suddenly they're being done over. I don't know where the Cameron government sends its Exocets; who knows?

So again, there's a structural issue about the resentment that's growing up in the BBC and how these things are handled and I think that in the end, Greg and Gavyn resign, which is pretty catastrophic in one way because it looks like a terrible crisis because they're not managing the relationship between the truth of the story and what's really going on above their heads well.

Q   Do you think it was politically possible for Gavyn Davies and Greg Dyke to say, "Look, we reject the Hutton Report. It beggars belief that the government was right about everything and the BBC wrong about everything."

A   That's really interesting. Yes, indeed, my husband from hospital, the last thing he wrote, was the thing defending the BBC and The Guardian about 10 days before he died.

"RED by James Hogan"

I wanted to say something else, which again is not at all helpful to the individuals in these terrible imbroglios, which is the capacity of the BBC to have its top decapitated is one of the reasons it's survived over the last 70 years and that sense that you can remake the BBC. I mean, it's very, very curious. We don't think that the NHS, somehow… we don't know who is the NHS, who is responsible for it. It doesn't have a head and it short of shambles along and we don't know quite where it is.

BBC we think of as one coherent thing because it has a head and certainly people like Julian le Grand, who works on the NHS, has always thought that the BBC's capacity to actually lose heads and have heads, lose directors general and have them… of course it matters, the quality of those people, the quality of the chairman, the quality of the director general but it's extraordinarily painful, unbelievably difficult for the people in those roles and has got more difficult. I mean, there isn't a director general since Alasdair or, indeed, for two, if not three… three directors general before Alasdair definitely went earlier than they expected or were effectively sacked. And all directors general since Alasdair, including John Birt, did not go when they wanted to go. This is such an exposed position.

So I'm saying as a historian, something that's not comforting to any poor individual caught up in the terrible fires, which damage them, sometimes, I think, forever. I mean, not Greg. I mean, he's risen brilliantly and we now think he's just absolutely defending British football, doing all the right kinds of things. It's wonderful. But it can be very, very, very damaging and I'd just say that's one of the mechanisms, as a historian, you can see the BBC survives by.

Q   As a student of directors general, do you think that George Entwistle had to resign over the BBC's handling of the allegations of historic sex abuse at the hands of Jimmy Savile?

A   I think he had to go, probably. I don't think it was fair. Everything I'm saying is that none of these exits are necessarily fair but the institution survives through them. I think it was terribly unfair because he was so new in. It was terribly unfair because he wasn't a vile man; he was rather a good man. It was terribly unfair because he was chosen not to be... he was chosen to be more demotic, less tricky, to grow into the job and he never had the time to do that and he was destroyed completely unfairly.

I mean, he's not an evil man; he's not done anything evil but the handling not of the historic sex abuse but of the programming over that autumn was a problem and I think there was a kind of panic. Poor man, he got a crisis too soon. He had no panic button mechanism in place. I feel fantastically sorry for him. But he'll be fine. He'll be fine. He'll re-emerge.

Q   Do you think the BBC knew about Savile's behaviour?

A   When it was happening?

Q   Yes.

"RED by James Hogan"

A   That is a very complicated question. None of the papers that I have seen, of which there are not many, but I have seen, as far as I know, all of the papers about Top of the Pops, about the payola scandal, which is quite early, '69, about Jim Will Fix It. I've seen all of those papers. There's one memo that with hindsight you would perhaps think was a bit iffy but only with hindsight. You would never in a month of Sundays have thought there was anything on paper. But of course, Light Entertainment didn't write anything down.

I think that I have very good evidence in my book, most persuasively from Helen Pennant-Rea, who I think has been a complete trooper, actually, very, very brave woman, who worked with Savile on Speakeasy for two years and is a completely good egg. She's a completely sensible, intelligent, motherly, concerned public service person. She worked with him for two years and she thought that he was very professional, particularly at giving working class young people a voice. She never noticed anything.

So I think in that sense, there were lots of people who never saw anything that they understood at the time to be abusive. If you look at Dan Collins' very, very good book on Savile, of course, this was true in other institutions, some of which… it was true in the NHS. It was true in the newspapers. It was true that Mrs Thatcher had him frequently to Christmas parties – not to Christmas day – but to Christmas parties, absolutely true in places like Stoke Mandeville that they somehow didn't see it.

Now, was there evidence that they should have noticed? I think you'd probably now say yes but if you go back to, say, that Paul Theroux interview with Savile, this is a man which is somehow the nearest one gets to a confrontation. I think that the BBC thought he was odd. I think that the music industry, which, actually, in a funny kind of way, he's not really part of. He's really pre pop industry, which is what is so odd about him. I mean, he's a DJ from Manchester. He's kind of too old for the pop industry as it really takes off. That had different mores around it.

I think lots of people can genuinely put their hands on their hearts, whether they'll be believed, and say, "I didn't see anything. I didn't understand." Some of those are incredibly decent, honourable people. Any of us have to assume that we might also… that we're no better than them, that we wouldn't have seen that.

That the BBC didn't take some of the evidence that was around more seriously, I think is a problem. That the BBC made two programmes, one of which was the World of Jimmy Savile in 1972, the other is a very, very troubled Anthony Clare, In the Psychiatrist's Chair, both of which go right to the edge of asking Savile really pertinent testing problems about his lack of a private life, about his devotion to his mother, about an abusive childhood. But almost by definition, they assume that the answer is he's a very sad and miserable person who is driven in an odd way to all these philanthropic goods, not that he's an abuser because they couldn't have gone out if they were abusive.

So the British public has a narrative around him, which is

that he's sad, not that he is utterly evil.

Q   Do you think the BBC turned a blind eye?

A   The BBC is quite good at sacking people if it thought they weren't good or closing programmes. I mean, there's an alternative narrative, which again is kind of very difficult, which is the Esther Rantzen's ChildLine. Did it... blind eye?

My concern about all of this is an odd one, really, which is that I imagine we are all now turning blind eyes to horrific abuses that we are not seeing, the most obvious of which actually is the export of sexual abuse on the internet to children in other countries, which has grown exponentially since the '80s. So there is an extraordinary area of abuse but we kind of are obsessed about the past here. So I think look for the mote in your own eye; what aren't we now looking at would be my problem.

So I think in as far as it did, it would be culpable... in as far as it didn't see things, it was culpable. I would like us to conclude from that that we have to be more rigorous about the abuses we don't notice ourselves.

Q   Was BBC talent untouchable in the period you covered?

A   Talent is quite often untouchable, owing to what talent is a bit rare. I think the BBC has a problem, which is distinguishing between the talent it makes and the talent that is really talent. The BBC can add Royal Jelly and exposure and paint political commentators, you know, DJs, presenters. It can paint them on lots of things and then they become…

So, if you looked at Jim Will Fix It, what's brilliant about Jim Will Fix It, to which the girlfriends of all my sons endlessly applied with dreams, is its most amazing format, its really brilliant BBC format, perfect, wonderful format, public spirit, public service, fun. Was Jim the only person that could have presented it? That's a 'what if?'

So I think the BBC… I think talent, as we've seen with Jeremy Clarkson, who I think is a real talent, though needed reinventing in some ways, talent is quite difficult to manage because it's not that ubiquitous.

Q   Why do you think the BBC self-censored the BBC *Newsnight* story about Savile's behaviour?

A   It's the most inexplicable, terrible decision made by the very nice, very decent BBC person because it wasn't concentrating enough. There are two real catastrophes; it's that and McAlpine. It was unbearable, the McAlpine, a dying man accused of paedophilia, just unspeakable. And he was then very magnanimous.

I think that decision – I am going to get into hot water here – I think that the material… my understanding is that the material had not been looked at properly and you would know better than me that you have to look at what the film shows you, not just hear the by-line on it. And when you saw the witnesses in that film, I think they were very compelling, particularly one of them, very compelling and very articulate. My understanding was that that material had not been properly looked at. That was a really big error. You always have to look at telly, don't you? You always have to look at it, please. And then the decisions get made too casually.

So I think that was really an awful set of decisions.

Q   I'd like to ask you just a few questions about the BBC today and the battle that is ensuing. Do you think there is a plot to kill off the BBC?

A   I don't know –

Q   Do you think there is a plot to kill off the BBC at the start of the 21st Century?

A   We'll see. I think that it's very difficult in the current climate to assert the national interest when the BBC stands in the way – I completely understand, actually – of the commercial interests, particularly online of a set of newspapers. I mean, it's completely legitimate that they object to that. Whether it's legitimate that the newspapers use themselves so uninhibitedly against the BBC, is another issue.

So I think there is a very powerful, much more powerful than before, commercial imperative which is being used against the BBC. I think that the public has almost no venues. I'm really worried about that. I think the public has… there is no platform for real public opinion to be voiced. Everybody always moans about the BBC, I suppose, because we love it and we own it. So that is another real anxiety. Where can we look around for a venue for the public to express their views?

I worry about the calibre of the discussions going on in government and a much denuded civil service about a bit of national kit and there are certainly a set of political enemies, including, as it were, the SNP and bits of the Conservative Party who coalesce in hostility to the BBC. People really don't like hearing the other point of view from their own. They find it really unpleasant and yet that's what the BBC is there to do.

For instance, we've now had two licence fee muggings, one in 2010 and one three weeks ago. Those were muggings. They were muggings because the Treasury needed to save money, the first time in 2010 for the Defence Review, this time because the government's got to save lots of money. And we live in a process driven world, all processes ignored; a mugging.

Did the BBC get the best deal it could have done? Yes, I think Tony Hall made a mistake by not saying, "This was an improper process but this was the best deal we could get," which is how I would have played it. We will see. But, I do not feel, which is part of the reason why the attack on my book is quite annoying because, in fact, in a funny kind of way, my book is poised to explain to you why you might want, nevertheless, to preserve this national bit of kit. And all of the attacks like, "Is it too big? Is it too popular? Is it a traitor? What's impartial news?" All of those things are investigated there.

I don't feel a strong coalition of defence and the lack of Liberal Democrats in the government… in the last government, the Liberal Democrats actually did defend… it did right back to the SDP, as a matter of fact. There's a long DNA of protecting the BBC, right the way back to the SDP, which is really interesting. We've lost that. So I look around and I wonder where the defence of the BBC will come from.

Whether there is a plot is another matter. Somebody once said to me "no Minister wants…" nobody wants on their obituary, "Under this man the BBC was finally killed." But you can kill the BBC in all sorts of little ways.

Q   Do you think the BBC will see this attack off?

A   I don't know. I mean I think it's the most… not least because the licence fee needs readjusting. I think it's the most challenging period since the period I wrote about. And the attack is more difficult for the public to identify. When it was Mrs Thatcher… even if people… biffing a bit, you see, even if the public agreed with the biffing, in a funny kind of way, they knew where it was coming from and they knew she had her interests.

Now the attack is much more amorphous, much more commercial, much more opaque for the public to identify.

Q   Jean, many, many thanks. Just pause there a second.

It's an outstanding interview.

End of interview

Chapter X

Peter Bazalgette

Chairman of the Arts Council and Non-Executive Director of ITV. Formerly Chief Creative Officer of the Global TV company Endemol which bought Big Brother to our TV screens.

Interviewer: James Hogan

A   I am Peter Bazalgette, I am Chair of Arts Council, England, at the moment. I have previously been chair of an opera company and a steam museum and before that I spent about 30 years in the world of television starting in the BBC and ending up as an independent producer.

Q   How did you start in the television industry?

A   I started in the television industry out of necessity. The necessity was I had a very poor degree, a Third, in fact, in Law. And since I seemed to have no option of entering the Law I thought I'd better find somewhere else to work. Probably, out of reckless charity, the BBC gave me a place on their news training scheme.

Q   What was the television industry like in those days?

A   In the 1970s the television industry was much like the rest of British Industry. It was dominated by two or three very large players whom you entered and, presumably, worked for, for life. And, if you behaved yourself, after about two or three years you'd get your own office. Then, after about four or five years, in the case of the BBC, you'd get curtains. But, after four or five years the curtains were false ones. Then, after six or seven years you'd get real curtains and then you were really living.

Q   What have been some of the biggest changes in television that you've witnessed?

A   The biggest change in television in my era is that the word, itself, is sort of oteus. Certainly, the word "broadcasting" is oteus because, what's happened is that we have with the internet multiple channels of distribution now. As a consequence the dominance of a small number of channels has disappeared. At first we had multi-channel television and now we have a limitless spectrum of means of distribution in the internet era. So, that is the most dramatic change.

Some of the funding models have changed to a certain amount in that content is still funded by a combination of advertising revenue and BBC licence fee money, State money that is in a way, but the addition since the late '80s has been…

A   But, the third means of funding content that emerged in the late '80s was, of course, subscription revenues, that is, initially BskyB but now, of course, it includes the likes of Netflix and Amazon Prime.

"RED by James Hogan"

Q   Why do you think that factual entertainment has become one of the dominant genre?

A   When I entered the world of television there were things that the Americans used to call "how to" programmes; programmes of immense earnestness and full of information and, frankly, rather dull. They were didactic, they were school ma'amish, and they taught you how to do your garden, do your house and lots of other things besides. But, a few people came along and said "we can make this factual information entertaining".

And the first person, perhaps, to do it in spades was Esther Rantzen who had *That's Life* which, at its peak, was getting 20 million viewers on a Sunday night. She was doing consumer investigations and human interest stories, all packaged together in a magazine. I worked on that programme, I learned a lot from her; and as a result of what I learned from her I was able to take food programming, DIY programming, gardening programming and, at its peak, get audiences of 12-13 million for it by adding human interest, by adding a story arc, in other words by formatting it.

Q   Can you describe the evolution of *Big Brother?*

A   *Big Brother* is a programme that was invented in Holland. It would never have come about if the public broadcaster in Holland, in fact there were about eight public broadcasters in Holland at the time but one particular public broadcaster had a hole for an entertainment show on the Saturday night and said to one of the leading entertainment producers, John de Mol, "can you come up with a new idea?" and that was the reason he got some of his best creatives around a table one evening, fortified by a little beer, to think up a new programme.

They were thinking around themes like the biosphere experiment where people have been shut in an eco-sort of bubble for a few months. They were thinking around some of the things that were going on, on the internet at the time, because I think with *JenniCam* where a student had put her life, put a camera, video camera linked to the internet in her room and put her life, as it were, or made it public via the internet. This was in the very early days of the internet in the 1990s.

They were talking around that and they came up with this idea of putting 12 people in a house and filming them 24 hours. And it was considered the most outrageous idea anybody had ever heard of and psychologists and politicians said "you can't do it" and no broadcaster would touch it until John de Mol decided to put it on a very small, youth oriented channel, called Veronica and agreed to take the risk, half the risk. In other words he said "if you don't sell any ads round this programme I will share your losses." Since he had a quoted company on the Dutch stock market at the time he was taking a very big risk with his own share price as well but he's a man of immense ambition who really likes to take big risks and that's how *Big Brother* was born, in the teeth of opposition from practically everybody.

"RED by James Hogan"

Q   Are you proud of *Big Brother?*

A   I was very proud when we imported *Big Brother* into the UK
in the year 2000 from Holland. I was very proud that it was
the first television programme, first entertainment vehicle
that combined the internet, television, the telephone and the
internet with its website. So, it was the first multimedia
entertainment property; I was proud of that.

I was very proud of the fact that because it started to relay
its pictures live 24 hours a day on the internet and, also later
on, on a TV channel it was the first programme in the
history of television that gave its rushes to the public so that
when you made an edited version in the evening the public,
that is the fans of the show, were arguing like crazy about
how unfair you'd been to Character A or Character B
because each of them would have edited it a different way.
That meant that it was the first programme to enfranchise its
audience, to show them the raw material and make them
realise that television programmes, those documentaries
that we heard so much about, which were meant to be this
bastion of objectivity were, in fact, the subjective view of one
director who edited pictures the way he wanted to. So, I was
proud of that.

The last thing I was proud of was the fact that some of the
winners of the programme were stereotyped individuals
who had been demonised by the tabloid press and, over
time, public came to see the warm characters behind the

stereotypes. I'm thinking of the gay winner of Series 2, Brian; I'm thinking of Pete, the Tourette syndrome sufferer; and I'm thinking of Nadia, the trans-sexual. All of them were stereotypes and the objects of demonisation in the press and the public took them to their hearts when they discovered what very nice people they were.

So, I'm proud of that but let me not make too great a claim for *Big Brother*, it was an entertainment show; it was made for a profit; it was made on a commercial channel, Channel 4 in order to attract advertisements; so, I'm not pretending that it was some sort of religious enterprise.

Q   What do you think has happened to the independent production section in the UK?

A   Well, the independent production sector has only existed since 1982, in effect, although there were a few independent producers before that, after the war. And, it got its opportunity when Channel 4 was told it could only commission programmes from independent producers, it couldn't have its in-house production, and its further chance when the 25% quota was brought in, in 1988. Both of these reforms were brought in by a Conservative government under Margaret Thatcher which liberalised the means of production in television and it brought a plurality to television. But, it did more than that. It helped create a production sector and helped create, I think, an important part of the creative industries.

Subsequent to that, the next significant thing for the independent producers was the 2003 Communications Act which gave them ownership of their programmes. They were allowed to own their IP, those programmes that were paid for and commissioned by the broadcasters.

It's interesting that our exports of finished programmes between 2003 and today have gone up from about half a billion to about 1.2, 1.3 billion, almost treble.

And, we now have about 51-52% of the international trade of entertainment formats. What does that tell you? It tells you that the independent production sector which started very emaciated, given its opportunity, very much a vassal of the broadcasters, has come of age. There has been a lot of consolidation and take-overs. Some of the companies are very large. Some are owned by American companies. And, they are able, now, to command some value because they own intellectual property and they own important sales relationships with broadcasters.

And it has been, I think, an object lesson in how you should intervene in a marketplace to liberalise it to create greater employment, greater creativity, greater economic activity.

Q   Do you think the indies self-censor in order to please the broadcasters?

A   To ask whether the independent producers in the UK self-censor, so to speak, to please the broadcasters is a very strange question because, actually, what you are talking about is merely the normal relationship between a buyer and a seller. And a seller tends to sell what the buyer wants.

In this case the broadcasters are the commissioners of programming and they wish to say "I want a certain programme on a Saturday; I want a certain programme on a Wednesday" etc., etc., and the independent producers are there to satisfy them. If broadcasters have the money to invest the independent producers sell the programmes. So, they are not self-censoring in any way, they are merely selling the programmes the broadcasters are requesting.

Now, whether the broadcasters are requesting the optimum mix of programming, when I say optimum, I mean optimum for the health of our democracy and the health of our culture as well as our creative industries; that's a different question. That would be a question for the broadcasters and not a question for the independent producers.

Q   Do you think that in today's television the broadcasters basically want entertainment and little else?

A   It's quite untrue to suggest that broadcasters only want entertainment today. In fact, the output of the BBC and the output of ITV and Channel 4 isn't even dominated by entertainment. It's dominated by entertainment in terms of the ratings but if you look at where the money goes into the programing and where the hours are, there are more hours in factual programming than entertainment and, then, that depends also on how you define drama. If you call drama entertainment, of course, a lot of money goes into drama, drama is very expensive but drama has a real cultural significance, I mean, the soap operas and some of the dramas on BBC and ITV are a really important part of our national conversation, our cultural language.

So, I can't actually remember what the question was, I've tied myself in a knock, old boy!

Q   Okay, I'll do it again. Do you think that in today's television the broadcasters basically want entertainment and little else?

A   Yes, I sort of answered it then, didn't I? I can answer again if you want?

Q   No, it's okay. we'll move on.

A   You'll probably find it out there somewhere.

Q   Do you think the indies are truly independent?

A   The term independent producer is something of a misnomer because independent producers are not entirely independent in that, on the whole, they don't own the means of distribution; the broadcasters own that. So, they tend to produce the programmes at a tariff that the broadcasters dictate and they tend to produce the sorts of programmes that broadcasters want so they are not independent in that sense.

Many of the independent producers are no longer independent in the sense that they are self-standing companies because they've merged, been taken over, often by very large companies, often by American studios. So, they're not independent in that sense.

But, they are independent since they are not broadcasters

and, in fact, to be an independent producer you cannot be more than 25% owned by somebody broadcasting a signal to the United Kingdom. Actually, about half of the output of the independent producers no longer qualifies for that either because they are companies that are owned by people broadcasting a signal to the United Kingdom.

Q   Do you think that the rebirth of the indies after 2003 came at a very heavy price, a dramatic narrowing of the type of programming that they can make?

A   After 2003 the independent producers got a massive shot in the arm because the 2003 Communications Act in the UK gave them ability to own their programming. That's been immeasurably valuable and has led to enormous growth, growth of creative output, growth of programme sales, growth of format sales; it's been good for everybody. Growth of creative ideas, so, it's all round been a positive thing.

I don't believe there is any connection between that and the sorts of programmes the independent producers are making. The only thing I would say is that if you want to have a solid business as an independent producer you are better off selling series that can be repeated. So, one off dramas and particularly one off documentaries have suffered because you can't really build a business around them. So, the only thing I would say is that as the independent production sector has matured, those programmes have been more difficult to make because it's very difficult to build a company around programmes like that.

"RED by James Hogan"

Q   Do you worry about what's happened to the indies in terms of democracy?

A   I don't understand the question.

Q   Well, when they were formed, as you said, in the '80s, the phrase was "let 1,000 flowers bloom" and they were very much seen as plural democrats, broadening the range and depth of programming that would be shown on UK television. Do you worry that the economics of broadcasting in the current era means that they have undoubtedly narrowed what they offered to broadcasters in order to get commissioned and make money?

A   If there has been a narrowing of the output of programming in the UK – if there has been – it is as a result of the broadcasters diktat not as a result of the independent producers' desire. The independent producers will make the programmes that broadcasters ask for. However, if you're going to debate whether there has been a narrowing of programming, you need to look carefully not just at the output of BBC, ITV, Channel 4, Channel 5, you need to look at the output of the hundreds of channels that are available on the television screen, most of which the critics of television who say it's too narrow haven't even discovered yet.

And, in fact, the output of programming and the choice of programming on offer on television screens but also, of course, on the internet now via any link you care to follow on the internet, YouTube or whatever, the choice of programming is wholly, wholly different to 20 years ago, and wholly larger. There has been no narrowing at all. There's been a bewildering proliferation of programming and choice. The difficulty, today, is finding what you want to see and finding the stuff you like out of the masses and masses that's offered to you.

Q   Do you think the indies are equipped to mount major hard hitting investigations?

A   Independent producers can make investigative programmes and the skill and the talent is there if they are backed and funded so to do by the broadcasters. I would say that there are fewer investigative programmes on mainstream British television now, than there used to be, just as there are fewer current affairs strands which used to carry some of those programmes.

There are, arguably, fewer such investigations going on in the newspapers. What does that tell you? It tells you there is more competition and it tells you some of those organisations that used to fund it have got challenges to their business models, certainly in the case of newspapers.

Having said that, in the mad rumbustious Tower of Babel world of the internet, there is more democracy, more investigation, and more openness going on than ever existed in the days of one or two *Panorama* investigations; so, again, if you look at the whole picture, arguably, there is a greater revealing of information and what's the purpose of an investigative programme? To reveal things that are hidden.

There is a greater revealing of things that are hidden today than there ever was when people used to make investigative programmes on television.

So, to go on about there being fewer investigative programmes on television is to over-emphasise the importance of television, is to make claims for it over and above the importance of the internet and other media.

Q   Do you think investigative journalism on BBC and/or ITV is dying?

A   There are certainly fewer investigative programmes on British public service broadcasting channels than there were but, by the same token, via things like Freedom of Information, via the extraordinary resource of the internet where 1,000 if not 100,000, if not 1 million self-appointed investigative journalists working from their homes and laptops are investigating things all the time, and making their findings public. In fact, I would argue that we have a more open society, today, than we ever did in the age of more investigative programmes being made on those very few broadcasting channels of the old days. It's better today than it was then. It's more open today than it was then; things are more transparent now than they used to be and there is more answerability now than there used to be. So, things are better today even though there may be fewer investigative programmes on television.

Q   Does the BBC have a special responsibility to carry out such programmes, investigative journalism?

A   The BBC has a broad range of responsibilities. For me, the most important thing the BBC should be doing is to be a trusted and reliable source of news and information. I think its news services are a cornerstone of our democracy. I think the fact that there is public money going into an independent news service that is free to investigate and criticise the government is evidence of a mature democracy. In that sense it is, absolutely, the responsibility of the BBC to investigate and, arguably, every night on the news it does just that.

Does it devote as much of its schedule to specific investigative programmes? Probably not. But, I would be far more concerned that we continue to fund a broad and plural range of news services that are cornerstones of our democracy than I would about worrying about a few *Panoramas* that may have gone by the board.

Q   Does the licence fee help or hinder the BBC in this respect?

A   The licence fee has a couple of peculiarities about it which it's worth pointing out even though it sounds like a statement of the obvious. One is it's compulsory. The second is it's hypothecated, unlike other taxes we pay; it's dedicated to the BBC or it has been. There are a few other uses at the edges like broadband at the moment but, broadly speaking, it's hypothecated.

So, for those two reasons, that it's dedicated to one purpose and we all have to pay it, it has a very special role in society.

For instance, the BBC is meant to be a universal service. That doesn't just mean it's available to everyone, it means it should have something on it for everyone as long as it remains compulsory to pay the licence fee.

At the moment the licence fee has now been renewed for at least, we don't know the outcome of Charter Review on the BBC yet, but we know that they have renewed the actual level of the licence fee so we know the licence fee is going to continue for at least five, possibly ten, years.

While it's possible for the public to accept the system, and it would appear at the moment there is no mass protest movement against it as there was, for instance, against the poll tax in the early '90s, while there is public of acceptance for it then it should continue.

It is challenged by, obviously, modern media. It is challenged by the fact that, at the moment, you can watch BBC programmes on iPlayer, on catch up, without paying the licence fee but the law will be changed to cover that. But, when or I should say if the public turn against it, if it doesn't command widespread support, then it will go and the BBC will be greatly diminished thereafter. I'm not saying it's a good or a bad thing but it will be greatly diminished.

So, at the moment, the system is good and the BBC reaching more than 90% of the population every week is an essential cornerstone, not just of our democracy in terms of its news services but also our culture, our national conversation, funding five orchestras and its radio channels and all the rest of it; and then investing in original programmes, there's nothing more important in the expression of a national culture than its TV shows made in their own language by their own talent, and on the question of talent bringing forward the next generation of talent.

Those are the key things the BBC does. It does the most easily with the compulsory licence fee. I just wonder, in ten years' time, whether that will be sustainable or will command public support.

Q   Is the BBC too big?

A   Phew! Is the BBC too big? According to the Director General of the BBC the BBC is too big because he has just announced 1,000 redundancies. He's currently got about 18,000 employees so it sounds as though he wishes to bring it down to 17,000. My guess would be that the BBC will be nearer 15,000 in five or ten years' time simply because of the plurality of media, all the different things that are going on, all the other ways of supplying programming to people. It can no longer have that quasi-monopoly position in the media world. I suspect it will have to be more efficient and operate with a smaller number of people. But, I hope it still has sufficient size to train the next generation of creative talent for our creative industries.

Q   What are your personal reflections about the Savile affair?

A   The most clear thing that comes out from the Jimmy Savile affair is that society has changed for the better in the last 30 years, that there have always been a very small minority of people who are known as paedophiles, who have a sexual attraction to under-age girls and boys; that's always been the case, always will be the case. The question is whether society dealt with it or covered it up. All societies tended to cover it up and now we are no longer covering up and we're no longer tolerating it. We've moved from a society, in quite a short space of time, that tolerated it to not tolerating it. That's the biggest lesson that comes out of the Jimmy Savile affair.

Q   Some people say everyone at the BBC knew about Savile. Did you hear rumours?

A   In 1978, as a very, very junior researcher working on a regional news programme, I was told by a director who worked by him, in the bar, gossip level, "oh, you know, Jimmy Savile, he likes little girls, you know". So, I was told that, I don't know, whatever that is, 35, 36 years ago.

But, you know, you are told gossip and rumour all the time about people, particularly when they are celebrities. Whether anybody actually knew, specifically, what he did, I've no idea because I never worked with him.

Q   Do you have any doubts that if the BBC knew that he was raping, brain damaged five year olds that they would have sent in the police?

A   That's a very interesting question and you're asking me and

I guess you've asked other people to speculate on how people, 30 years ago, would have reacted to information. I like to think if they'd had hard evidence of what was going on, they'd have acted on it. I can only imagine that something as shocking as what you've just described, the abuse of mentally or physically handicapped children at a very early age, defenceless children, I'd like to think they would have acted on it. I can only think that the people who knew about it on the front line didn't bring the hard evidence to the people who could have taken action. I think that's probably what happened.

Q   Why do you think the BBC self-censored the *Newsnight* investigation into Jimmy Savile?

A   Why did the editor of *Newsnight* not run an investigation into Jimmy Savile? There are two explanations in this world for those sorts of mistakes. One is cock-up and the other is conspiracy. Most of the time I believe in cock-ups rather than conspiracies; most of the time people make a series of mistaken judgments. The tragedy of *Newsnight* was that having made that terrible error and having not run an investigation that they had paid for, that had been done, that clearly was valid, we know now with hindsight, and that ran very successfully on ITV as a programme, having not run it they then, shortly afterwards, over-reacted by trying to prove their journalistic credentials and ran a story about McAlpine that was palpably untrue and had been discounted and devalued several times in the past.

So, they didn't show one error of judgment, they showed two errors of judgment; one of omission, one of commission.

That's pretty tragic.

Q   Do you think the subconscious was at work; do you think the BBC didn't want to believe the allegations against Jimmy Savile so they didn't want to publicise them?

A   I love to hear people talking about "did the BBC want to do this; did the BBC want to do that" as though it's some sort of single organism with a single brain, sitting there making plans. The BBC is like all other organisations, it's a huge sort of box of frogs. It's a huge number of people with differing opinions and whatever was happening in the BBC around that time with Savile and *Newsnight* and the rest of it was a result of a whole series of decisions taken by individuals quite a lot of whom would have disagreed with each other; quite a lot of whom didn't seem to be talking to each other when they should have been talking to each other.

So, it was a sort of 'bugger's muddle', if you like. But, I don't think it was a sort of malign conspiracy that "Jimmy Savile is one of our heroes, we want to run a hagiographical documentary about him; we're going to censor investigations." I don't think the BBC, I'm afraid, is that well-organised (laughter).

Q   Do you think, however, that it was inevitably a very uncomfortable story for the BBC and that discomfort played a part in the self-censorship?

A   To say it was an uncomfortable for the BBC is absolutely true. As it was, and is going to be, for all the other institutions he worked with. The Royal family, he worked closely with; Stoke Mandeville Hospital he worked closely with; a lot of treasured institutions worked closely with Jimmy Savile. It's uncomfortable for all of them. But, to suggest that is why they might not have run the story, I think, is probably wrong and the reason I think it's wrong is that all the people who really worked with Savile, who made all the radio programmes with him, who made all the TV shows with him, they're long gone, half of them are dead. Those big shows were made by him in the '60s and '70s and '80s. So, there wasn't anybody left in power at the BBC who had a massive investment in their own personal reputation and having worked with Savile. They weren't around anymore.

Q   Why do you think they scrapped the programme rather than just postponed it?

A   You're talking about *Newsnight* aren't you? Why did *Newsnight* scrap the Savile investigation is an incredibly pertinent question. It was a big error of judgment not to run the investigation and if they thought it wasn't ready they had the resources to hold it over, put a bit more investment into it; but, to scrap it, that is the single most questionable decision that was made by the editor of *Newsnight* at the time and I've never heard a proper explanation of why.

Q   What do you think about Channel 4 these days?

A   Channel 4 continues to be an invention of genius. The idea that the State would set up a publicly owned corporation that is nevertheless funded commercially but with a very strict remit to only commission programmes from independent producers rather than have an in-house production unit and to make programmes for unpopular and unlikely points of view, minorities, younger people, and an organisation that will stimulate young, creative businesses which it does not just now in terms of television production but also games and other sorts of internet product, that's brilliant. And I think Channel 4 remains true to that.

The pressure on Channel 4 is the pressure that exists on all of the heritage broadcasters. That is, they are selling a mass audience in an era when mass audiences are declining and when there is much competition for our attention from the internet.

Channel 4 has a particular challenge. In 1982 when it was set up, it was the sort of sullen adolescent in the broadcasting arena; it was the alternative view; it was the way out; youth oriented; outré sort of channel. In the era of the internet where anything is possible and everything is possible, that slightly changes your positioning. Channel 4 still expresses itself in that way, they still say those are their brand values but it's difficult to sustain that in the era of the internet. And, the only thing I would say about Channel 4 is it's possible that it needs to revisit some of its brand values because it, in a sense, is now part of the mainstream. It may

286

be, and it does, successfully deliver a younger audience even today and it does some marvellous programmes.

I was watching *Not Safe at Work* last night. Have you watched it? Brilliant comedy, absolutely brilliant, brilliant comedy; absolutely touches a button about the way that life is in the office today. But, it's part of the mainstream now so there is a dissonance between its brand values and its positioning I suspect. That's something it will have to work out over the next few years.

Q   Do you think it should be privatised?

A   I think it would be a pity to privatise Channel 4 right now. I think it's unlikely that it will be privatised. What happens with Channel 4 is that every time there's a new government they go into the Treasury and say "give us a list of the government assets we can privatise" and the Treasury dusts off the list that it always brings out of the cupboard and Channel 4 is always one of the government assets on the list.

However, here's the thing. If you privatise Channel 4 but make it keep all its public service broadcasting responsibilities then you won't get a very big price for it; I don't know, maybe half a billion. If, on the other hand, you relax those public service responsibilities you can probably get more than one billion for it. What's the point of privatising it for half a billion? It's not even worth it; and, if you did relax its public service responsibilities, we'd be losing something of value. So, there's, if you like, a tension between those two positions. And I think that tension will mean that Channel 4 will not be privatised, not in the near future.

"RED by James Hogan"

Q   What do you think about Channel 5 these days?

A   Channel 5 is a channel that Richard Desmond bought cheaply and sold on rather more expensively. He sold it on more expensively for two reasons. (1) He had commissioned *Big Brother* to go on the channel which turned around its ratings and brought it some younger viewers. (2) He has sold the channel to its new owners, Viacom, having committed his newspapers to taking advertising on the channel for some time. So, the headline price he got for it is not exactly, if you like, all things considered, the price he got for it.

So, it is a channel that has been revived. With *Big Brother* it competes quite effectively against Channel 4 and ITV2. And it does also commission some quite enjoyable documentaries and arts programmes; I hope it continues to have that mix.

Q   Let me ask you about the internet and then I'm going to ask you about the Arts Council. What, in your view, is the likely future impact of the internet?

A   Well, let's talk about the impact of the internet on the television industry. The most obvious impact it's having right now is that younger viewers, say aged between 16 and 25, 16 and 30, they like the output of the television, the traditional television industry, they like the programmes as much as they ever did but they don't really want to watch them when they're scheduled. So, they've become, they're becoming schedule avoiders. They want to watch programmes on their mobile phones and on their tablets and, indeed, on their connected TVs whenever they want. They call it, don't they, Martini Media, any time, any place, anywhere. And that is the biggest effect the internet is having, is that as a distribution medium it means you can deliver content at any time when you order it.

So, what is critical for the broadcasters, so called, and they shouldn't be called broadcasters for much longer because "to define their business by their means of distribution is a very odd thing to do because it is the programme, stupid", I'd say. But, they need to make their programmes available as they are beginning to online in any way they can.

Having said all that, and that is quite a shift of the tectonic plates, it's not the death of the schedule, it's the reduction of the importance of the schedule. I'd like to say I'm a great believer in Riepl's Law, and you will say to me "what is Riepl's Law?" And I will tell you, Riepl's Law is named after a German economics professor of the early 20th century and, just before the First World War, he came up with his Law of Innovation in Media. And, simply put, it is that innovations in media tend to add to what went before rather than replace it. Innovations in media tend to be like the car and the train, not like the car and the horse.

And, we hear soothsayers say that YouTube is going to obliterate TV and it's going to obliterate this, that and the other, that the internet is going to obliterate... Actually, it's adding to it; it's more choice; more possibilities; more ways of distributing content. So, nothing is going to disappear in the next decade but there is going to be a changing relationship between it.

Let's remember that if you're a traditional broadcaster producing programmes as well, which the BBC does and ITV does, the internet is an exciting new form of distribution both your programming and your broadcast signal. So, it's an opportunity as much as a threat. So, there are big changes coming to the television industry as a result of the internet. You could say it's digitally challenged but in that challenge there is as much opportunity as threat.

Q   In such a world, how important is the Arts Council?

A   The Arts Council, financially, is less important than the BBC. If you add together the Arts Council's tax payers' money to its Lottery money, it gets about one sixth of what the BBC gets in the licence fee. So, the BBC is a much more significant intervention in the country, in the culture, in the creative industries, in the democracy than the Arts Council.

Having said that, the Arts Council is a National Development Agency, for arts and cultural organisations. It does invest 600 million a year and it enables a lot more than that. For instance, if you take the larger funded arts organisations, Arts Council funding, national, public funding represents no more than about 25-26% of the income of those arts organisations. So, what it does is it enables the rest of the income, commercial income, the ticket sales, the hospitality offer, fundraising, local authority funding, so there are all sorts of diverse revenue streams and we're trying to develop new ones like social enterprise investment as well.

And so, the Arts Council's greatest significance is that it is public funding for arts and culture which is like seed corn investment that enables a whole lot of other things to happen and greater value to be delivered.

Now, why do you do it; why do you put money via the Arts Council into arts and culture? Four main reasons: The intrinsic value of arts and culture; personal identity; national identity; the development of empathetic citizens; sense of sheer entertainment, delight and insight; those are the intrinsic values of arts and culture which you wouldn't necessarily want a dismal economist to reduce to numbers. That's more a statement of philosophy.

Then, you have the benefits to society. Go into an old people's home, go into a hospital, wherever you go, go into a prison and you will find arts and culture doing great things, giving people new frontiers and new opportunities and new insights and pleasures in their life. In fact, in health, where we spend more on curing obesity than we do preventing it, we have to completely turn it around and, in future, doctors will prescribe people to go and sing in a choir rather than give them Prozac. That is the sort of thing, role, that arts and culture is going to play for society.

Third, is education. Primary, secondary, tertiary, lifelong learning, massively important. Symbiotic relationship between arts, culture and education.

And the fourth, and we mention this last, is the economic benefits. We don't put money into arts and culture because there's economic benefit but, we should point out, there is an economic benefit. What are the economic benefits? Urban regeneration; tourism; the development of talent for the creative industries; and, just as importantly, the reputation of British creativity and culture around the world. British Council has research that says that people who trade with Britain... sorry, people who come into contact with British culture are more likely to trade with Britain. So, it's massively important to our reputation around the world.

So, those are the reasons we put public money into arts and culture and I say them as often as possible and I write about them as often as possible, because I found when I became Chair of the Arts Council that half the people I spoke to in government and the civil service have forgotten why.

Q   Is the Arts Council safe in this government's hands?

A   I believe that this government has a commitment to funding the arts. I believe the cuts that have been made in arts funding, while regrettable, and how we've argued against them, would have been made by any government since 2010 dealing with the credit crunch. I note, though, that government tax revenues are now increasing; I note that we can see a bit of light at the end of the tunnel; and I hope that the infinitesimal sumps of money going to arts funding – and just to put that in context, the tax payer dollar as a proportion of government spending, less than 0.01%, it's a tiny amount of money. Arts Council gets from the tax-payer about 300 million a year. National Health Service, 120 billion a year and counting. You get the picture.

So, it's a tiny amount of money; it doesn't make much difference to the nation's finances but makes a huge difference to the nation's health, culture and national conversation.

Q   What has been the most inspiring thing you've learned as chairman of the Arts Council?

A   The most inspiring thing I've learned as Chairman of the Arts Council is that arts and culture has a more profound effect on society than I had ever imagined. I knew I enjoyed it; I had helped run arts organisations; I had raised money for arts and education organisations; but, I hadn't realised how profound it was.

I have just been doing some work on an idea I call "The Empathetic Citizen". I've just been researching the way in which arts and culture are essentially the telling of stories about humanity, human stories, human interest stories, stories that touch us. They are, in fact, us exercising our empathetic muscle in our brain. They are that profound. In other words, they have a contribution to make to the glue that holds society together. That sounds like a bold claim; it's true. And that's the sort of thing that's inspired me hugely being Chair of the Arts Council and thinking more deeply about why we do it.

Q   And is there one worry you have about the Arts Council

that keeps you awake at night?

A   My biggest concern is that the public will and the government maintain the desire and continue to see the value for investing publicly in arts and culture and, at the same time, that we manage to diversify the funding for arts and culture to keep our arts and culture as strong as it currently is.

Q   Many, many thanks.

A   Pleasure.

End of interview

Chapter XI

Sir Trevor Mc Donald

Sir Trevor McDonald is one of the best known faces on British television having presented ITN's News at Ten for many years. Hugely popular and authoritative he continues to present ITV documentaries of quality and exclusivity.

Interviewer: James Hogan

Q   With me today is Sir Trevor McDonald. Trevor, many thanks for taking part.

A   A pleasure.

Q   How did you get started in TV?

A   I started in television in Trinidad, in the West Indies. Television had come into the island in the '60s. I was a radio journalist. I thought I was rather good, especially since I got a plum assignment to London in the early '60s to cover the Trinidad and Tobago Independence Conference at Marlborough House. When I got back to Trinidad thinking I had covered myself in great glory, because no other radio journalist had been sent, and so I had the field to myself, hence the glory, nobody else competed, television came in and I naturally wanted to gravitate to the television world.

And, I applied and wasn't immediately successful. And

then, wasn't quite sure I wanted to do television, I was enjoying radio so much. So, I agreed to do the news on television at seven o'clock at night and later on to do a discussion programme called *Dialogue* which attempted to inject an element of controversy into rather placid West Indian political life.

Then, I came to London to work at the BBC at Bush House and boasted to my colleagues there that I had been involved in television in a peripheral way in Trinidad, and they said to me "if you think you're so good why don't you apply to this new place called ITN?" And I went to ITN and was given an audition and I was employed. I was probably the most surprised person in the world! I never thought I had a chance. I did it because I thought my career at Bush House was not going as fast as I thought it could and, in any case, there was a sort of perception that Bush House was a kind of end game, you didn't move on too far from there and I wanted to get out. So, I applied to ITN and that's how it happened.

Q   What were your first impressions of the TV industry?

A   I was astonished at the TV industry when I joined ITN. It was all a big, big surprise to me. I knew so little about television in a large country like Britain. I started doing the news on television in Trinidad. Trinidad had a population, then, of about a million and a bit. Broadcasting to the United Kingdom was an entirely different proposition. And, of course, I began by getting involved in the Northern Ireland story at the time of the Troubles, that wonderful euphemism for the mayhem that went on in Northern Ireland in the late '60s, 70s and 80s. And, of course, that immediately gets you noticed quite nationally.

So, my first impression was about just how important an element in British life television was. People watched the news. They set their time by watching the news and they actually digested what you said and listened very carefully to what you said. So, I was surprised by how very, very quickly, you were recognised as somebody who was on television. And, of course, I was a black face, there weren't any other black faces on television so I was noticed and those were the bits that surprised me.

Q   Tell us about you and *News at Ten*.

A   Well, working for *News at Ten* was the highlight of any young journalist's television life. *News at Ten* had established an enviable reputation. I think, first of all, because nobody thought that you could schedule news at 10 o'clock at night. In those days, 10 o'clock was regarded as very late in the evening for television. And, I think, ITN was rather given *News at Ten* or the time of 10 o'clock as something which the companies had to do to satisfy the broadcasting regulations.

ITV got the contract by saying that you had, at some stage of the day, or several stages of the day, to have national news broadcasts to compete with the BBC. ITN were given 10 o'clock because they thought it was a dead time and they soon made it into the most watched time on British television, or certainly one of the most.

I think that had to do with its style, they had these bongs, you know, Big Ben. I think it had a lot to do with the strength of the editorial content; it was very well driven. I think it had a great deal to do, too, with the personalities. They had this idea of two newscasters and these people became household names; Reggie Bosanquet, Andrew Gardener, Anna Ford, Alastair Burnett, Robin Day did interviews. I mean, all the biggest names in British television appeared on *News at Ten*. I was absolutely delighted beyond words to have a walk on part in what had become, even by the time I joined, a great, great British institution. It was absolutely wonderful.

Q   You became the brand, didn't you, you became in later years, the embodiment of *News at Ten*.

A   Well, I don't' think I was ever the embodiment. I mean, I think the reputation of *News at Ten* really preceded me. I got, again, much to my surprise, the job of being the sole anchor of *News at Ten*. In other words, there were always two newscasters. I got the job of being the sole anchor and that was a great, great surprise to me. When it was being decided I was thinking "what am I going to do if I don't get this job?" because if you have two newscasters then you have several combinations; if you have a single anchor then you have a single anchor. And if you don't get that job then you are in a spot of bother, really.

So, I contemplated what I would do if I didn't get it but I was lucky, I got the job and I thought it was probably the most important journalistic thing that has happened to me because to be able, well, let me start again, I've always thought the whole business of the dissemination of news to be an essential part of what we like to call, and we proudly call, our democratic process. We tell the people in Afghanistan, Iraq and Syria, "you must be like us; you must be a democracy; you must … there must be freedom of information; you must let people know what is going on." To have a role in the dissemination of that information I always thought was a crucial, crucial part, beyond television, beyond social life, essential element of the way we live, of the way we are governed, of the traditions that this country is so proud of.

So, I thought to have a part in telling people what went on and trying to make it interesting, accessible, so that people can really… why are people watching something about Syria or Uganda or India? You have to be able to catch their imagination to make that interesting. So, I always took the job terribly, terribly seriously because I thought it was very, very important and *News at Ten* managed to do that.

Q   What were the landmark moments for you as the anchor or *News at Ten?*

A   Oh gosh! I mean, there are so many. I suppose the death of Diana is one that comes to mind. I don't think most world events have a kind of genesis you can… there is a sort of a bit where you can see the problem beginning to emerge; you can perhaps forecast, sometimes badly, what the course of events is going to be and what the end game might be, if you're lucky, you get that right. The death of Diana just came out of the blue in Paris with Dodi Al-Fayed, these two people who were, apparently, having a serious relationship, and so on. And, quite out of the blue.

The other thing, of course, was that she was extraordinarily well liked by the public; she was, as Tony Blair or Alastair Campbell liked to think they coined the phrase, "the people's princess." She did capture people's imagination. And, to think that at that young age her life had suddenly been cut off was the most tremendous shock for people. I got a call about three or four in the morning, or something; and I went in to London and I never left for a week. I stayed there doing a variety of programmes about her. And the shock of it all was beyond words. And I remember that as one of the things.

Q   And the fall of Margaret Thatcher?

A   The fall of Margaret Thatcher had almost the feel of a slow motion part of a film, really, because I was in covering something in Brussels - or some other part of Europe or some other bit of the EU or the Common Market as it then was, for all I remember – and she, there was the first ballot and she was not in London, she had been at a meeting in Europe and, of course, rather surprisingly, she didn't do as well in the first ballot as everybody thought she would. She stormed out of this meeting, well, she came out of the meeting and said "I fight on, I fight on" and was terribly resolute about what she'd do.

Margaret Thatcher had dominated the political landscape in this country to such an extent that when she said "I mean to go on, and on, and on" people thought "you know, this might just be possible; this might just be possible". She was such a commanding figure, a controversial one; she was hated by some parts of the people in the country, the miners for example, and so on. And she was very divisive in many of her policies but she stood head and shoulders above everybody else.

We never understood, I think, how deep those cross-currents inside the Party were, the Conservative Party has never been a champion of feminism, and I don't think... that many people didn't take very kindly to having the lady who bossed them around. So, it was a big, big, big shock and the images that I remember so well, not only that bit about going on and on, and on and "I fight on; I fight to win" not only those but the final, the epilogue of her walking out of Downing Street and you could clearly see moist-eyed; unforgettable. You never thought that she would (a) go; and not in that way.

Q   Tell me about you and meeting Saddam Hussein.

A   Saddam Hussein was, strangely, a very good interlocutor. I was terrified of the whole prospect of meeting Saddam Hussein. We had an exclusive interview with him and were given a pretty rough time by the security people. He, himself, was very, you know, straight laced; you didn't agree with what he said but he was very forthright about what he'd done in Kuwait; he thought the Kuwaitis were stealing his oil; he thought they were a bunch of corrupt princes who cared nothing for their people and cared only for themselves; who lavished all the money the country had, not only on their families and on themselves but also spent a lot of it in European casinos. He really had a kind of grudge against the Kuwaitis and it all came out.

The other thing about it was that the Iraqis never quite understood why the Americans would attack them. There had been, preceding that invasion, an Iran/Iraq war in which the Americans had supported the Iraqis against the Iranians and, in that culture, you don't switch from being a friend one day to be an enemy. What I remember most persistently being asked when I was there was "why are the Americans doing this? Two days ago they were our friends." And in that culture you don't switch sides so easily. So, there was a general consternation about what the Americans were about to do. They didn't quite understand it.

Q   Was it a very big decision to decide to interview Saddam Hussein?

A   That's a very, very good question. I was shocked to learn that there were some people, I thought propelled, mainly, by jealousy, by the fact that they didn't get the interview, there was a minor fuss in Britain about whether Saddam should be interviewed. Absolute garbage in my view. Of course he should be interviewed. And I was asked to respond a lot to questions about whether he should be interviewed. And, at one stage I got quite exercised about having to, you know, justify this thing over and over again where I thought no justification was necessary. I said, "look, one of the things I would have liked to have done if I were around in 1939 would be to ask Adolf Hitler what the hell he was about, what he was doing."

I've always thought information is key; it is much better to have people express their views widely so that you know what they are than to have them, somehow, secreted under a carpet, under a blanket, and then it suddenly arises that "do you know this German guy who doesn't like the Jews?" Well, it would be much better if somebody got him on television to say "would you explain to me your policies about what you are doing, about taking these people away in carts and sending them to concentration camps. How do you do that; how do you justify that?" The fact is that any society which resembles any kind of civility must have a certain openness and that applies to Saddam Hussein as it applies to anybody else. All these questions are relevant; people are players on an international stage; they must defend their actions. We, as journalists, if we're lucky, get the chance to put those questions to them and we must always, it's a foundation principle of what journalism is all about.

Q   What have been some of the biggest changes in television that you've witnessed?

A   Speed, brought on by the technology. When I started, I would do a film in India and take the cassette to a kindly pilot at the airport, British Airways, and ask him if he would hand it to one of my colleagues in London. In the meantime, I had a chance to carefully compose what I was about to say over this rubbish we'd shot over the last two days. I think that gave us time to make, perhaps, occasionally, a better, more well balanced assessment of what was going on.

You have to be very careful about this because, sometimes, we like to look back and think that everything we did in times past, in the early days, is much, much, was much, much better than it is now. That's not necessarily true. But, there is no question about the fact that you got a little more thinking time to decide what you were going to do.

Now, you are shown the pictures of you are on the spot, at the same time that they can be seen by our office in London. And you have to react and make a judgment and talk about it. I think what you occasionally lose, and I know some of the best journalists today are still capable of doing it very professionally, some of what you lose is you lose a little thinking time, a little time to reflect. The kind of priority given now to instantaneous news, to speed, does not always work out to the benefit of the viewer.

I was watching something on American TV the other day in New York and they said, they had a caption saying "breaking news" and under the breaking news caption they had sort of "happening now" now, instant, let's do it now, you know. Sometimes you lose a little bit of reflection in that. I'm not saying that everything one did then was more balanced and more better judged, I'm not saying that at all; but, I'm saying that, just occasionally, events are… international events can be quite complex and you need a little thinking time, you need time to work out what's going on and when your priority is always speed, getting it done, must be done now, must be done quickly…

I once talked to a colleague, a friend at the BBC during the Iraq war, the first Gulf War, he was doing pieces for a variety of BBC programmes, every hour on the hour and he said to me "what have you been doing?" I said, I've been walking about and trying to meet a few people and talk to a few people. And he said to me "you know, I haven't had the chance to do that today because I have to do the 10 o'clock and the 11 o'clock and the midday news and the one o'clock news". Sometimes the necessity for speed, breaking news, keeping up with the times, keeping up with the schedules, can be difficult. It's a great professional task to be able to do that well, these days.

Q   Do you think the internet will eventually kill off television?

A   I'm very bad about making any assessment of what these new technologies will do. I think it's already changed television beyond recognition. One of the problems I have about the internet and this vast array of information with which one is confronted every day is, you know, the old BBC dictum about accuracy, balanced, well fact-based, that's gone out the window. I'm not saying that everything on the internet is rubbish but who checks that stuff; who guards those guardians, do you know, of this accessible information? There's no question that it has helped television to become much more proficient at doing what it does but, in the end, it's a huge swathe of information out there which can, occasionally, be unchecked.

Q   Tell me more about the way in which the internet has changed television out of all recognition, in what ways?

A   I think it's been a big competitor to television. I think it's people don't need any more to pick up a daily newspaper or to listen to the news on television to find out what's going on; they can now click on. A lot of this information is absolutely splendid. Not all of it is. I was talking once to somebody who worked in the White House who said "we have a guy who gets up at four or five in the morning just to check what goes out on the internet about what the President has done or what the policies are likely to be and so on. And we have to do that early in the day because if you let that stuff go out there, you're dead, you can't call it back. if you don't counter it, if you don't respond to it you're in trouble." And so that's a great competitor to whatever the television stations do.

The generality of the television industry still believes in making a kind of digest of what goes on in the news and telling people, at various points in the day, a reasonably well-judged view about what's happening. I don't think the internet is under any such constraints. Their thing is instant information and speed. But, you know, you can't ignore what a vital part it's playing in our lives. I know young people who don't watch television news, don't read newspapers. It's all there. it's all on your iPhones these days, it's all there. So, it's given television a lot to think about.

I think one sees it in the way television operates these days. Television operators are now acutely aware of the fact that, in this internet age, to get somebody's attention for more than 15, 20, 30, 40 seconds, you've got to do something pretty jazzy. Maybe not the news but a lot on television now has this flash, this jazz, because they are terrified of losing people.

Q   Do you think that has been to the great detriment of investigative journalism on television?

A   I think the whole question of investigative journalism is almost a separate one from the internet. I don't think one can blame the internet for that. I think television reached an age where investigative journalism seemed, for reasons which are occasionally beyond me, to go out of fashion. There were programmes like *World in Action*, the *Panorama* programmes at the BBC, *World in Action* on Granada Television and ITV, which set out, deliberately, day after day, to go behind what was happening in the news.

Now, we're much more news driven and the speed at which it all happens seems to mitigate against this idea that you can do three or four weeks investigating something that has really happened. It's gone out of fashion slightly and, I mean, I think it's a change in the times. People don't spend so much time doing things anymore. There is this priority of, kind of, instant access and getting things done quickly.

And, I suppose that has been to the detriment of some investigative…

I still remember with great fondness the big disclosure things on things like *World in Action, Panorama.* And, you know, it still occasionally happens but if you were to go and talk to television executives today and say to them, "and what about your investigative journalistic part?" I think they will probably put their hands up and say "well, we don't do as much of this as we used to."

Q   Do you think that the teams, like the one in *World in Action* which was the standing army when they investigated the Birmingham Six and they came back to it over a period of years, do you think those teams exist in television anymore?

A   I don't know. I'd be very surprised if they did. I am always surprised when you see programmes where it's palpable that people took a long time to get to this point, especially in television journalism. I don't think there are as many dedicated teams as there were doing that sort of stuff anymore.

Q   IS your point that in this new world of television it's very good at the visible but what's missing is the invisible?

A   It's probably well put. For very good at the visible I read what you can see at the moment. I tell you when you see it most dramatically. You will see somebody on television at an event, something is happening, breaking news, something is happening and they are focusing on it, maybe a scene outside Downing Street, or something. And then there is a call about a traffic accident in Birmingham and, immediately, what was going on in Downing Street was probably reasonably important and relevant to our lives but the fact that the television is now primed to do instant things, they will immediately break off and go to the fact that somebody has been killed on the M6. Now, it's a very tragic story, somebody being killed on the M6, but there's absolutely no reason to break away to do that then; absolutely none; but, the reason it was done is that that's the theme of the television age, you have to, you can't be late on a traffic accident in Birmingham anymore because instant news, breaking news is what it is.

So, yes, you lose, occasionally, a little reflection. I still think there is… most of the television stations still have a time of day when they sit back and tell you, in a kind of summary form, with some sort of contextualising, what has happened during the news day. So, there is still that and I think that will always exist. But, we are hooked on speed, today.

Q   What do you think about the BBC today?

A   I think the BBC is what it always was. It's a great, great organisation which commands a sort of view internationally that is unparalleled. I remember as an ITN reporter turning up on stories, and one particular one was a siege, many, many years ago, in the Hague; some French diplomats were being held by some Moroccan gunmen and I was questioning the Dutch police about why they wouldn't tell us more about the negotiations and so on. And they said – I was working for ITN – "because if this gets, it would be on the BBC all over the world and the gunmen here and in Morocco and everywhere else in the world would know what's going on." The BBC is the pre-eminent news organisation in the world.

I don't think it's surprising that an institution, an establishment that has this relationship with the public in that it's supported by public money, comes occasionally under scrutiny; I think that's absolutely natural. I think it's always going to happen. I think all governments would be extremely wary about what they do to an organisation as eminent as the BBC. I think, though, on the other hand, the idea that you could somehow stand back and exclude yourself from any kind of scrutiny – and I'm not talking about interference now in the malevolent sense of the word – I'm talking about interest, scrutiny, the fact that any government would be interested in what happens to its £3 billion a year or whatever, is not entirely surprising.

And, one hopes that caution will prevail and whatever is done to the BBC does not, in any way, impair its great, great, great influence around the world.

Q   Bearing in mind your description of the world that television now finds itself in, what do you think is the special role that the BBC has moving forward?

A   I've never been too sure of this special role of the BBC. The

BBC is now in competition with all the other television stations. I don't know whether it has that special defined role anymore. I suppose because of the way its funded it must always bear the responsibility for being… I talked about that dictum before about being thoroughly responsible, being accurate, being well balanced and representing that kind of public interest. Public interest derives from the fact that you take public money, that's a given. But, it's in competition with everybody else.

I don't entirely buy the argument that it shouldn't do popular programmes because it should always err on the serious side. I don't.

Q   Do you think that investigative journalism is a key part of the BBC's public service role?

A   I would have thought that investigative journalism should always be an important part of the BBC and I would have thought particularly so if other people are not doing as much of it as they used to. Then I would like to think and I would hope that the BBC would continue to do it. I would have thought that would be part of their kind of public remit. The bit where the BBC, then, is special is that it could probably, given the way it's funded, devote more time to some things that some of the commercial… you know, you can't leave the future of television to people who make money by selling ads. They have a different prerogative. I mean, they do their job responsibly; they still have to make sure that they are governed by regulations, Ofcom and the rest of it but, basically speaking, commercial organisations are there to survive in a commercial world, they are there to make money.

Q   Do you think the BBC licence fee helps or hinders its
     journalism?

A   I don't know; it's a tricky one. The BBC licence fee is an
     inescapable part of the whole argument about what the BBC
     does. If it's funded in that way there will always be a call by
     governments, or by the public, for it to do things in a certain
     way. I'm always struck by the fact that if you move *The
     Archers* by 10 minutes there is almost a kind of national
     outcry. Now, that only happens, I think, because of the way
     it's funded. People think they own it. It's not "the BBC." It's
     "my BBC because I pay the licence fee". And, by the way,
     they're hoping to change this, or thinking of changing this
     but, under punishment if you don't' do it, you can be
     charged for not paying your licence fee. So, "it's my BBC".
     Once you are in that area, people expect certain things of
     you by the fact that they are responsible for your well-being,
     for you being funded in this way and you will always have
     that.

Q   Do you think it would have been politically possible for the
     BBC to break the MPs' expenses scandal?

A   I think the BBC would have done. I think the BBC would
     have done it. I'm not in the school which believes that the
     BBC would deliberately hinder something like that because
     it's politically embarrassing. I don't buy that. Yes, I think the

BBC would have broken the MPs' expenses scandal.

Q   Do you think they would have broken the phone hacking scandal?

A   Yeah, I think they would have broken the phone hacking scandal, yes. I think they are... I think one of the problems we have when we think about the BBC, we think of it as a kind of monolith, a sort of one... they are a number of, you know, brilliant people there; fiercely independently minded. It would have been extremely difficult organisationally for the BBC to suppress journalists who were intent on breaking the phone hacking scandal or the MPs, yes, I think the BBC would have done it.

Q   Why do you think that the BBC self-censored the *Newsnight* report into Jimmy Savile's child abuse allegations?

A   I have no idea. I don't know how that happened. I have no idea. I tell you the one thing that people failed to understand about that, if I may say, and this is probably peripheral to your question, it's the structure within which the BBC operates. That man who was told about this and said "thank you for telling me" instead of saying "what the hell's going on!" That's the way it functions. You have different structures. And it goes down almost to sort of Tennysonian precedent to precedent, it goes down the line.

So, that executive would then have been told "okay, that must go to this department, the other department must look after it..." And that he would have seen his responsibility in an entirely different way to somebody in organisations which are structured differently. It was a classic case of what can happen in some structural circumstances.

Q   Why do you think that they dropped it all together rather than postponed it?

A   Pass. Puzzled. Don't know.

Q   It's a puzzle.

A   It's a puzzle.

Q   Let me ask you some questions about Channel 4 if I may. What do you think about Channel 4 these days?

A   Oh, I think Channel 4, when I had the honour of being part of the team that started the *Channel 4 News* and I have grown, I didn't at the time, I have grown to like the idea of having a news bulletin which doesn't always go after the sort of multi-million audience but which tries, instead, to devote more time to single subjects and to explore them in greater depth. I know Jeremy Isaacs and Liz Forgan and the people who have brought this into being initially were very, very set on that.

We had arguments about it when I was involved. I said "I want my stuff to be seen by the widest number of people". And it was pointed out to me that that is not always the aim of all television programmes; it is possible to do programmes where you choose subjects, you go into greater depth and make these still watchable. And I think it does splendidly today.

One of the things, I mean, this is perhaps not terribly profound, one of the things I admire most about it is the fact that it started out at seven o'clock, and today it's at seven o'clock. Fantastic. Every other thing has chopped and changed, we had an awful time with *News at Ten* when it went to ten whatever, *Channel 4 News* has stuck to its time and to its remit and it's absolutely brilliant for that.

Q   Do you think that the growth of digital channels has created a crisis of identity of Channel 4?

A   That one's beyond me; I don't understand enough about the digital world to comment. I'm not dodging, I just, there's nothing I can add.

Q   Do you think Channel 4 should be privatised?

A   I don't really know what the implications of that are. It's past my bedtime, that one.

Q   Do you want to make any comments on the independent production sector at all?

A   I think the independent production sector is a very important sector in television. You need people outside the ring, outside the box to think of ideas. No one television company is the custodian of all the good ideas. It's great to have other people out there who are, you know, in competition for work and so on, who are thinking up things. I've been fortunate to do things with independent companies which I think have worked out terribly well. We got into American prisons where people hadn't been before, in that way. We got a chance to go into Death Row in Indiana. We recently had a chance to go and talk to people about the mafia and to say to them "why do you think it's part of your job or remit to put a gun to somebody's head and blow his brains out and not be terribly accountable?" And some of these ideas came from the independent sector.

Nobody is a custodian of all the great ideas for television. An independent sector, striving to compete with the established sectors in television can only be good. And I think that's recognised, now, in the BBC and by ITV who actively court the independent sectors and say "come up; tell me your good ideas; let's run this" it can only be good. It's certainly worked for me.

Q   One last question. If you had to have a wish for the next stage of the development of the television industry, what would that wish be?

A   James, I don't know; and I'm wary of wishes, you know. I love that line "if wishes were horses, beggars would ride". I am. Wishful thinking is not my strong point. I hope that… I think there's a great, great tradition in British television. I now have travelled a lot around the place and I have watched, and I wouldn't be specific about particularly what but I have now watched television in a number of countries and I don't think anybody does it as well. The tradition about television here…

We can learn a lot. I think we borrow constantly. I mean, one of the great tricks in life is to see what your competitors do, what they do well and then steal it and make your own thing much better. But, I think in broad terms, the traditions of the television industry are just superb and I say one of the prime movers in that, still, is the way news is done in this country. And I say it again. It's part of the tradition that we boast about, we tell the Iraqis, and the Syrians, and everybody else "do like us; you must have this rigid independent, vibrant, unafraid sector which holds truth to power" that old cliché, "you do that, you must do like us." I think generally speaking we do that and do it quite well.

Q   Trevor, many, many thanks.

End of interview.

Chapter XII

Adam Boulton

Adam Boulton is one of the best known and most authoritative presenters working in British television. He has blazed a trail as an innovator and commentator working for Breakfast TV and Sky News. He also writes extensively for newspapers having written for The Times, Sunday Times, The Guardian, Spectator and New Statesman.

Interviewer: James Hogan

A   I'm Adam Boulton. My current title is Editor at Large, at Sky News and I present *Sky News Tonight* from 7 – 9 Mondays to Fridays.

Q   How did you get into television?

A   I was quite lucky inasmuch as after university I went to university in England and then in America. I came back at one of the periods of expansion in television that, in the early '80s, as well as BBC and ITV, there was the launch of Channel 4 and there was the launch for the first time ever of breakfast television and I managed to get employed largely

318

because at that stage the mantra was "we want fresh young people with new thoughts; we don't want the old school of broadcasters."

So, I went to a company called *TV AM* which was - difficult to think of now - a front page story for about three years. A lot of famous people involved at the beginning, didn't hit its commercial targets, they all left or were sacked and, actually, it was a very good place for a young person to climb quickly because the levels above you kept on getting cold.

Q   Tell us a bit more about what it was like in those early days to be working on breakfast television.

A   Well, I think the most striking thing about television then was it was heavily unionised and so there was a lot of demarcation between jobs, the National Union of Journalists operating as journalists, the ACTT operating with some producers and cameramen and soundmen and then a different union doing lighting. And so, an awful lot of trying to do television was based around trying to manage those very much competing sections.

Breakfast television was great for me because it had never been done before. The BBC could have done it at any point in its history but only decided to compete when ITV got a franchise or a licence to do it. And, we pretty much invented it. You know, we started out with a rather sort of high minded *Mission to Explain* that had been jointly written by John Birt and Peter Jay, former Ambassador to America, then known as the cleverest man in Britain. And I remember having discussions as to whether we should do a programme, an item about what was then called female circumcision, now called female genital mutilation, at eight in the morning and we did do it.

And at that early stage there wasn't that much concentration on things like showbiz and then what happened was because breakfast television, *TV AM* in particular was in bad commercial trouble there was a switch where long term professional television investors came in, rather than funds looking for a quick return; they brought in a man called Greg Dyke, initially from ITV, he identified the audience which, by and large, was young mothers with children, and we then recast the programme around that.

But, what was interesting was that the licence, the franchise, depended on having a strong current affairs element so we always stuck with having our own news operation and, certainly, what tended to happen was the first hour of the programme was very heavily news dominated and then throughout the hour towards 9.30 when it came off air it became more lighter and magazine-y. And, really, what you see as daytime television in this country now, not just BBC *Breakfast* but also the morning show on ITV that Philip Schofield does, and elsewhere, that style of television had not really been done to any great extent on a national basis in the UK before and that's what we pioneered.

Q   Did the idea of 24 hour news come in at the same time?

A   No. The Channel 4 and breakfast television started at the beginning of the '80s. 24 hour news, in this country, came in at the end of the '80s and it came in after the launch of CNN, about six or seven years after CNN. And I think there are two reasons for that. The first – and they are related reasons – was the practicalities of doing it. Very, very difficult to do rolling news with the then union arrangements and demarcations and *TV AM* actually went into a major strike in 1986 – I think – '85, '86, when the management kept the channel on air during a very bitter strike and, effectively, broke the ACT union in a similar way to which the Wapping dispute had broken the print unions.

But, the second reason why 24 hour television rolling news became possible was because of the technology, that it became possible and even cheaper to go live or show live pictures than to do the traditional thing of go out, shoot them, edit them, bring them back. I remember conversation ahead of the 1983 election when Greg Dyke was there and realised that, to cover the election, we needed to have a live capacity. And we bought a fifth-hand van, famously known as the ice-cream van, which was our only live link vehicle and Greg Dyke effectively had to write a personal guarantee for the £75,000 that cost because, at that stage, the company was broke.

Now, increasingly, we do everything pretty much live or not at all and that process of editing and turning round finished reports is not something that happens in 24 hours news. So, we needed the technology to catch up with us, really.

Q   What has been the influence of 24 hour news?

"RED by James Hogan"

A   Well, it's quite interesting inasmuch as I remember *Sky News* went on air and the BBC didn't, in fact, go on air for another six years after that and I remember saying to a senior BBC executive "why does the BBC need to go into 24 hour news? You have your flagship bulletins, *Nine O'clock News* which became the *Ten O'clock News, Six O'clock News,* and he just said to me "well, because the audiences, we've done all the research and the audiences for news bulletins are going to go down like that."

Now, actually, that's turned out to be apocalyptic. There are, although audiences have dropped steadily, there are still millions of people who watch *News at Ten* and the *Ten O'clock News* in a volume which is not typically what happens either here or in America for rolling news. My own view is that, as in the world of sport, 24 hour channels have certainly given people much more access to information to make their own decisions. So, I think there's been a shift from, if you like, a kind of authoritative, ex-cathedra, this is what's happening in the world today, to "we know you're interested in what's happening in the world; we will give you the best information we can, in as near to real time as we can so you can draw your own conclusions."

So, for example, I don't think it's any accident that *Sky News* started and was actively involved in the discussions for the arrangements for televising the Houses of Parliament, for televising parliamentary committees, we've been involved in discussions about getting cameras into court and they are now in the Court of Appeal. So, it was that shift from – which interestingly, I don't think British audiences have still quite got their heads around – "we're going to tell you how it is" to, "we're going to tell you to the best of our ability what's happening" and almost assembling the news on air through the hours.

And, I think frankly, the authority of traditional news bulletins was sometimes over-estimated. I mean, when that was all we had, they were actually often wrong and we've learned how to deal with information which is incomplete, has many sides to it, in a much more intelligent way.

Q   What have been some of the most important breaking news stories you've covered?

A   Well, we were lucky right at the beginning because there were two very major stories, the first was the first Gulf War and that began the embedding and broadcasting live from the field with advancing forces.

The other one was – for me it affected me more – the fall of Margaret Thatcher. And, really, that goes all the way through to the 2010 election and the formation of the Coalition in the world of politics and in more general news; certainly, the various Middle East wars that have taken place, we've been able to cover live firefights and really bring home to people what happens in war.

We had big audiences for court room trials, Louise Woodward, OJ, Michael Jackson, the various Michael Jackson trials. And, again, this is giving people information to draw their own conclusions. And, for us, 24 hour news,

"RED by James Hogan"

you've got breaking news, giving the information as quickly as possible; but, what you also have, very importantly, is analysis. You have to have the journalists who can, are confident enough and informed enough to analyse and tell people the implications of what's going on or the reasons for what's going on and really to be prepared to do it off the top of their head.

And, you know, if I've made any difference at all in journalism, it is that prior to *Sky News* people used to treat British politics with kid gloves. It would be "such and such a Minister said this; such and such a Minister said that" often indirect reporting because we didn't have television pictures, and then a very, very cautious piece to camera summing it up. And, I had been in America in the early '80s, I'd seen how they did it in America and I felt confident to – partly I suppose because we were a start-up channel, we didn't have that bigger audience – I felt confident enough to go on television to give people my analysis within impartiality as to what was happening. I always liken it to being a bit like a sports reporter and although I don't want to overdo this, I think I set a style which was then picked up on. So, people like Andrew Marr and Nick Robinson did what they do after I started doing it; let's just put it that way. I'm not saying... perhaps their analysis is better than mine, I'm not saying that, but I think we did make that change in political coverage and I think that, then, affected the coverage of other matters.

I mean, a major story for Sky which I wasn't really involved in was Madeleine McCann but the depth which Martin Brunt, our crime reporter on the team, went into with that story right at the beginning, certainly helped establish the McCann's and Madeleine McCann to the point that it became a story of national significance and importance, as it should have been.

Similarly, when you get big changes in public mood where, if you like, the news agenda and the public agenda, the public is engaged in that news agenda, in Sky's time, the death of Diana, for example, or the rise of New Labour, that is when it's most rewarding to be doing breaking news because you not only have this front row seat bringing the story to people live but, sometimes, because you're paid to do it, you should be able to spot the currents and significances, sometimes, before a general audience has realised.

Q   Would you say, therefore, that *Sky News* has its own particular persona?

A   Yeah, I think all channels have a persona. I mean, people always talk about this question of bias in television. I don't think… I think by and large the British channels, Channel 4 perhaps is the exception, but by and large the British channels behave honourably in terms of they don't have an agenda and they don't push an agenda. But, I think the BBC is inevitably of the public sector and has a slight mentality which is that the public sector is generally good and that the profit motive and business is suspicious. I think we, because we know that we're part of a commercial operation, part of a commercial business, are perhaps more sceptical about the public sector, the public provision, more willing to question it and, also, perhaps less negative towards business and the profit motive and all that.

In the case of *Sky News* there's no doubt about it, *Sky News* would not exist if it wasn't for the commitment of Rupert Murdoch and the personal commitment he has to news. He has never, in my experience, tried or sought to influence the news or to tell us what to do or to tell us what editorial line. But, there have been times when the company, particularly in the early days, was not doing well commercially where a lot of business people were saying "we need to get rid of the news channel" and he said "the news channel is very important." But, that does mean that because Rupert Murdoch does have an editorial voice elsewhere in the news businesses that he's concerned with, it does mean that to some in the public we're seen as "just Murdoch news". I defy them to show any evidence that we do show that bias and I think our coverage of the phone hacking scandal and the subsequent enquiries, the Leveson Enquiry, showed us to be pretty fearless as far as our editorial priorities go.

But, one does have to accept that people working at the Sun or the Times, they are our cousins and even if they get themselves into trouble, one understand the motivation of what they are doing.

Q   What was the target audience for *Sky News* in the early days?

A I think the target audience was… I mean, basically, when Sky started we were offering vertically streamed channels, sports channels, entertainment channels, news channels. So, what we were saying to people was rather than sit at home and have a programme controller assemble your viewing, you can have your own, you can make your own menu of what you watch when. And we also discovered that, really, the USP of all television these days, in an age of video cassettes and all that, is live, the live event, that you can't see a football match or you can't see an election result or you can't see a television debate between politicians any other way than watching it live. And so, our job was to cover the agenda but rather work towards a bulletin to be producing stuff of quality across a 24 hour cycle.

I think we always accepted, and this was the crucial difference about 24 hour news and a crucial difference about what's happened within television, is that Tony Hall, at the BBC when he was in charge of their news said rather plaintively "we can't force the public to eat their greens anymore". By which he meant that in the days when the BBC had a monopoly or even in the duopoly with ITV people would want to watch, well, take the *Six O'clock News*, *Neighbours* was very popular for about a decade, and one of the tasks of the editor of the *Six O'clock News* was to hold as much of the audience that he inherited, or she inherited from *Neighbours* through the *Six O'clock News*. And, in fact, what happened is they lost about half their audience in the first five minutes.

But, we never had those pressures because we always knew that people would only switch to a rolling news channel if they wanted rolling news. We weren't going to get accidental viewers who were waiting for *Coronation Street* or *East Enders* to pop up. So, I think that did mean that right from the start we weren't looking for a particular demographic but we were assuming that our audience was interested in the news in a way that, perhaps, with a daytime audience, a breakfast television audience, an early evening audience, you can't necessarily make those assumptions.

Q   Did you deliberately and do you deliberately target key influences? I'm thinking of the fact that, for example, the audience for *Sky News* may still be relatively small but, everywhere you go, the banks, the institutions in the City, communications companies and so on, I find that *Sky News* is invariably the one they're watching.

A   Well, *Sky News* has never had a big marketing budget because it has been a shop window into the subscription, the paid TV model and by and large has been … well, we can talk about it later, but it had pretty much free to air although a lot of people don't know that. So, talking about actively seeking audiences is never really done because we've never really had a marketing director, or whatever. The only kind of explicit efforts we've made in that area were to get people to carry the channel abroad, which has been an important revenue stream.

But, I took the decision and, you know, I was running the political department, I think, I had just got the job, I was just 29 and I took the view that, you know, we needed to be impactful in Westminster because media companies have influence, perhaps, above their weight in commercial terms because they matter to politicians; you want to be in a situation where politicians want to come on your channel to make their case and, in the early days, we did have some stand up rows with some politicians or departments who said "what's the point of doing you; I can do BBC and ITV" and we had to literally, physically fight, sometimes, to get our cameras into the room to do the interviews.

So, it was important for us that we could offer a competitive service and we could offer it ahead of the traditional news bulletins and there was an element, certainly, I mean things have slightly changed with the expansion of the internet, but there was still a strong element of agenda setting that the political parties and politicians are fighting for the air time through the day because they know the television channels and opinion formers are watching the rolling news. So, when it comes to the evening, the person who's set the tone during those exchanges during the day is likely to be the person who comes up best in the evening news bulletins.

Q   To what extent has social media had an impact on *Sky News*?

A   Everyone will tell you that the impact of social media is that you get an immediate response from your audience; that it certainly can provide new sources of information very, very quickly. If we hear now that there's been a big explosion in York, possibly the first eye witness reports, the first pictures will come in through social media, although one has to be extremely cautious because what we can do in professional news organisations is curate and aggregate and verify the information which is coming in, and there are well-established cases of people spoofing or trying to spoof the news media – not just Sky – through the use of social media.

Social media also means that you can do things in different ways. For example, the internet and Twitter, now, are very important in assembling panels of questions or, indeed, audiences for some of the political debates which we've done. And, now, I think we're moving through a phase where analysis of big data, analysis of social media, is another part of the news analysis which you can offer. How many people watch something who… how people responded to what they were hearing on television in terms of a yes/no vote, you know, those types of things.

So, I see social media as an extra tool and I also see social media as an additional forum where we can reach new audiences by having a presence, whether it's in Snapchat or Twitter, or on other platforms. Half of the people who access the *Sky News* website now access it through mobile phones. So, there are constant changes of interacting with audiences. And there's no doubt that our generation, my generation, grew up with the assumption that in every home there was a television in the corner and that was one of the focuses of households. The generation growing up now, there are lots of screens around but there isn't that same focus on the television and what the broadcasters are operating. So, as a news organisation we need to find as many ways as we can of connecting with that audience while, in my view and fortunately this is the view of *Sky News*, not losing sight of the fact that the spine of our news operation is our television channel.

Q   Can you describe the successful campaign that you ran for the televising of the leaders' debates in the last two general elections?

A   Yes. I over the years, with my different employers, have always felt that really it's an affront to democracy that we haven't had big televised debates during general elections because, it seems to me, we know that television certainly has been and is still the biggest source of information that the public have and the public use. Therefore, I've frankly found it disgusting that politicians in this country have not been willing to debate and have found various, spurious in my view, excuses for not debating.

But, when we discussed the matter about two years before the 2010 election, the head of *Sky News* John Ryley was, actually, more concerned about public engagement and lowering turnout and lack of interest in politics which had been manifested in a decline in audiences since 1989 for our coverage and everyone else's coverage of the elections. And the initial problem which John raised was how we could increase voter engagement in the political process which we thought was a good thing. After discussions, we came down to the view that the most important thing that television could do to get voter engagement was to get television debates and John and I and the company started campaigning for them.

Now, at that stage, really, the whole question of TV debates was almost a matter of commercial competition that the BBC, quite possibly looking after their own interests, took the view that it was not their role to campaign for television debates; they took the formal view that to campaign for television debates would be an interference too far in the political process and that they had to be particularly cautious about that.

ITV, which going back then historically was not in a particularly happy state at the time, really had quite a dog in the manger attitude to debates which was that they didn't really want the debates because they weren't sure they would get a decent audience in prime time but, if debates did happen they felt that they should pretty much have an exclusive on holding at least one debate and they weren't, frankly, particularly interested in actually having a collaborative approach to trying to bring debates about.

Now, the big stick, if you like, in trying to bring debates about seemed to us to be the threat of the empty chair. We had no intention of empty chairing anyone if we could avoid it but, if you got to the point that two of what was then seen to be the three main parties, two of the three main parties agreed to participate the biggest threat was to say "okay, given the way in which electorate rule has loosened up we will stage a debate with the Liberal Democrat, Conservative and it's up to you whether you turn up or not." But, to get there you had to get to the point where you had, at least, a relationship with trust with two of the parties such that they were prepared to take part in a two-legged stool debate. And, what happened was that we did secure from the Conservative Party the commitment that if it came to it David Cameron would simply do a debate with the Liberal leader. We had an agreement from the Liberal leader and that, therefore, meant that Sky credibly could say "okay, we will hold a television debate; it's up to the leaders whether they turn up."

Now, *Sky News* was probably the only channel that could have done that inasmuch as prime time air time on the BBC or ITV would never, credibly, be given over to a two-legged debate, firstly; and secondly, the political risk of being seen to campaign for that and being seen to put pressure on one of the parties, probably only Sky had the balls to do at that time, and I mean it when I say that. It's partly because we are, were, a more edgy news organisation. Some people would say we had less to lose, or whatever.

And, what happened was we were quite open with all the parties about what we were doing and the other position which we took very early on was that we felt it was important that debate should happen. So, any debate which we had, we declared right at the outset that we would not seek to make commercial gain by doing it exclusively; we would make it available to everybody. Again, you could make an argument and say it only made sense because the audiences for rolling news compared to the audiences for terrestrial are disproportionate. I will leave people to draw their own conclusions on that. So, we said we'd make it available to everybody, live, as it happened. So, in that sense it wouldn't be a kind of overtly *Sky News* event.

So, as soon as Gordon Brown put out his statement saying he would take part in 2015 leader's debates which, basically, Sky had secured unilaterally, we said "okay, fine. What we're going to do is do this collaboratively with the other broadcasters." So, at that point Sky rolled our debate, if you like, which we had secured single-handedly, into negotiating with the BBC and ITV on one side and the three parties on the other side, with a kind of in our involvement of Channel 4 which we didn't resist because as you can see in the most recent election we did a co-production with Channel 4. And that... So, we, if you like, we got our foot in the door but we then took the decision to work with the other broadcasters to achieve it and, duly, we got three.

Q   And how important were those debates, did they determine the outcome?

A   I've always thought that it's very difficult to say what the influence of the debates are and I've always been slightly on the conservative side as to whether they really change people's minds. I think what they tend to do is reinforce people's minds. I think what was important about the debates and, as you know, there's been a lot of academic research on this including a pamphlet done by Reuters and

Leeds University called *Leaders in the Living Room* and what is important with about the 2010 debates is that they engaged the public, they engaged the section of the public it was most difficult to reach, the under 25s, that fractionally by two or three per cent turnout went up, as it's gone up again in 2015.

Did they have political influence? I think quite a lot of myths have grown up afterwards, largely centred around the Liberal Democrats. Labour and the Conservative right wing say that, including Nick Clegg in the way that he was included, bigged him up and cost the Conservatives their overall majority and, therefore, helped the formation of the Conservative/Liberal Coalition.

The counter argument to that is that, actually, the Liberal standing in the opinion polls at the start of the campaign before the debates and the score they got in the general election was pretty much the same. So, I would say, well, actually, you can't show there's much influence. The Conservative conspiracy theorists say "ah, but had there not been the debates, the Liberal Democrats would have tanked and they would have gone down whereas the debates helped them even at a fairly high share of the vote."

I don't think that will ever be known but, certainly, this argument was a big factor in the really pretty brutal and unsatisfying confrontations which took place to bring about the debates in the 2015 campaign.

Q   Tell us about that.

A   I was less directly involved, to be honest, this time round.

Mainly because I took the decision that if *Sky News* was doing another debate I wouldn't do it, certainly for the sake of variety, having done the one in 2010. And, basically, what happened was the broadcasters tried to negotiate on the same basis as in 2010 but the Conservatives prevaricated about coming to the table and one of the things that we'd always felt was that because the political temperature, competitive temperature, tends to heat up when you get to near an election time, that it was important to start agreeing the debates as far out as possible from the general election date. And the Conservatives basically said they weren't willing to sit down until the last party conference before the general election and so, somewhat reluctantly, everyone put everything on hold until then and then, basically, the Conservative side didn't sit down which left the broadcasters trying to effectively move forward on their own with some kind of formulation.

I also felt that having delayed so long to the point that UKIP had won the European elections, that meant that it was much more difficult to exclude UKIP from a debate line up which you could have done on the basis of performance in the last general election and it became clear fairly rapidly that the Conservatives were going to use the rise of the other parties as a way of saying, arguing that a two-way debate or three-way debate wasn't a good idea because "what about the Scottish Nationalists; what about the Greens; what about..." So, it became a much more complicated business for the broadcasters to sort out.

Others are writing the history of what happened in the debates but my understanding is two-fold, that, first of all, it was not really getting anywhere and James Harding, the head of news at the BBC, the former editor of the Times, went behind the back of the negotiators, including his own negotiators, and dealt directly with Downing Street and said "well, what is acceptable?" And, what they basically agreed was fundamentally a series of events where David Cameron would never actually come face to face with his opponents. And at that point – and this is exclusive if you like, you may not have heard this before – we on behalf of *Sky News* said in that case we would not participate and would publicly withdraw and not, wouldn't support the proposals, we'd say that they were… and as a result of that the one seven-way face to face debate with David Cameron took place but it was in the most diluted form because, obviously, it was with six other leaders.

But, had Sky not done, effectively, what it did in 2010 say "we're not playing if we don't get a debate" a debate wouldn't have happened. And, in fact, what happened, I think very unsatisfactorily, was we had the first programme jointly done by Sky and Channel 4 where the leaders were interviewed and faced an audience but separately, that was Miliband and Cameron; then we had the seven-way; then we had the five-way without Cameron which was the original plan for the debate format. And then, finally, we ended up with the Question Time again where the leaders faced the audience separately.

My view, I think on balance, I think the broadcasters got about 20 to 30 per cent of what they should have got in terms of having live debates but I think the Conservatives while they fought a cynical but successful election campaign. But, I think British democracy is the poorer for it because I just think I'm not sure debates change that much but because five to ten million people will sit down and watch them, I think they should take place because I think the election should be the time when politicians ask the people to support them by showing themselves.

Q   What do you think history will say about the effect of television of the coverage of the 2015 Labour Leadership contest?

A   I suspect not much, actually. To be honest, I don't think television saw what was happening any more than anybody else. And I don't think the rise of Corbyn has had anything to do with the coverage that he's had on television. So, obviously, it depends what happens but I think that with hindsight people might say that it shows that the thing which I believe in, which is impartiality and treating people with fairness, can sometimes be something which renders you rather impotent. In other words, our job as I see it was to say, okay, they have a nomination process and as soon as Jeremy Corbyn is nominated you treat him equally to the other candidates and you have to, in a sense, have a sense of deference where you can't say that if Jeremy Corbyn has been nominated it basically shows that the whole direction of the Labour Party has been thrown out the window and that, basically, the Party has gone bonkers.

And, I think that Corbyn has benefited from a kind of deadpan treatment of equality on television but, overall, I really don't think that television or, come to that, the newspapers have had much impact on what's happened within the Labour Party. I think it's much more about the sort of collected nervous breakdown of the Labour Party post-Tony Blair and a failure of the mainstream political party to field an attractive candidate.

Q   What qualities do interviewees need, or politicians need, to come across well or most effectively on 24 hour news?

A   That assumes you actually want to come across well. I mean, I think one of the problems which actually relates to the obstacles thrown in the way of the TV debates in 2015, one of the problems is that now the default of media handlers and spin doctors is not to seek to gain anything from going on television. It's not to drop any negatives. And, therefore, most politicians these days, certainly people, Ministers, people who have handlers, are fundamentally defensive. They don't want to go out and make an argument; they don't want to – with some exceptions – by and large they don't want to make their case. What they want to do is to tell you what they're doing and not drop any bricks which undermine their position.

I often say that the most depressing thing after you've interviewed a politician is when you hear them going out of the studio with their handler, for some reason they can't turn up on their own, they always turn up with handlers;

and when they are walking out the studio the handler, if you ever hear them, it hasn't happened to me very often but if you ever hear them say "I thought that went very well; I didn't say anything". That is actually the mentality with which they are, by and large, coming into the studios. And I find that deeply frustrating and I find it deeply frustrating that all the political parties…

Q   What are they scared of?

A   They are scared of making an error, of saying something that is too lurid or which contradicts, or of being made look a fool. And, I have done interviews where I have made Ministers look fools because they've been advocating a policy that they clearly haven't thought through or, in some cases, just haven't seen the logical flaw in that policy. That's what they're scared off and, what I'm basically saying is that, I suppose, I feel that most politicians and most PR people, special adviser, whatever the hell you call them, handling politicians see the downside of engaging in public argument much more than they see the upside, which is bad and is a change over the 30 odd years I've been doing this job.

Q   Does that mean there's…

A   In a sense, the attraction of Jeremy Corbyn or Boris Johnson is that they do appear to say what they think and they appear to say what they think without, necessarily, too much premeditation as to what the angles might be.

Q How important is the sound bite?

A Well, of course, one of the differences about rolling news is that we do have more air time and so we do or are able to give people, five, six, seven, eight, nine, ten minutes to make their case and, sometimes, several times in a day if a story is really hot. I've always felt that this notion of sound bite politics and just reducing everything to a sound bite, I really don't think it's true. That said, I think if you can produce a phrase, either spontaneously or by calculation which is striking and which sounds like your position, what is it "tough on crime and the causes of crime" then I think that's very important. But, I would say, for every sound bite which flies there are probably 3,000 which still just don't really strike through.

Boris Johnson is an interesting case in point. Does Boris Johnson really have a sound bite? He doesn't. What he has is an argument and a spontaneity, apparent spontaneity which people find engaging.

Q Is your chief competitor BBC News?

A Yes. I mean, the BBC is the biggest broadcaster in the country and it keeps plugging away on its various channels and various mediums and all that. And we are the biggest commercial independent broadcaster in the country, by which I'm not disrespecting ITV but ITV is still a model which works towards bulletins in the evening and, therefore, the amount of news they do, including Channel 4 news, is quite limited; so, they can afford to pick and choose;

whereas, we and the BBC are the two organisations which are running news gathering operations that have to be out in the field covering stories which may not make.

The interesting question is, in a sense, technically we are in competition with the BBC news channel, BBC 24, as was. I personally have never felt like that. I know that the relative audiences and how many homes we're in and all that are important, but I see myself as in competition with the BBC, with Nick Robinson or Andrew Marr or Jeremy Paxman, or David Dimbleby when we do an election night programme. That's where I see the focus of the competition. I don't think that... ITV is a very successful entity, some ways ITN has been the most, over the 5 or 60 year cycle at least as impressive as the BBC and one of the big drivers but, at the moment, I see our primary competition as being the BBC. Although, when we talk about competition, it's by and large very wrong to see the competition as being the front page that we are trying to sabotage each other's efforts.

A lot of the battles that we fight for access and for information we are fighting alongside each other rather than, necessarily, against each other. Nonetheless, I want to produce and I hope the people I work with want to produce news which is crisper, sharper, fresher, than what's on the BBC.

Q   Does *Sky News*, within the Sky organisation, see *Sky News* as a public service broadcaster?

A   I've always hated that phrase. I really, really resent it because I think that all broadcasters are trying to serve the public in one way or another and, if you take a capital P and capital S then Sky is not a public service broadcaster inasmuch as it doesn't have privileged access to either revenue or the airwaves which is what BBC and ITV have. And, therefore, it correspondingly doesn't have the obligations to do the same thing.

Is our job absolutely to serve the public and to be on the side of the public? Yes, it is. And have successive chief executives and heads of *Sky News*, going all the way up to Rupert Murdoch himself, taken that view? The answer is "yes, they have." Very early days the first time I was offered the job as political editor at Sky I said to the then head of news "look, just before I commit myself here, let's get this absolutely straight, we both know what the law is but is there any intention to do the news with a twist, with a bias? Let's be honest about this." And his reply was extremely comforting. He didn't say "oh no, of course not; we're going to set up an independent news board headed by Lord Dacre" his reply was "you know that wouldn't work."

And, the reason is that in the culture which the television culture, the ecology which has grown up from the monopoly of the BBC, through the duopoly of ITV, heavily regulated, the public appetite in this country is for impartial, balanced, comprehensive news. And, anyone in the mainstream who goes outside that will quickly find themselves in the position where, either Labour or the Conservatives or the Liberals, or someone, refuses to speak to them; or the police won't trust them. And, if that happened, then your news product would be inferior to those news channels who do have access to all those people.

So, the history of the BBC and the history of the duopoly, I think, has created a fantastically healthy news culture. But, I also think that the advances – and you know about this, you've written books about this – the advances in news in serving the public have come from competition. It was ITV which took on the 14 day rule about covering politics and covering by-elections; and it was ITV which first put journalists and professionals in charge of writing and presenting the news. It was ITV which did the first breakfast television. It was independents, us, who did the first 24 hour news. It was us who came up with, as I say, the style of live analysis of events in a confident way.

So, you say do I see the BBC as the main competition? Yes, I do but, if you like, it's within a – to use the Russell Brand word – a paradigm which has evolved from the way in which broadcasting has evolved from the BBC in this country.

Q   Could you ever envisage a time when *Sky News* would be given free?

A   Well, *Sky News* is given free. No-one knows this and I thought you might ask this question and I was a little bit taken aback, *Sky News* is available, it was available on Freeview; it is available on Freeset; and, you can get it streamed on the web; and, our phone app and things like that, are at cost or anything else. We're not really making a profit out of that and that's because Sky... one of the truths, I think, about the electronic news business is that you can't do it on your own. Basically, if you want to be in television or electronic news, you need to be part of a bigger company which has other media interests, predominantly in entertainment.

So, *Sky News* has persisted, now, for 26-27 years, never been a major profit centre within BskyB, well, Sky, then BskyB and now Sky again, always received a subsidy of some kind from the centre but has expanded its own earnings through sales to satellite, through commercials, through everything else like that. But, I think, if you say why does Sky have a news channel, perfectly good question. I think you would say "for several reasons." And it has a news channel, bearing in mind that it's not a public service organisation so it's not like ITV which has to have news, Sky doesn't necessarily have to have news for its licence.

I think it does for several reasons. The first reason is that I genuinely think it's not called a news corporation for nothing. It is in the bloodstream of the Murdochs and the people who run it, they think news is important. Secondly, as I say, I think if you're involved in the news business and I think if you're dealing with politicians as a total entity you are more visible, more influential and probably more courted than if you were just putting on entertainment shows. Thirdly, and this is very important, *Sky News* has always been an ambassador for the other channels. So, in our commercial breaks we run adverts for the dramas, the films, the sport which we are showing and tell people about what *Sky News* does. But, also, *Sky News* is a calling card saying "look, this is a quality media organisation; the quality of our news which is available is proof that we are serious; we're not downmarket and all the rest of it."

Now, I think that's less important now because people understand that but when we started there was a lot of stuff about tabloid telly, lowest common denominator, all of that, and doing an upmarket news channel which Murdoch once referred to as BBC Light was proof of where we were in the market in terms of wanting to offer a complementary service to the intelligent, committed people who were brave enough to do that extraordinary thing of commit to subscription television.

Q   Thinking about investigative journalism, just wanting you to comment about that, some people say that television today is very good at showing the visible but what's missing is the invisible. Would you like to comment on that?

A   I think it's certainly true that when I was growing up I kind of thought if I'm going to work in television that the documentaries, *World in Action, Panorama* and all that was where one wanted to be. But, I think that technology has really undermined that. What you can turn round in a day in terms of analysis, explanation, relevant archive, not in a day but in a matter of hours, is what it used to take people two weeks carefully crafted to assemble and there are an awful lot of, well, everyone has a camera in their pocket so images are out there. What we can do, as I've said already, we can aggregate, analyse and try and make sense of all that data coming in.

But, I do believe that television as a medium is best at examining things when it shows them and asks questions as near live as possible. If one thinks about John Freeman or Dick Cavett or David Frost, those were near enough live events. The skill was in getting there and finding the direct question and that's why I say that the analysis and the persistence of what we do, I think it does, it ends up making what you're calling the invisible visible. I do genuinely feel that the documentary, what you are doing, in areas of mainstream interest, things like politics and health and all that, struggles a bit. I think what the documentary can do is shine a light in much greater detail on something that's away from what they used to call – what did they call it – Al Gore called the super highway, or whatever. But, if you're in the super highway of news I think it's quite difficult for documentaries to compete with those.

Q   Do you think that British television will ever see another investigation like the *Birmingham Six* which took years to make and they had a standing army on *World in Action*, they came back to it again, and again, over a period of several years. Do you see that happening again?

A   We are trying and we see it as important, partly because there's more offline viewing growing up and, partly, because where the competition is, we are trying very hard to develop long form journalism. But, I would say that the things I'm proudest of that we've done is our battles for cameras in courts, our battles for television debates, leaders' debates, our battles for access. I think all those things have been very important but we've certainly been involved in exposés, we've got currently if you go back to the *Birmingham Six* my colleague Ian Woods is currently in Indiana on a death row case of someone who's due to be executed in 10 days' time who didn't' pull the trigger and is almost certainly totally innocent. I think we do those things but I think things get exposed in different ways.

Probably, the biggest two stories of recent times in my world have been the MPs expenses and the phone hacking and all of that but I think those required a combination of skills that some came through newspapers, some came through information leaks and then others came through television cameras seeking people out and getting them on the record or facing them and confronting them with difficult circumstances.

So, yes, I think it's a pity that current affairs doesn't work so well but I think it is partly because the waters are over-fished, I genuinely do. I think all that is covered. Going back to Jeremy Corbyn, John Ware is a fantastic documentary maker but, basically, I saw it very elegantly put, eloquently put, on his programme *Panorama* last night but I didn't actually learn anything about Jeremy Corbyn that I didn't know or, indeed, I hadn't reported or seen reported elsewhere.

Q   And one last question…

A   I should add, you've asked me about news events and
things that I've done and highlights for me. A big highlight
for me was the Good Friday Agreement and the whole
Northern Irish peace process and I do feel that our
persistence in, basically, sticking with that story, committing
me, our main political guy over there, of doing that
particular incident over five days without sleep, and
obviously we didn't achieve the peace agreement but I think
what we did do was raise it up the agenda and we took it
out of the ghetto in national broadcasting and I think that
was a very constructive thing to do.

Q   Thinking more broadly about British journalism, print and
TV, do you think that we should be worried about the fact
that we missed the historic sex abuse scandal stretching
back over 50 years?

A   No because I interviewed Johnny Rotten yesterday and we
reminded each other how, in 1978, he was banned from the
BBC for saying that everyone knew Jimmy Savile was
dodgy. I think there have been allegations against people. I
actually see it the other way around which is that I think a
lot of the reaction to the undoubted abuses of Jimmy Savile,
which only emerged after his death and which I see are
primarily a problem for the BBC, I have to say, that was the
organisation which promoted Jimmy Savile and which
protected him to a certain extent. And I think rather than
focus on that I think this has become a rather blunt
instrument with a sort of slightly sensationalist press media
generalising the story with, as yet, no evidence and I do

think that, sometimes, the media gets involved in a kind of mood of hysteria and witch hunt, along with others, along with politicians and police and all that, and I think we are having a bit of that at the moment.

I think it's important, this issue, but I think it needs to be treated with caution and I think it's not our job to stop people doing it but I think if you look at a man standing out and the police chief standing outside Ted Heath's house and making allegations like that, I think, rightly, one's analysis of that should include comment that this might perhaps be a rather outrageous thing to do.

Q   One last general question, quite a lot of people say, in fact a lot of people say, there are too many channels on television but there's nothing to watch on TV. How do you respond to that?

A   I think it's a bit like a library now, it's like saying there's nothing to read. There is the world at your fingertips. You can download it, you can get it on your Kindle, there are still public libraries. There is an awful lot out there. And, I personally... okay, I'm very radical about this. I personally think there is an awful lot of good quality out there. I don't think that the bulk of it is being produced by the BBC.

And, I think that the idea of having this publicly funded entity, basically producing middle brow and low brow culture is not good for our society and I personally,

personally, make myself incredibly unpopular. I think the things that I actually think are rubbish and I would never consider watching are the things that are most popular. They are things like *Top Gear* and *Bake Off* and *Strictly Come Dancing* and all that. And I, from my elite, snooty, blah, blah, I just think all that stuff is rubbish and I think if people want to watch it, it would doubtless have a commercial future but I think saying that you look down the schedules and there's nothing that any sane person would want to watch on BBC1, BBC2, ITV and Channel 4 which has some sort of body distortion programme or something, I think in terrestrial television there probably isn't anything to watch a lot of the time but I think good quality visual and sound images available on screen, I think there is probably more than ever before.

Q On terrestrial television, tell me why you say there probably isn't anything to watch.

A Well, because I think we've accepted and we're accepting it now with the BBC's slogan of "for us all; there for everyone" or whatever it is, we're accepting this notion that mass audience is public service and, therefore, I do think it goes back to... I remember being in a Royal Television Society and News Awards and they gave ITV an award for best news, or something, the same year that it was moving the *News at Ten* out of the *News at Ten* slot and cancelling *World in Action,* and I just thought "this is hypocrisy gone mad." The view is mainstream terrestrial television wants to maximise its audience for as long as possible and there has been a collective decision that the way to do that is to go from being middle brow to low brow. You know, it used to be *Morse,* and now it's David Walliams in some crappy adaptation of Enid Blyton or something, Agatha Christie, which is more about style than substance.

Q   And is this why we've seen the tremendous growth of factual entertainment?

A   I think one of the reasons for the growth of factual entertainment is the fact that when you can go and get a box set of Jacob Bronowski or the James Bond films, or whatever, what do you watch television for? I would argue that news is actually one of the stronger brands because you watch it for live events and factual television is, by and large, live event television.

Q   Adam, huge thanks.

A   I hope I agreed with your thesis.

Q   You are very brilliant, fantastic. You do.

End of interview.

Chapter XIII

David Montgomery

David Montgomery is one of the most experienced and visionary newspaper executives in the UK and Europe. A former editor of the two Murdoch owned National newspapers; the News of the World and Today. He served as Chief Executive of Mirror Group Newspapers (1992-1999) where he rescued the business from bankruptcy following the late Robert Maxwell's raid on its pension fund. In 2000 he founded the MECOM Publishing Group and later launching Local World.

Interviewer: James Hogan

Q   David, many thanks for taking part. Can I just ask you first of all to introduce yourself, your CV?

A   Well, I am Chief Executive of Local World which is a company that I founded and we acquired the titles from Northcliffe and Iliff families three years ago.

Q   And how did you get started in the media industry?

A   As a journalist in Belfast while I was at university.

Q   Is it true to say that you've pioneered radical change throughout your career?

A   Radical or just through necessity is hard to argue which is which. Obviously, the most contentious episode was the reform of the Mirror group after Maxwell's death; the company had been plundered of 500 million sterling and we had to restore the pension fund and we had to make efficiencies and that was a reformist action; whether it was radical or not is highly debateable. It was necessitated by the economic circumstances of the business, it either was going to survive and the national papers were going to survive, if there was radical restructuring, or they could have been closed and the banks would have simply liquidated the business. We chose to make a radical reform of the business which was very controversial because quite a few journalists were dismissed at that point.

Q   In your blueprint for Local World and the future of local journalism you say the role and scope of the journalist needs to be redefined. Can you elaborate?

A   Well, it is being redefined because, today, we are all journalists. And if you look at how our children use technology they're communicating on a number of devices all the time so, in essence, the community have all become publishers and we need to harness that and create journalism from it because everybody has the power to communicate and when I started in the industry tabloid newspapers were, really, the only vehicle where you could communicate across the mass of the country and it was very effective and it was very structured and disciplined. And, of course, it was confined by physical limitations and print and geography. Today, there are no such confinements, no such limitations and everybody wants to join in. It's become a two-way street.

So, journalists have to change their role to become Editor-in-Chief or publishers themselves and harness this power of communication within the community and make sense out of it. And that is a very overwhelming challenge for the industry and, if we don't do it soon, somebody else will do it for us.

Q   In your blueprint you say "there will be just one command layer within the modern content department." Can you say more?

A   One command layer is, effectively, the journalistic resource which will not have the structure of vetting and sifting and rewriting that the current industry still engages in. The world does not wait for that process. The world wants instant gratification. They want the community to produce the content and for that to be published instantly. It doesn't necessarily have to go through journalistic hands in the first instance but, once it has been published, then the idea is that the journalist can intervene and manage that content and make it more effective and make it mature over minutes or hours, or even days, but the first job of the journalist will be to make sure it's published, that the world can see the content and, therefore, the idea of journalists as publisher will emerge, I think, from the restructuring that's going on in the industry at the moment.

Q   You say news editors will be defunct. Why?

"RED by James Hogan"

A   News editors *are* defunct because the traditional role of the news editor is to come in with a list and tell everybody what he/she considers – mainly he still of course – what a good story is and rank those stories; they're defunct because the audience tell us what content they're interested in and, very often, that is a surprising judgment by the audience. It may not be a rape or murder or drugs raid, it probably isn't, what they will be interested in will be things that are much more community minded, much more general interest, much more lifestyle.

So, for instance, one of the top ranking stories on this very day is not murder or mayhem, it is the opening of a John Lewis store in Cheltenham; that is the big story in one of our regions because it enhances the lifestyle of the people who live in Cheltenham. They're making a choice "we don't need a news editor to tell us that anymore".

Q   You say only a handful of content managers will be office bound; how come?

A   Because this is something that has existed for many years in my thoughts. Stories, content, is not in a newspaper office. The stories are out there in the community. We need to have our journalists, publishers, embedded in the community; we don't need them through modern technology to be sitting in an office chatting up the secretaries and keeping warm by the radiators in December. They should be out being part of the community and it's not just the traditional beat that a reporter would cover, it's their entire lifestyle, their network, everything that happens is content and is no longer confined by 48 pages or 64 pages; everything is publishable, every journalist that we employ will and does produce pictures from their mobile phone and video, and upload it; and it may not conform to the old definition of news but it is something that's happening within the remit of any local publisher and we need to publish more of it. We need to be comprehensive.

And the industry getting, moving the industry away from this idea of vetting everything and sifting it and then narrowing it down into a very particular agenda, we need to change to be more comprehensive and publish everything that moves in the community; we need to be a one-stop-shop.

Q   You say the old fashioned publishing structure that acted as a hydra-headed nanny will no longer exist. What does that mean?

A   I suppose it's the old argument about how many pairs of hands does content have to go through before it reaches the public? My answer to that is we must dismantle any of those structural impediments to instant publication. And the operating model that we're devising here at Local World will allow the community to go directly to publication without going through that editorial structure.

Q   Is your vision a stripped down, virtual newsroom?

A   Well, I think newsroom is an expression of the past. I think where you had the philosophy that the community provides the content because everybody is capable of providing content; I think that doesn't require a newsroom. It does require individual journalists to cover particular segments of activity, for instance, schools or policing or traffic, or even weather, or even bus timetables. The journalists will preside over those segments and they will preside over geographical areas as well but they will do that like an all-embracing publisher so the old idea of a newsroom, again, with the news editor is not really relevant to this modern view of local publishing.

Q   Is the driving force cutting costs?

A   Absolutely not. The driving force is much more to do with local publishing re-inventing itself as the only place the community needs to go to engage in an activity driven by content. In the past newspapers lost the plot. You know, they lost the plot because they were confined very physically in how much content they could run; they had to make a judgment of what content people were interested in; and gradually, they lost touch with this structural change that was going on where instead of making an appointment with the newspaper or, indeed, making an appointment to watch broadcast television, people sought content out for themselves. And if they couldn't get it from the confines of the Leicester Mercury or the Nottingham Post they would go elsewhere.

And that is very evident in our children who are not

interested in having TV sets in their bedrooms. They're interested in sitting with their laptops and accessing content, whatever content they want; and using that content to communicate with each other. We as a publishing industry have been too slow to join that revolution. We're not the masters of content anymore; the public are the masters of content and we need to facilitate that.

Q   Is your vision the end of journalism as we know it?

A   No, the journalistic skills are still the fundamental requirement of any journalist publisher. And we shouldn't forget that, of course, journalistic skill has been absent in some of the great national newspapers that we have in the UK and has led to considerable errors of judgment. And, I think, fundamentally, those journalistic skills have never been more important but they're only a very small part of what people need to do. So, the discipline and the training needs to be there but the skill set has got to be widened into a job which has greater responsibility... and that's not happening in certain quarters.

I imagine that if I was to go into a tabloid national newspaper today, the sub-editorial culture would still be there where a journalist does a very minute amount of work in contributing to the paper. In local publishing (a) we can't afford that luxury; and (b) it doesn't do the job effectively. So, I'm saying that as well as the journalistic skills, what we need is journalists to be much more able to make publishing judgments and direct content towards publishing without having to go through that structure, that rigid structure of vetting and sifting and then publishing. The world is moving too fast for that.

Now, in highly refined national newspapers I'm sure this culture of sub-editorial vetting will continue but, in local publishing, our job is immense to cover all the territory. And, of course, we have the ability to publish instantly online. So, I think getting the message to the public is much more important than adhering to those old-fashioned restrictions of the typical newsroom.

Q   What drives you?

A   I think this is the most exciting time in publishing that we have faced in decades. It does empower the journalist to be very much more than a cog in a machine. So, I say to - and I see it in the young journalists – I say to them "you've got potential now to do something that really will give you job satisfaction; which will make you feel that you're in command of your audience; that you will be able to handle many times the amount of content you would handle as a reporter in the old days in the '70s, '80s, or '90s. Today you can comprehensively serve your community across many different elements of content and we can rebuild local publishing to be a force in the land but not in the old-fashioned manner. It is different but this is a job, as a journalist/publisher, you will be able to command more responsibility and, ultimately, you will earn more money as well because the productivity will hugely increase, our audience can be built beyond anything we've imagined so far."

So, with defining print circulations audience can build many times what it is at the moment. And we've demonstrated that in the three years of Local World where we've quadrupled the audience with the same number of staff because we are now bringing in content we would never have dreamt of publishing previously. So, this is the most exciting era in journalism, certainly in my career.

Q   Have you modelled yourself on Rupert Murdoch?

A   I have been influenced by Rupert Murdoch, as I think everybody in our industry has been; now what are those influences? I think the… it's basically entrepreneurship, that you're not satisfied with circulation at its current level; you're not satisfied with audience at its current level; there is a willingness to compete against other media.

Now, I'm not sure the industry has, to a man, followed that. And, of course, there is a great deal of criticism of Rupert Murdoch, even contempt for Rupert Murdoch. But, the lessons we learn from him of competing as media operators rather than simply thinking we've got some mission in life as some journalists and some media organisations that don't need to make a profit, they will continue along that path, their existence is a God given one, whereas I think Rupert Murdoch considers media as like any other business and you have to earn a living.

So, I think those lessons and influences are important and I have certainly learned by them but I think as a role model you probably wouldn't pick Rupert Murdoch; as a businessman and the example that he's set in terms of building media businesses, then I think it's a very valid exercise to follow some of those lessons.

Q   Does waste disgust you?

A   I think disgust is not the right word. But, clearly, wastefulness in any activity, and we're all guilty of it because we don't necessarily use our time to the optimum; you can't perfect your working day to get the most out of it every day in life; but, yes, I think productivity and endeavour needs to be part of any business practice. And waste is a tragedy, particularly in the media because time is important and clarity of communication is important and, to some extent, striving for perfection is part of what we do in the media and, of course, there is not, it's not the same as some other cultural efforts.

If you make a great movie, people will remember it in 10, 20 or even 50 years. You make a great front page and we're just looking at the front pages of John Lennon because it's the anniversary of his death coming up, but those front pages, and I was involved that day in the newsroom, I can't remember what the front page was. Was it a good front page? I think it actually was and we were comparing front pages. So, you strive for perfection, you strive to be efficient, and I think that is part of the media industry. But, of course, it is true of all cultural pursuits. If you are involved with music or cinema or theatre, you are always striving for something special, aren't you? And I think the media is part of that and wastefulness will act against achieving a good result at the end of the day.

Q   What did you learn from working with Mr Murdoch while you were editor of the News of the World?

A   Well, I did learn something that people probably would be surprised about. He is not an interfering proprietor despite all the stories. I think I heard from him only on two subjects regarding content in three years or so. And if you expand that to the eight years I was an editor because I was an editor of Today as well as the News of the World, in those eight years it was still only twice that I heard from him about an editorial matter; once was when I objected and, indeed, killed a column by Woodrow Wyatt because it was in support of a apartheid and although I respected the views of someone that I didn't necessarily agree with, the second week he attempted to run a pro-apartheid regime column I killed it because it was a very strong link between Woodrow Wyatt and Margaret Thatcher. Rupert wanted to know why I'd offended Woodrow Wyatt by killing his column and I told him. And the column didn't appear. So, he was interested but he didn't overrule the judgment I'd made as his editor. And I consulted him only once about an exposure to give him a warning that he might be approached to try to kill that story. He was approached and he didn't kill the story.

So, my encounters with Rupert as a proprietor with me as editor I could say, honestly, that he wasn't interfering.

Q   What was the other story?

"RED by James Hogan"

A   The other story was about Jeffrey Archer who was, of course, exposed. And we lost a libel action and then 20 years later the damages were repaid and Jeffrey Archer went to jail.

Q   Were you surprised when Mr Murdoch shut down the News of the World?

A   Yes, I think it was a bad decision.

Q   Why?

A   Because the News of the World was much bigger than any scandal and very dear to the hearts of people in the UK and it would have recovered from the phone hacking scandal. And I think Rupert had a lot of things to think about; he is famously decisive. He clearly thought this was a way to deal with the crisis. I don't agree with that judgment.

Q   Were you sad?

A   Yes. I have the distinction of having edited two papers for Rupert Murdoch, both of which he closed down because he closed Today some years earlier. And I think that, also, was a mistake because 300,000 buyers of Today just walked across the street and bought the Daily Mail instead and it was the greatest gift to the Daily Mail so I think Rupert Murdoch should have stayed in the middle market and Today should have survived. But, again, that famous decisiveness on both those occasions I didn't agree with those decisions but that's Rupert. He makes a fast judgment and he makes the decision, and he's in the position to do that.

If, you know, you are working in a publicly owned company in this country, as I did with the Mirror group, for instance, then those sorts of decisions wouldn't be possible. You would have to consult many people and get a Board to endorse that sort of decision but Rupert Murdoch is an extraordinary colossus who doesn't need to consult people for what, effectively, is quite a small decision within a great global empire that he's built up.

Q   What was the biggest challenge you faced when you ran Mirror Group Newspapers?

A   The initial challenge, of course, was to revive the company after the abuses that Robert Maxwell had brought to the business. The newspaper and the various titles and there were five national newspapers, still are, in the Mirror group, those titles were in relatively good health but the corruption with a small 'c' throughout the business that he had effectively infected the business with, which was people living high on the hog and the offices were very much structured to support a management that was dependent on the proprietor, all of that had to be dismantled and a different, if you like somewhat puritan, streak had to be injected into the company to resuscitate it.

And, inevitably, that was – and I think it's been described as a brutal process and perceived, certainly, as a brutal process – nevertheless it had to be done and not everything we got right as a team but, you know, within a year we had relisted

60% of the company that the banks owned; we had in 18 months moved the company out of Fleet Street to Canary Wharf, that had a therapeutic effect on the business; and it went on, then, to acquire regional newspapers and move on a journey towards being a much more broadly based publishing company than it was when I went in after Maxwell.

So, it worked and whether the methods were unnecessarily harsh is arguable; but we stabilised the company and it's gone on to be a stronger company despite the fact that there's been constant structural change. the business is strong; at the moment Trinity Mirror is debt free; it's got a pension fund deficit but then all mature publishing companies have got that; but, nevertheless, all the titles are intact and in pretty good health. So, when we did this 20 odd years ago, it was emergency measures because of the larceny of Robert Maxwell.

Q   What were you trying to do with Live TV?

A   I believe that, obviously, to diversify using a tabloid skill that we had was important and at that point, 20 years ago, there was room for other broadcasters; I felt that was for certain. And Live TV was an attempt at entering that market cost-effectively and it did cause a stir and it was entertaining on a shoestring. What would have happened if I had not left the Mirror group, I simply don't know. But, yes, television was an ambition, efficiently funded, of the Mirror group at that stage. And I feel that it could have led somewhere.

Q   Was Live TV before its time?

A   It clearly was a beginning of an exercise that might have led
     to a much more refined TV strategy. And it broke some
     rules, which is always good. Like many entertainment
     propositions you have to make yourself different and
     whether it was before its time or just different I'm not really
     able to make a judgment about that but I think it deserved a
     longer run than it got.

Q   What do you think about the BBC at the start of the 21st
     Century?

A   If we are at the start of the 21st Century. We seem to be well
     into it. But, the BBC has got the most exciting potential and I
     think that requires someone at the BBC, or possibly a
     combination of government and the BBC to be very bold
     and my personal feeling is that the big opportunity is within
     the cultural segment. That is, we in the UK have got a very
     rich cultural life across theatre, cinema, music, the arts,
     museums; we have just the richest tapestry to weave here in
     broadcasting. Therefore, the BBC, to me, should be less of a
     broadcasting corporation and more of a cultural
     corporation. The BBC should become the custodian for all of
     those arts, culture-driven activities that are going on every
     single day in life throughout the country.

     Broadcast only scrapes the surface of those things. We have
     many talented people in all these cultural spheres; they
     never see the light of day and are striving in every
     community up and down the country. We need to have a

broadcasting organisation which acts as the curator of those cultural events and pursuits and the BBC can fill that role.

Now, people will say that's an elitist thought, where you're saying you put serious music, opera, visits to museums on the agenda, the top of the agenda for the BBC. But actually, I think we should be we should have a national broadcaster who does have an objective to raise the attention of the public to these levels. It's not elitist. It is, I think, something that provides a genuine public service. And the material is there and we need somebody to harness it. I don't see there is anybody better than the BBC to do that.

You know, we all have our thoughts about future funding, the technology exists to have premium BBC channels; I would personally pay for high grade cultural programming and I think a lot of other people would as well. So, you can be very inventive with what you do with the BBC but I think its greatest mission should be to promote and protect our cultural heritage and there is no lack of material.

Q   Is the BBC too big?

A   Well, I would say it was too big because, you know, I could say any good media manager can take 10-15%, 20% of the workforce away and still have a very similar output. So, yes, there is always room for reform; there is always room to pare down management, remove bureaucracy, direct people to the front end of the business. I would say that's what we've done in Local World and other newspaper companies that I've been involved in.

So, there is always scope for that but I think the essence of reform of the BBC is about its content. That's what the BBC should be about, content. The debate should be much more about content than funding or efficiency. If they get the content right I think everything else can be forgiven.

Q   Do you think the licence fee helps or hinders BBC journalism?

A   Journalism in the BBC is a very different matter to other content. And the BBC will always be subject to scrutiny, both internally and externally because it's funded by the licence fee. I personally prefer a free market where you have competing news organisations and then the public can make the choice which programming they care to watch in terms of reporting. I make a choice every morning when I flick through the channels which news service I will consume on a given day but I continue to have to pay for the BBC service. Should we not have a choice as to which news service we want to consume and which news service we want to pay for; and would that strengthen the proposition of news reporting in this country?

If you dropped all of the so called safeguards for integrity and also balance I don't think there's a perfect solution. And I don't think the BBC, by the way, can ever hope to be perfect in terms of balance because even the judgment you exercise in how to lead a news bulletin is subjective. So, there is a bit of pretence here that only the BBC can deliver impartiality. I don't think that's true. I think all news broadcasters who are credible and are thought of attempt to reach some balance and they all have their own procedures and protocols to do that. So, relying on the BBC as the one impartial news broadcaster is not a very practical thing. People are people and they make judgments and they will exercise those judgments from their own personal prejudices from time to time.

I think that's pretty intolerable for any news organisation to be subject to scrutiny on the basis that there's a licence fee. So, it's an imperfect world but I think it's going to persist and then... but, fortunately, there is some choice; there is Sky News; there is ITN; you do have some choice, possibly not enough choice.

Q　As a funding model would you favour a basic service for a basic licence fee and then a second offering which is a subscription premium channel offering from the BBC?

A　I think, certainly, there is room for a mixture and I think people will pay for BBC services independent of the licence fee. And if you capture that thought and you also capture the thought about how does the BBC develop its content along these cultural grounds that I'm suggesting, I think there is a very exciting future for the BBC. But, they've got to get out of this defensive attitude.

The idea that a manager in the BBC can cajole the people who appear on the BBC, the actors and the other people, who are paid by the BBC, cajole them into writing petitions to save the BBC that, frankly, is nonsense. They should be bold enough to say, the BBC had this phenomenal history, it's got this capability, now what are we going to do with it in the modern era? What does the market not supply; and how are we going to fill that need?

Now, I think that's beginning to happen. And I think that the fresher minds within the BBC are moving towards an innovative approach to content. For instance, I understand that there is an effort now to fill the democratic deficit of reporting courts and local government and the BBC will help to fund that and that content will be made available to all bona fide local media organisations in collaboration with the regional newspaper industry.

Now, that is a very bold move; it fulfils a public service need; it is good for democracy to expose courts and local government to this sort of detailed professional reporting. We're beginning to see a movement in the BBC which is much more creative in terms of changing the content agenda. So, I'm optimistic and I think given there is also technology where the BBC can charge a premium for certain content, to certain people, that's an opportunity as well.

Q   Do you think the internet will eventually kill off television?

A   I think broadcast, making an appointment to view in the old way is unlikely to be the economic model of the future. Content on demand is what I see the younger generation engaging in. They find content, the content they want, at any given time; it is very rare that my children will actually say "oh, there's a programme I want to watch at eight o'clock on Sunday evening." You know, you get the flurry of activity and communal interest in things like Downton Abbey but it's not a daily routine anymore as it used to be.

So, I think what people want is access to content when they want it and they very often choose content that might be obscure, not mass popular at all; and they fill their hours where they're communicating in different ways than picking up a newspaper or switching on the TV.

We're on a journey in this respect. It's a journey where there is immense opportunity for conventional broadcasters and for conventional or traditional publishers but we have to move very rapidly or somebody else will take away our living whether you are a broadcaster or publisher.

So, the means of communication through the internet is certainly going to dominate how we behave as broadcasters and publishers in the future.

Q   And finally, thinking about terrestrial television do you have any sympathy with people who say there are too many channels but nothing to watch?

A   I think that says more about the people concerned. Also, the myth of American television is just that; lots of channels, nothing to watch. The Americans make good television; let's face it; we broadcast it in the UK so some of it must be good; some of it's on the BBC so some of it must be good. And, again, people dismiss the Italians or the French. They all

372

make good programming. They make good detective series. The French have their gritty version of Morse and so do the Italians. The Germans make excellent cultural programming.

So let's be a bit real here, there is some sort of myth that only the British can make good television and only the BBC can make good television. This is not true. The rest of the world is out there and they make good television, they make good programming and they make good content. So, that's something we should dwell on. We're in a competitive global world and we have to do it better all the time.

Q   Many, many thanks.

End of interview.

Chapter XIV

Epilogue

Blasting of the Royal Cannons.

I find TV too cumbersome and too crowded with 600 plus channels in the UK, at least the news channels have vastly improved in Britain thanks to Sky news, Al-Jazeera and an array of new formats on RT news.

Without FOX we would never have had the Simpsons, American Dad and Family Guy and some may well see the cartoons as just brilliant current affair programmes!

TV became too obsessed with Reality TV. Repeating the same format over and over again.

I use and watch the internet: verified and unverified news. VICE news, The Young Turks, TheLipTV, AnotherClip and anyone's own face page amongst a myriad of others.

Viewed through this angle it may be a mad world out there where 21st century broadcasting and communication is concerned but we will perhaps be spared the fate of George III and exchange total nonsense for enlightenment.

What ever happened to TV?

By Nick Peterson, September 2015

"RED by James Hogan"